ZIONSVILLE PUBLIC LIBRARY

W9-CBS-294

ZPL

WITHDRAWN

DESIGN
HISTORY

DESIGN HISTORY

UNDERSTANDING THEORY AND METHOD

Kjetil Fallan

Oxford • New York

Hussey-Mayfield Memorial
Public Library
Zionsville, IN 46077

English edition
First published in 2010 by
Berg
Editorial offices:
First Floor, Angel Court, 81 St Clements Street, Oxford OX4 1AW, UK
175 Fifth Avenue, New York, NY 10010, USA

© Kjetil Fallan 2010

All rights reserved.
No part of this publication may be reproduced in any form
or by any means without the written permission of
Berg.

Berg is the imprint of Oxford International Publishers Ltd.

Library of Congress Cataloging-in-Publication Data
A catalogue record for this book is available from the Library of Congress.

British Library Cataloguing-in-Publication Data
A catalogue record for this book is available from the British Library.

ISBN 978 1 84788 538 8 (Cloth)
978 1 84788 537 1 (Paper)

Typeset by Apex CoVantage LLC, Madison, WI USA

Printed in Great Britain by the MPG Books Group, Bodmin and King's Lynn

www.bergpublishers.com

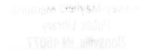

Contents

Introduction

'Everyday things represent the most overlooked knowledge . . . Quotidian things. If they weren't important, we wouldn't use such a gorgeous Latinate word. Say it,' he said. 'Quotidian.'
'An extraordinary word that suggests the depth and reach of the commonplace.'[1]

These are the words of the stoic, wise, old Jesuit priest Father Paulus in Don DeLillo's 1997 novel *Underworld*. In all its simplicity, this statement epitomizes the motivation behind this project. Throughout his epic account of the recent history of the modern world, DeLillo lets the minute, mundane events and the grand, great narratives resonate in a proposal for an 'underhistory'. And as the quote demonstrates, it is not only everyday *events* that rise to prominence in his philosophy of history; everyday *things* are just as essential to understanding society and culture. This little reflection on the importance of learning from quotidian things inspires the writing of a design history that recognizes the extraordinary significance of the ordinary.

But what can quotidian things say about our culture and history, and how? Ben Highmore claimed that 'the ordinary elements of the designed environment orient us, and orchestrate our sensual and social worlds. And it is the ordinary, the ubiquitous and established rather than the brand new that demonstrate this social orchestration most complexly and most vividly.'[2] In other words, design culture is not elite culture, but everyday culture, and it is best explored through historical analysis. Perhaps the most interesting aspect of design as a field of historical inquiry is its many guises of inherent ambiguity, its essential tension between ideology and practice, between mind and matter, between culture and commerce, between production and consumption, between utility and symbol, between tradition and innovation, between the real and the ideal.

The design of everyday things can also function as a lens, allowing observers to better see some of the most prominent paradoxes of modern society and culture. Everyday products—and the ideas that shaped them and the meanings they mediate—constitute a rich material and fertile ground for cultural history.

Design history today is no longer primarily a history of objects and their designers, but it is becoming more a history of the translations, transcriptions, transactions, transpositions and transformations that constitute the relationships among things, people and ideas. In a sense, then, the questions that underpin and frame the new design history are, as phrased by Bill Brown;

> questions that ask less about the material effects of ideas and ideology than about the ideological and ideational effects of the material world and transformations of it. They are questions that ask not whether things are but what work they perform—questions, in fact, not about things themselves but about the subject-object relation in particular temporal and spatial contexts.[3]

Whereas Brown's wording here might seem to imply something of a dichotomy in the causal connection between the ideal and the real, This book argues for a greater emphasis on the relational and reciprocal dynamics of idea and object, mind and matter, ideology and practice in historical studies of design.

Design history as a field or discipline is a relatively recent phenomenon. Generally speaking, at least if compared to many other humanistic disciplines, it must still be characterized as having reached only a quite modest degree of professional dispersion, organization and institutionalization. Whereas the field has achieved a certain degree of autonomy in some select places—notably Britain—there is still precious little indigenous knowledge regarding the theoretical aspects of design historical scholarship available to emerging scholars in the field or to those entering or approaching design history from more general or neighbouring disciplinary backgrounds. This book should serve its primary purpose as an introduction to some of the most important theoretical perspectives and frameworks informing and transforming design history today.

Two decades have passed since the publication of the first—and last—books intended as introductory surveys of the theoretical aspects of design historical scholarship: Hazel Conway's *Design History—A Student's Handbook* (1987) and John Walker's *Design History and the History of Design* (1989).[4] Although by then design history was established as a discipline or field of study in its own right, the two decades since have seen the discipline develop remarkably through an upsurge in publications, heated debates, improved institutional footing and increasing interdisciplinarity—in short, through radical changes in design historical practice and theory. Thus, it is high time that the pioneering work of Conway and Walker is supplemented by new studies focusing on the more recent discourse. This book is intended as one such contribution.

But first, what is this thing called design? In other words, what is design history the history of? This used to be a fairly simple question. Design history was conventionally considered the history of designed objects of high (aesthetic) quality and the designers, ideas, movements and institutions that conceived those objects. Such topics continue to be studied in design history today, but the subject matter of the discipline at large has become much more complex and multifarious for several internal and external reasons. First, design history has matured considerably as an academic field, a process characterized, for example by an increased interest in an array of material far beyond the gourmet objects once considered core concerns and by a heightened attention to such issues as consumption, mediation and use. Perhaps design history today is better described as the history of design culture, a history that encompasses a wide gamut of practices and phenomena. These developments within the field of design history are explored at some length in chapter one.

Other contributing factors to the increased complexity and multifariousness of design history's subject matter are external to the discipline itself, stemming instead from changes in the public perception of design, changes in design practice and changes in design research. The first and probably least important of these influences comes from how the term 'design' is perceived and used in the public sphere. Design has become such a buzzword lately, especially in marketing and media, that it seems to have taken on a positive value in itself, transforming ordinary products, as if by magic, into exclusive, stylish objects. Thus, there is 'design furniture'. As opposed to what? Furniture brought about by industrial manufacture's equivalent of spontaneous combustion or immaculate conception? The same line of reasoning has turned pretentious hairdressers into 'hair designers', and expensive dildos and vibrators into 'designer sex toys' (a term used by Lelo, a Swedish manufacturer of 'pleasure objects' set up in 2003 by designers Carl Magnuson and Eric Kalén and engineer Filip Sedic with the expressed aim to tap into a new market segment of 'Women and couples with money to spend . . . open to acquiring erotic toys as lifestyle accessories' through the explicit invocation of the Scandinavian design heritage.[5]) The eclectic and discriminatory use of the term 'design' in these examples has no place in design history, where the mundane, the cheap, the amateurish, the flawed and the garish elements of material culture feature alongside the usual suspects of good design.

A factor that—at least potentially—has greater impact on design history's subject matter is the changes that have been and are under way in the practice of design. Although the world never was as simple and neatly defined as it might appear in retrospect, there can be little doubt that the massive changes in industrial structures, manufacturing technologies, market organization, consumer behaviours, communication technologies, visualization techniques and so on over the past few decades are of vast importance for the restructuring of design practice. Design history will have to engage with these dramatic developments, which most likely will require the reconsideration of many conventional categorizations and terminological traditions underpinning the discipline. In doing so, design historians may also fruitfully question some of the habitual labels used to pigeonhole different types of design work and, thus, destabilize the inside/outside divides built in this manner. Even established domains and professions, such as architectural design, engineering design and graphic design, are not all that straightforward in their relationship to design history and its subject matter as they might appear at first glance.

For instance, when an architect designs a standard phone booth manufactured in the thousands, as Georg Fredrik Fasting did for Oslo Telefonanlegg in 1932, it may technically be a building, but it is nevertheless also a work of industrial design and can easily be claimed for design history. When architects design unique villas or public buildings, on the other hand, it is probably best left to the realm of architectural history. Then there is a borderland between comprising the design of prefab housing, standard houses and so on.

Similar, but more complex considerations can be made in the case of engineering design. When engineers design cog wheels to go in the power transmission of a drill or brake discs for a car it would seem material more at home in the history of technology than in design history. However, when engineers design drills or car bodies their work is of more immediate interest to design history. It may seem that the crux of the matter is the degree to which the object as an entity interacts directly with users. A brake disc does not, as its function is mediated by other actants and its appearance is hidden from view. A car, on the other hand, requires heavy interaction from its users and even from its beholders. What is complicating the matter in the case of engineering, however, is its anonymous omnipresence. In design history, the design of a product is habitually attributed to one or a few persons with professional training in some sort of design discipline. In the vast majority of cases, however, a number of other persons—often engineers—have made essential contributions to the product development, though their names never appear in marketing material or exhibition catalogues. Behind every great designer stands a great engineer (or rather, a host of them), one might say. A case in point may be when the oil and gas company Statoil in 2000 launched CompLet, a new liquefied petroleum gas (LPG) container for the leisure market. CompLet, made from an advanced composite material of polymers, fibreglass and resin, replaced conventional steel containers. The design office Ghostwriter Design was hired to complete the final design and detailing only after four years of product development involving an array of actors, including engineers from the container manufacturer Raufoss Composites and researchers from the Norwegian University of Science and Technology's Department of Engineering Design and Materials. The material technology is here such an integral part of the product design that drawing division lines between scientists, engineers and designers would be futile, misleading and artificial.

The last example of border-area design domains and professions is graphic design. The history of graphic design is often considered a more or less self-contained subfield to design history. This makes sense insofar as graphic design has traditionally engaged with different types of artefacts, generally two-dimensional rather than three-dimensional, and with paper as the pre-dominant—but by no means the only—medium. But when graphic designers work on packaging, product graphics or interfaces, such a segregation would seem far less appropriate.

Had only the real world of design practice been as simple and schematic as depicted in these examples. Meticulous and conscientious attention to the real multidisciplinary and interdisciplinary and collaborative nature of most, if not all design work in full detail is, if at all possible, a massive challenge to design history. Take the Apple iPod. The patent for the 'ornamental design' (patent lingo for 'form') of the first generation iPod nano launched in 2005 lists fourteen persons as 'inventors' (patent lingo for 'designers'), amongst which are Apple's now famous senior vice president of industrial design Jonathan Ive and company co-founder and chief executive officer (CEO) Steve Jobs, but also (in alphabetical order) Bartley Andre, Daniel Coster, Daniele De Iuliis, Richard Howarth, Vincent Keane, Duncan Kerr, Shin Nishibori, Matthew Rohrbach, Peter Russell-Clarke, Douglas Satzger, Calvin Seid, Christopher Stringer, Eugene Whang and Rico Zorkendorfer. The point here is not to identify the contributions of these individuals but simply to indicate the fragmentation of competences and tasks in design practice. What's more, being an electronic device, the design of the iPod would not be worth much without the work of Ben Knauss and his colleagues at PortalPlayer, the

I When engineering, material science and design amalgamate: The interdisciplinarity of design processes increases with the complexity of products. Raufoss Composites for Statoil, CompLet liquefied petroleum gas (LPG) container, 2000. Design: Ghostwriter Design (Mats Henriksen), Raufoss Composites (Jens Økland, Trond Inge Flønes and Gaute Jensen), and the Norwegian University of Science and Technology (Professor Claes-Göran Gustafson, et al.) Copyright Norwegian Design Council

company that developed the electronic guts of the product for Apple. Then there is the host of anonymous engineers of different denominations. Add to this the importance of the media player's acoustic and haptic qualities, its graphic interface, its packaging, its panoply of available accessories (both authorized and non-authorized), its extensions into computers (for battery charging and music synchronization) and the Internet (online music store) and so on, and the intricacy increases even more. In a sense, though, multi-disciplinary collaboration is nothing new in design practice. What seems to have changed is the scale and grading of such multidisciplinary collaboration. When Elektrisk Bureau in 1932 launched the world's first telephone made entirely from Bakelite and with the handset cradle integrated in the base unit, the product development was led by the company's design manager Johan Christian Bjerknes. He coined the conceptual design, but as a technically rather that aesthetically trained man he called upon the artist Jean Heiberg to refine the exterior shape. Such collaborations are fairly manageable, even in historical analysis, but as products, manufacturing technologies and design processes grow increasingly complex, it becomes more and more difficult to maintain or establish neat definitions and categorizations of what makes up the subject matter for design history.

In addition to changes in the perception and use of the term 'design' in the public realm and changes in design practice, a third external factor contributing to the increased complexity and multifariousness of design history's subject matter is found in the realm of design research. As design education has become more grounded in theory and design practice has become more reflexive, research in design is also gaining ground in academic contexts. Design research is a rather fuzzy term and a confusingly heterogeneous field, but the branches most proximate to the social sciences and humanities—and thus also to design history or design studies—have cultivated a broad discourse on basic but profound questions regarding the nature, scope, responsibility and potential of design. One argument that has been pushed far and fervently in this discourse—perhaps because it by implication empowers design, highlights its role in society and legitimizes design research—is that design knows no limits. The most infamously universal definition of design

2 Multidisciplinary collaboration in design is nothing new: The world's first telephone made entirely from Bakelite and with the handset cradle integrated in the base unit resulted from a cooperation between a technician and an artist. Elektrisk Bureau, telephone, 1932. Design: Johan Christian Bjerknes and Jean Heiberg. Copyright the Norwegian Telecom Museum, Photographer Cato Normann

stems from Herbert Simon: 'Everyone designs who devises courses of action aimed at changing existing situations into preferred ones.'[6] Victor Margolin offers another highly inclusive, but somewhat more elaborate and discerning, definition:

> By 'products' I mean the human-made material and immaterial objects, activities, and services, and complex systems or environments that constitute the domain of the artificial. And I intend 'design' to denote the conception and planning of these products. As I apply the term 'products' in this essay, I refer not only to the outcomes of professional design practice but also to the vast results of design activity that everyone engages in.[7]

Such an all-embracing definition of 'product' and 'design' may seem sensible, refreshing even, to design historians eager to move beyond the limited subject matter of conventional design history—especially its attention to amateur design practice, user participation and creative consumption. The problem is that a definition that does not exclude anything is of little or no use. Reconsidering demarcation lines and conceptual categories is a sound and rewarding exercise but eradicating them altogether can easily become a disservice to design studies. If the only differential definition design can be given is against the natural world, there is a risk of emptying the term of any substantial meaning. When now even intangible phenomena such as software, services and sounds are said to be *designed*, rather than programmed, planned and composed as they used to be, it may be liberating in a design studies context, but for design history it is probably more confusing than constructive. If every artificial aspect of our world is best defined as a designed product, then every form of history except natural history becomes design history. Even the time-honoured genre of political history must be usurped by design history, because what is political history if not the history of how political systems have been designed? Clearly, this is no viable solution to the problem of defining design history's subject matter.

It would seem that not every colloquial use of the word 'design' belongs to design history's subject matter, just like the most stubbornly universalist definitions of the term 'design' from the field of design studies seem less transferable to design history. But which demarcations can be made without falling into the elitist or sectarian pitfalls of past programmes? Perhaps the best answer is to keep asking the question. Ostensive definitions can only take one so far anyway. As Ludwig Wittgenstein argued through his unsuccessful attempt at finding a satisfactory definition of the word 'game', the meaning of words and concepts are inextricably linked to their use and cultural context. His point, though, is that a lack of a definition does not prevent a congruent and meaningful use of the concept. Likening what he calls a 'blurred concept'—such as game—to a blurred image, Wittgenstein asks: 'Is it always an advantage to replace an indistinct picture by a sharp one? Isn't the indistinct one often exactly what we need?'[8] Given the difficulties in making clear-cut distinctions in the examples discussed previously, it is tempting to consider design a blurred concept. This is not to say that design historians should stop asking what design is, but rather that the search for a distinct definition may be better left to others, and an indistinct picture may provide a more rewarding image of design history's subject matter. Perhaps the better option is to say with Henrik Ibsen: 'Don't press me, friend, to act the necromancer; I'd rather ask; it's not my job to answer.'[9]

These brief musings on what design is and thus what constitutes the subject matter of design history clearly leave a lot to be desired. But a deeper understanding of what design history is can only be achieved through a discussion of the discipline's theory and method—a discussion that is the topic of this book. The book is structured in three parts devoted to each of the following three aspects of disciplinary reflexivity: historiography, theory and methodology, and epistemology.

Chapter 1 is a historiographic survey. First, it presents a brief outline of the development of the field before discussing in more detail some major approaches in recent design history. Although histories of design have been around for a long time, design history as a distinct, academic field of study in its own right it did not emerge until the 1970s. The first section shows how this new field was established as an offshoot from art history at a time of turmoil and radical renewal and discusses some of the more problematic aspects of the heritage from this parent discipline. These tensions were particularly acute amongst design historians whose chief interests were with the popular culture, consumer goods and ordinary objects. The second section traces some of their efforts at promoting a design history better suited to this type of subject matter. The third section examines one of the most important historiographical debates in recent design history, in which a key question was whether design history should be considered primarily part of design research or primarily a branch of historical research. Ever since branching off from art history, design history has declared an interest in interdisciplinarity. An important effect in this respect has been the field known as material culture studies, whose influence is explored in section four. The last section of this metahistory presents a few examples of what design history could look like if design were treated not as some sort of minor art, or given a privileged position, but rather as a cultural phenomenon on par with others. It is thus a proposal for a cultural history of design.

Chapter 2 discusses a selection of recent theoretical perspectives and methodological concepts appropriated from neighbouring fields of study and how these may benefit design history. Suggesting that design, as a cultural phenomenon, has more in common with technology than with art, the first section introduces the history and sociology of technology as a rich reservoir of theory and methodology for design history, too. The second section explores actor-network theory (ANT), one of the most widespread yet controversial theoretical developments from the field known as science and technology studies (STS), and focuses on how ANT may heighten design historians' sensitivities to materiality, relationality and process. The third section presents script analysis, a methodological tool—also appropriated from STS—that holds great promise to design history in facilitating better and more dynamic understanding of how meaning is transported and transformed through the material. The fourth and last section is devoted to the third STS-derived concept to be treated here: domestication. Domestication was coined as a concept aimed at describing how media and information technologies are simultaneously adapted and adapted *to* when integrated into our homes and everyday life practices, but it can easily be applied to other domains of the material culture as well and thus represents a welcome aid to design historians interested in the intriguing relationship between what design does to people and what people do with design.

Part 3 discusses some basic epistemological questions related to historical studies of design. Primarily, it seeks to investigate the rather intangible notion of (modern) 'isms' as a categorizing concept and analytic tool and to develop an understanding of design ideologies as parts of cultural modes. The first section offers a brief outline for a terminological clarification regarding a cluster of key concepts: modern, modernity and modernism. The second section explores the nature of isms as a categorizing concept and argues that isms can be seen as cultural modes and that design culture—as experienced and articulated through isms—can be conceptualized as a dialectic between or co-production of ideology and practice. The third section considers isms as dynamic discourses, highlighting their historicity and transitional character.

Questioning how isms are transformed through space and time also invites reflections on how they and their manifestations are to be treated as historical material. The fourth section reassesses Thomas Kuhn's notion of paradigms as a structuring device in the history of science and asks whether such ideas— which were originally derived from art history—may be brought to bear on the dynamics of historical change in the history of design. The fifth and last section pursues this topic somewhat further by outlining what a differential paradigmatic system would look like in design history. It concludes the epistemological discussions by calling for a design history more sensitive towards its own terminology and reflexive of its own conceptualization principles.

Needless to say, like any work of its kind, this book cannot be, nor does it aspire to be, definitive and complete. As an introductory survey focusing on selected issues of great importance in the recent and ongoing development of the field, it is deliberately brief and partial—in both senses of the word.

I

Historiography

Design history is fairly brief compared with the history of many other academic disciplines. Surely, designed objects—and their conception, manufacture, meaning and use—have been subject to historical studies for a long time in older fields such as archaeology, art history and history. Yet design history in its own right is a relatively recent phenomenon—at least when measured by the degree of professional dispersion, organization and institutionalization. Its historiography, theory and methodology are thus still in flux and in need of discourse. This chapter will first present a brief outline of the development of the field before discussing in more detail some central approaches in recent design history. Next, the chapter will critique design's heritage from art history, discuss the formation of an industrial design history proper, analyse the theoretical and methodological debates in the field, and assess the influence from material culture studies. The chapter concludes by arguing for a cultural history of industrial design.

Comprehensive historiographies of design are in short supply, though some brief but informative outlines have been published.[1] Attempts to summarize the historiography of design tend to start out by discussing Nikolaus Pevsner's 1936 *Pioneers of the Modern Movement*, sometimes pausing at Sigfried Giedion's 1948 *Mechanization Takes Command*, before moving on to Reyner Banham's 1960 *Theory and Design in the First Machine Age*.[2] The merits and shortcomings of these works have been debated thoroughly for several decades, so there is no need to repeat that discussion here.[3] Although all three authors were trained as art historians, and the bulk of their work was dedicated to architectural history, their contribution to design history is indisputable. However, three books in the course of a quarter of a century can hardly be said to make up a separate discipline.

Scholars generally agree that Great Britain led the way in the development of design history as an academic discipline. Both in terms of publication volume, educational programmes, organizational structure and the number of academic appointments and other practitioners, Britain may still be considered the heartland of design history today.[4] This situation dates to the 1970s when many of the country's polytechnics and art colleges established courses in design history, partially to supplement and support their art, crafts and design programmes. The development in other countries should not be disparaged, but volume and organization do matter. As John Walker puts it:

> The awareness that a distinct discipline exists occurs when a sufficient number of practitioners become self-conscious about their activities and begin to join together to discuss common problems and interests. It is usually at this critical conjuncture that a professional organization is formed. In Britain the Design History Society was established in 1977 even though, of course, histories of design were being written long before that date. Once an organization exists, the trappings of an academic discipline soon follow: elected officers, a newsletter, a scholarly journal, an annual conference.[5]

The *Journal of Design History* did not appear until 1988, but 'got off to a good start' and has established a reputation as a renowned and essential publication.[6]

Looser organization and a wider scope characterize the development in the United States. A Design History Forum (renamed Design Studies Forum in 2004) was founded in 1983, and the journal *Design Issues* was launched in 1984.[7] These communities are important arenas for design history, but, as the journal's subtitle—*history | theory | criticism*—suggests, its scope exceeds that of history.[8] This is true also of the Design Studies Forum's own journal, *Design and Culture*, launched in 2009.

In Scandinavia, the discipline of design history remains small and loosely organized, despite the establishment of the Nordic Forum for Design History (*Nordisk Forum for Formgivningshistorie*) in 1982. However, biannual conferences organized by the Nordic Forum and the *Scandinavian Journal of Design History* have helped generate some sort of community for the few design historians scattered across the Nordic countries.[9]

More recently, design historians in other regions have also organized academic forums. The Design History Workshop Japan was founded in 2002 and began publishing its annual journal, *Design History*, in 2003. A Turkish Design History Community (*Türkiye Tasarım Tarihi Topluluğu*), set up in 2006, organizes annual conferences with published proceedings. One of the latest additions to the organizational flora is the German Design History Society (*Gesellschaft für Designgeschichte*) established in 2009.

Outside the realm of organized societies, the city of Milan has hosted two international conferences of the historiography of design: *Tradizione e Modernismo: Design 1918/1940* in 1987 and *Design: Storia e Storiografia* in 1991.[10] Since 1999, the International Committee of Design History and Studies has organized biannual conferences, bridging activities within the various groups mentioned previously and others. Thus far, meetings have been held in Barcelona, Spain (1999); Havana, Cuba (2000); Istanbul, Turkey (2002); Guadalajara, Mexico (2004); Helsinki/Tallinn, Finland (2006); and Osaka, Japan (2008).

This short introductory survey of the field does not aspire to be a state-of-the-art report on design history but instead is meant to convey a partial picture of an academic discipline in rapid development. Before embarking upon a discussion of the theoretical frameworks and methodological questions of design history, a brief review of the problems regarding the subject matter of the discipline is warranted.

Design history is not the only discipline concerned with the cultural meanings of historical artefacts. In various ways this interest is shared, for example by archaeology and the history of decorative/applied art. Where the subject matter differs the most between design history and these other disciplines is when design history leaves the spheres of artistic creation and craft production and focuses on the realm of industrial manufacture. The general field of design history, however, is normally thought to encompass a far wider subject matter, including pre-industrial and non-industrial manufacture, and spanning graphic design, fashion, textiles, interior design and craft. Such a diverse subject matter makes it difficult to shape a common theoretical framework and methodology. It should be fairly clear that studies of fifteenth-century court dress and studies of twentieth-century automobiles have little in common in this respect. This multitude of interests is reflected in the *Journal of Design History*, and the two most commonly known books on design history methodology—those by Hazel Conway and John Walker—try to tackle this problem.[11] This chapter will not take on the arduous task of following Conway and Walker in proposing universal frameworks for design history at large but, instead, will reflect on theory and methodology first and foremost in terms of the history of design for industrial manufacture. These reflections may very well be relevant to other aspects of design history as well.

The Heritage from Art History

We can forgive a man for making a useful thing as long as he does not admire it. The only excuse for making a useless thing is that one admires it intensely.[12]

In direct parallel to how Oscar Wilde succinctly and poignantly explains how design is not art, design history is also not—or at least should not be—art history. Even in Britain, however, where design history has come the furthest as a distinct academic discipline, the field's origin in art history is not only acknowledged but is still felt today. As already mentioned, both Pevsner and Banham were trained in art history, but even now, when degree programmes in design history exist, the heritage from art history is highly present. This is even more true outside Britain, where degree programmes in design history are rare and many of those working in the field come from the field of art history.

In Britain, the heritage from art history was handed down not only through the precedents established by Pevsner and Banham but also because most new courses and programmes in design history were set up in departments of art history. In addition, many of the new degree courses combined design history with architectural and art history. Furthermore, before the Design History Society was founded in 1977, design historians met as a subgroup of the Association of Art Historians at their annual conferences.[13] When Middlesex Polytechnic established the first postgraduate course in design history (a master's degree), it was not only run by a department of art history but was explicitly 'formulat[ed] . . . around approaches that were to be identified later with what became known as the "New Art History"'.[14]

Another important initiative that grew out of the same institution was the journal *Block*, which was established in 1979 (and discontinued in 1989).[15] Inspired in particular by French social theorists such as Pierre Bourdieu, Jean Baudrillard and Michel Foucault, this new journal spanned art history, cultural studies and design history and 'argued for a rejection of prevalent and established academic approaches of art history influencing the subject in favour of radical alternatives that sought to understand the social and existential meanings of things'.[16] Despite the radical attitude and pluralist approach, the fact remains that most of the editors, writers, articles and readers of *Block* were deeply rooted in art history and art studies. From the very start, however, the journal did feature some important articles presenting truly fresh perspectives on design history.[17] Studies of posters, advertisements, film and television also made their way into *Block*. Thus, the journal strove to break down the traditional barriers between so-called low, commercial and applied art and fine art but did not seem to intend to get rid of *art* as the common denominator.

However, the shift from high to low was by no means massive and unisonous in the field at large. As Jonathan Harris stated, most art historians still studied traditional subject matters—canonical paintings, drawings, prints and sculpture—but the more radical art historians did so in a new way, asking new questions and applying an analytical apparatus highly influenced by the radical political and social criticism of the time.[18] A recent case in point might be Caroline Jones's work on how meaning is constructed in art. Discarding the notion of meaning as inherent to the art object and ready to be disclosed by the viewer/critic, she sees the meaning of art as a social construction—or perhaps more aptly, as a co-construction—invoking both artist (or rather, the artist's paintings) and critic (or perhaps, the critic's texts) plus many other more or less peripheral actors. Jones invokes the work of Bruno Latour, a persistent advocate of collective construction of meaning in science and technology. The protagonists of Jones's case study, however, are archetypal heroes of conventional art history: the painter Jackson Pollock (and his paintings) and the critic Clement Greenberg.[19]

The tenacity of art history conventions in design history is apparent in a 1980 *Block* article by Fran Hannah and Tim Putnam, which asserted that efforts at contextualization and interdisciplinarity had thus far not done design history much good:

> All too often . . . art-conventional notions of design still pass as the substance of the subject while context amounts to eclectic dippings into new fields. Bits of business history, history of technology or social history find their way into an account without consideration of the problems proper to those histories . . . 'Context' is not really established because we are still in thrall to certain categories which present themselves as the self-evident substance of any history of design. Such notions as 'designer', 'school', 'artefact', 'medium', 'style', continue to be taken as starting points even when they have been the subject of critical discourse in Art History. Far from being a greener pasture free from the contradictions of Art History, Design History is in fair danger of becoming an academic backwater.[20]

Hannah and Putnam went on to claim that '[m]ost Design Historians approach the subject from an art historical or design medium background'[21] and did not seem to have high hopes of design history as a sovereign discipline. Nor did they seem to have much faith in design historians' abilities to draw value from other disciplines or apply approaches to historical studies of design from disciplines other than art history.[22] In other words, design history was still largely presented as an art history of design—albeit one in dire need of revitalization and improvement.

This view is consolidated in the introduction to the 1996 compilation of *Block* articles, which described the journal's view on design history as an attempt to 'treat design, like art, as an ideologically encoded commodity, the value and significance of which were dependent on dominant modes of consumption.'[23] Although the introduction also claimed that 'This approach was in opposition to prevailing notions of design writing which adopted un-transformed art historical notions of univocal authorship, inherent meaning and received hierarchies of value',[24] it did not challenge the idea of art history per se as the basis for design history. The authors were critical of how design history and art history had traditionally been approached but still saw no reason to study design in a different manner than studying art. In fact, the authors saw design history as 'the undergrowth of visual culture' then becoming visible from what is half sarcastically described as 'the lofty vantages of art history'.[25] This mode of expression might now be interpreted as rather condescending, insinuating that design history was a lowbrow field in which highbrow art historians could go slumming. So, inasmuch as *Block* renewed design history, its contribution was to moving from an art history of design to what might be called a new art history of design. Still, the editors did publish a few articles that clearly broke the mould, such as those by John Heskett and Tony Fry—but then these writers did not come to design history from art history but from economics and design and cultural studies, respectively.[26]

It should be clear, then, that despite an articulated criticism of the traditional art history approach to design history represented by such critics as Pevsner, art history—albeit new or radical—has remained influential in the further development of design history. This heritage from art history is problematic. Why? The simple answer is that design is not art. This is true at least of the vast majority of design work in industrialized societies, and pre-industrial and non-industrial design probably has more in common with craft than with art. In this connection it is useful to recall Tomás Maldonado's statement that 'industrial design is not art'.[27] He made this remark in 1960 in his capacity as director of the German school of design Hochschule für Gestaltung Ulm. The fact that Maldonado was an artist by training makes his statement all the more interesting. The logical consequence for historians is of course that if industrial design is not art, then art history can hardly be the best basis for historical studies of industrial design. Maldonado dismissed the design history of his day on the grounds that it ignored every sector and aspect of design that could not be squeezed into the configuration of art history.[28]

Three problematic tendencies in design history have arisen as a consequence of the patronage of art history. This bias is by no means universal, but to a certain extent generalizations are necessary because of scope and acceptable because of representativeness. So in broad strokes, the three major problems of writing an art history of design are as follows:

First, an excessive attention to aesthetics overshadows the many other aspects of design. Value judgements of aesthetic quality have often been the art historian's principal selection criterion. The discriminatory dimension to this practice has been heavily criticized, especially by design historians with an interest in the more anonymous and profane areas of design, such as engineering design.[29]

Second, there is a tendency to view designers as artists or authors and products as creations or oeuvres and to consider the best of these the primary subjects of study.[30] This tradition is what Hazel Conway calls the 'Heroic Approach', and as much as her criticism of it is highly commonsensical, it is also eloquent and to the point: 'In general historical studies we no longer concentrate solely on kings and queens and battles and conquests.' She goes on to state that, in contrast, 'The design of goods that most people live with is important' when writing design history.[31] Jan Michl wielded another good argument against the personality cult, pointing to the collective and cumulative dimension present in most, if not all, design.[32] This is no new way of reasoning: David Lowenthal quotes Wilhelm von Humboldt's 1836 statement that 'No . . . individual can ever be purely original: "since each has received material transmitted by earlier generations", creative activity is never "purely innovative but rather modifies the heritage".'[33] Besides being highly elitist, disturbingly mythopoeic and contributing to panegyric personality cult, this

3 Conventional design history's predilection for beautiful objects for the home has left out a vast array of material from other spheres, such as military equipment. Båtservice Verft AS, Tjeld-class (Nasty) Motor torpedo boat, 1957. Design: Jan Herman Linge. Copyright The Royal Norwegian Navy Museum

bias towards creation/production has also resulted in a neglect of use and consumption.

Third, for a long time, design history has considered only a very restricted subject matter, largely limited to object categories that have traditionally been affiliated with art (decorative art, applied art and industrial art). To sum up then, design history has rarely bothered with objects historians did not consider to be of high aesthetic value, objects that could not be attributed to an author or objects outside the domestic sphere.

The heroic approach has also had a great impact when design history has moved outside the object/creator domain: there are countless studies of the so-called great schools, organizations and institutions promoting great design, but slim pickings when it comes to studies of their more mundane or reactionary counterparts. A recent and notable exception is Paul Betts' history of German design, where he is as equally concerned with the heroic organisations such as Deutche Werkbund and Bauhaus as he is with the un-heroic organizations of the Nazi era, such as Amt Schöheit der Arbeit and Kunst-Dienst.[34]

Despite reservations regarding generalizations, it should be mentioned that these biases have been criticized and challenged within the realm of design history and in the parent discipline of art history for a long time. Jonathan Harris has noted that

> If the notion that the 'works of art themselves' have axiomatic qualities has been thrown into fundamental doubt because it is recognised that *any* act of description or analysis is necessarily partial and preferential, then equally doubtful now is the idea that all art historians should properly involve themselves with artefacts instead of, for example, the study of institutions such as art galleries or government funding bodies.[35]

But Harris acknowledges that old habits die hard: 'The traditional and still predominant art-historical conception of human agency has been in terms of art's immediate and individual producers . . . Authorship remains, then, a necessary but problematic idea within *both* conventional and radical art history.'[36]

In one way, Sigfried Giedion's *Mechanization Takes Command* may, as its subtitle *A Contribution to Anonymous History* suggests, be seen as an early attempt to challenge the conventional predilection for chronicling the great designs by great (or famous) designers.[37] Although the book thus can be said to be fairly modern in this respect, it is not equally progressive by other standards. Jean Baudrillard has offered a thoughtful and pertinent critique:

> [T]he simultaneously formal, functional and structural analysis which Siegfried [sic] Giedion offers us—a kind of epic history of the technical object—notes the changes in social structure associated with technical development, but scarcely addresses such questions as how objects are experienced, what needs other than functional ones they answer, what mental structures are interwoven with—and contradict—their functional structures, or what cultural, infracultural or transcultural system underpins their directly experienced everydayness.[38]

In architectural history, Bernard Rudofsky offered an important criticism of and alternative to the personality cult in his 1964 *Architecture Without Architects*.[39] About the same time, George Kubler criticized the biography as the habitual format for art history because biographers notoriously overstate the significance of personal genius.[40] Much in the same way, Nicos Hadjinicolaou later disparaged the monographic approach based on the argument that the history of art was more than the history of artists.[41] Ideas like these found theoretical support and inspiration in such fields as Marxism, feminism, postcolonialism, semiotics and psychoanalysis, and participated in forming what is now known as the new art history, which, as we have seen, came to the fore in such places as the pages of *Block*.

The new art history of design has produced a considerable body of sound research. Most notable, perhaps, are the studies inspired by social history and feminist history.[42] These have applied fresh perspectives on design history in terms of political views and analytic approaches, although many still have not disengaged design history from art history. In this vein Carma Gorman has criticized some self-proclaimed feminist contributions to design history for being methodologically reactionary, striving to recover great female designer heroines from oblivion and plot them onto a disturbingly conventional and canonic chart of design history alongside their long since deified male counterparts: 'familiar tales of artistic heroism have been reworded to apply to female designers rather than male fine artists, but the stories and the questions that generate them remain largely unaddressed'.[43]

Although the heritage from art history is still very much present, recent developments have shown an increasing acceptance of design history influenced by or written from the perspective of other disciplines. Furthermore, the past couple of decades have seen the construction of a body of research that perhaps is taking on an identity as a distinct academic discipline—a discipline where there is interest in objects that historians do not consider to be of high aesthetic value, objects that cannot be attributed to an author, and objects outside the domestic sphere.

4 Design history is beginning to take an interest in design produced and consumed by alternative actors. Self-taught entrepreneurs as designers and children as users are among the less explored and most interesting of these. Rustadstuen Snekkerverksted, Fjellpulken children's pulk, 1963. Design: Egil Rustadstuen. Copyright Norwegian Design Council

Nevertheless, the more traditional art history of design still prevails, especially in the more popular publications. A recent case in point is David Raizman's *History of Modern Design*.[44] Although some attempts are made to expand the subject matter, treating for instance transport design at some length, this book is still largely based on an art history template. Within this genre, though, it is a quite thorough, nuanced and insightful book, as it pays more attention to the social and cultural contexts of design than many other publications. But it still reads as a design history based on the established canon of great designs and great designers. Raizman makes the occasional attempt to revise that canon by including the odd humble product and discussing some topics that have been frowned upon and disregarded by conventional art histories of design, but the museum pieces, celebrity designers and elitist cultures still dominate. Books like Raizman's might leave the impression that art history proper has become more radical than the art history of design. Fortunately, a growing number of design historians do not subscribe to this way of writing design history.

In contemplating the relation between art history and design history, Mirjam Gelfer-Jørgensen posed the rhetorical question 'Has Design History anything to do with Art History?'[45] Being herself an art historian by training, her answer is hardly surprising. Whereas she recognizes one of the core problems in an art history of design by stating that 'design history based on the methods of art history probably adheres to the traditional view of artefacts, so that the focus is on the process and the designer's creative ability' and admitting that 'the result has become a far too uncritical concentration on the design-historical icons', Gelfer-Jørgensen still appear to profess an art history of design.[46]

Gelfer-Jørgensen's defence of this approach is based on two arguments: First, with its traditions of studying both the near and the remote past and of paying more attention to artefacts' properties/meanings than to their modes of manufacture/distribution, art history can serve as an antidote to what she considers to be an unhealthy bias in design history towards *industrial* design (or, as she puts it, design since the Industrial Revolution). This is a sound argument, supported by her assertion that 'interesting relationships can arise traversing chronological and geographical boundaries'.[47] However, her concern that design history runs the risk of becoming synonymous with industrial design history is not shared here. To illustrate, it should suffice to quote Jeffrey L. Meikle's address on the occasion of the twentieth anniversary of the Design History Society:

> [T]he *Journal of Design History*['s] . . . articles have ranged across time from the sixteenth to the twentieth centuries, and across cultures from Algeria and Japan to Hungary and Italy. It has entertained discussions of Betty Boop and Le Corbusier, Harley-Davidson and Charles Babbage, and devoted special issues to craft, to graphic design and to green design. Most important, the Journal has remained open to a wide range of theory and method—narrative history, intellectual history, economics, stylistic analysis, anthropology, culture studies, reader-response theory and documentary—thereby encouraging authors and readers to accept the widest possible definition of design history.[48]

Gelfer-Jørgensen's second argument for an art history of design is that 'What links art history and design history is the fact that no discourse, no theoretical approach can ever replace the need to consider the actual core of the area, that is to say the artefact.'[49]

Although the artefacts themselves constitute essential sources in design history, and this is a concern shared by art history, the analogy is not complete. As John Walker noted, 'since *function* is a key aspect of design, ideally goods should be *used* as well as scrutinized'.[50] The importance of hands-on experience in the writing of design history and the history of technology has also been discussed by Jeffery Meikle and Joseph Corn.[51] Furthermore, art history is not by any means the only discipline that shares design history's concern with artefacts as sources—so do the history of technology, the history of science, archaeology and material culture studies.[52] And these fields study and interpret artefacts in ways that may be more rewarding to design history than those cultivated within art history—be that new or radical or not. As Steven Lubar and W. David Kingery claimed, 'Only a small minority of art historians have investigated beneath the perceived surfaces of the artifacts, and most have placed the artistic creations of the past in a category separate from less purely aesthetic creations.'[53]

It is hard to disagree that 'design history [has some]thing to do with art history'—much like design, even most industrial design, clearly has something to do with artistic aspects (which is a far cry from claiming that design is art). The meeting points and similarities between art and design seem to be most evident within the realm of what Peter Dormer has called 'high design', that is elitist, exclusive design—but not even here is the analogy unproblematic, as '[t]here are important differences between the economic framework within which art, as opposed to design, generally operates'.[54] Nevertheless, attempting to purge design history of every trace of art history heritage would decisively be an ill turn.

This fact should not preclude the search for alternative, additional and complementary references in the development of a theoretical framework for design history. Because, as Tony Fry wrote in *Block* in reply to the aforementioned article by Fran Hannah and Tim Putnam: 'Viewing design outside the shadow of "art", it is important to proceed on a basis of the "aesthetic" being of variable significance and not always an essential feature of the design object.'[55] Therefore, Fry states his 'reservations as to the centrality of aesthetic evaluation in addressing some of the social constructions of the design object.'[56] He further warns that '[u]nless we acknowledge design beyond the aesthetic, and the social transformation of design—not only does the topic of Design History become a political hobby for winter evenings, it also becomes politically impotent for contemporary or future use in increasing our understanding of design'.[57] Fry's reaction may seem a bit exaggerated today, but it may still serve as an important reminder. And although art history clearly has much more to offer than aesthetic analysis, and although the field of design history has matured considerably since then, it is worth mentioning that John Heskett still—twenty-four years after Fry's scorching criticism—finds it necessary to demand 'design [history] to be moved out of the shadow of art history'.[58]

Industrial Design History

Even though we all know well that the 'historic avant-gardes' from the beginning of the [20th] century—futurism, cubism, purism, prounism, constructivism, De Stijl etc.—have been of vital importance for the subsequent development of the visual arts—and thus not only painting and sculpture but also architecture and furnishing—I do not believe, to be honest, that the study of these movements are worth much when it comes to the industrially produced object.[59]

These words by the acclaimed Italian art historian and design critic Gillo Dorfles, uttered at a 1987 design history conference in Milan, are well suited to illustrate a shift of attention towards a more specific discussion of design history. Despite the brevity of the outline presented in the previous section, the broad lines of the formation of design history as a discipline and some of the principal problems regarding its heritage from art history should be clear by now. Of course, art history is more than the study of avant-gardes. Nevertheless, studying design in the industrialized era engages a subject matter only remotely related to art and Dorfles's assertion can thus be seen as the historian's logical consequence of Tomás Maldonado's statement that 'industrial design is not art';[60] in other words, if industrial design is defined broadly as design for industrial manufacture, design history is not art history. The following section outlines some of the attempts that have been made during the past couple of decades at advocating the writing of a design history better suited to a subject matter made up of ubiquitous, mass-produced, mundane, industrial products rather than precious objets d'art.

One of the first attempts at writing a survey history of design that was not based on the idea of museum pieces or a canon derived from art history was the 1980 book *Industrial Design* by John Heskett. Here he strongly criticized what he perceived as the formalist methodology of the conventional art history of design for creating an iconology of objects that disregarded or greatly underestimated the various circumstances of their production and use.[61] But he also cautioned against what he saw as a potential contextual determinism of the 1970s trend towards social histories of art and design.[62] Seeking to portray 200 years of historical development in 200 pages, Heskett's book shares many of the problems generally associated with survey books in terms of case selections, emphasis, and so on, but its strong standing is nonetheless deserved because of its refreshingly balanced representation. The book's chief merit, though, is that it is an attempt at writing a history of industrial design on its own terms rather than as an art history of design. In other words, Heskett writes industrial design history—not industrial art history.[63]

Heskett was neither the first nor the only one struggling to construct a design history less dependent on the art history template. The past two or three decades have seen the publication of many monographs on national or international survey histories with an emphasis on design in industrialized society. Amongst these are books by such authors as the German Gert Selle, the Brits Penny Sparke and Jonathan M. Woodham, the Australian Tony Fry, the Italians Paolo Fossati and Anty Pansera, and the American Jeffrey Meikle—to name but a few.[64] Any individual historiographic analysis of these books is of course not possible here. This omission may perhaps obscure their considerable differences in many respects, but they have one important common trait that merits their mention, however briefly and inadequately: they all aspire to an understanding of industrial design on its own terms rather than as some sort of industrial/decorative/applied art. The major achievement of books like these, then, is that they represent a growing body of literature on genuine industrial design history. Surely, survey histories intended for a broad audience are rarely the place to look for the most progressive research in any discipline. If the discussion had shifted towards publications dealing with more particular subject matters and more unconventional delimitations, there would be more radical and challenging ways of writing industrial design history. Conducting such a discussion is, however, a far too arduous and comprehensive task for the present context.

Heskett's advocacy of an industrial design history on its own terms is carried on in his contribution to the 1987 design history primer edited by Hazel Conway. Here Heskett states that '[i]ndustrial products are . . . elements of our material culture, tangible expressions of individual and social values. This means objects cannot be studied simply in terms of visual characteristics and qualities, or as ends in themselves. Instead, visual analysis needs to be supplemented by questions exploring wider reaches of meaning.'[65] Elaborating on where such wider reaches of meaning should be sought, Heskett identifies two basic contexts; the contexts of production and the contexts of use and consumption. Like conventional art history, design history has traditionally focused much more on production than consumption. In addition to exploring the neglected sphere of consumption as a subject field, Heskett argues that design history must also broaden its horizon when regarding the sphere of production in order to elude the all too often myopic studies of design processes and the resulting mythopoeia. For design history to rise above the mere connoisseurship represented by the artists and oeuvres approach, Heskett asserts,

> a wider range of investigation [is required]. This may involve business structures, professional and industrial organization, economic and political policy, social influence and impact, which should enlarge and enhance understanding of the design process and designed artefacts. To emphasize the latter as an autonomous activity is to ignore the element of social formation and effect in industrial design. Conversely, however, to reduce human creativity simply to an expression of social or material factors is to diminish this essential feature of our humanity.[66]

Taking this call for reciprocity one step further, Heskett argues that there is much to benefit from combining the spheres of production and consumption in studies of design history.[67] This point has also been made by John A. Walker,[68] Suzette Worden and Jill Seddon,[69] and Grace Lees-Maffei—the latter, concerned with advice literature as design historical sources, claiming that 'Currently, design history is becoming increasingly preoccupied with *mediation* as a point on the continuum providing a focus for studies attentive to both production and consumption'[70] [italics added]. Similarly, seeing flaws with both the traditional production-oriented and the newer consumption-oriented approach, Johan Schot and Adri Albert de la Bruheze have outlined a perspective built on 'a focus on the mediation process between production and consumption', a process they define as one of 'mutual articulation and alignment of product characteristics and user requirements'.[71] Studying such arenas of mediation is a fertile strategy for better understanding the negotiations not only between production and consumption, but also between ideology and pragmatism, between theory and practice.[72]

A topic that is easily derived from the concern for use and consumption is an interest in the kinds of objects most consumers actually use, and it should be fairly evident that these are not necessarily identical to those favoured and promoted by the design elites. The concern for democratic design, then, is closely related to the issue of selection criteria governing design history's subject matter. As discussed earlier in the chapter, the criticism of how the creations/oeuvres tradition inherited from art history has created a problematic bias in the selection of objects to be studied in mainstream design history. This tradition is responsible for the ignorance of a vast range of object categories outside the domestic sphere and an equally vast array of objects not conforming to the aesthetic canon of good design. Many design historians—including John Heskett, John A. Walker, Hazel Conway, Rainer Wick, Fredrik Wildhagen, Peter Dormer and Jonathan M. Woodham—have pointed out this problem and have argued for an industrial design history more focused on everyday objects.[73]

Making a case for why design history should shun aesthetic value judgement as selection criteria, Judy Attfield has gone so far as to claim that '[t]he material culture of Modernity in the [post-World War II] reconstruction period was in distinct contrast to the theory of good design'.[74] However, such a strategy requires more than just incorporating new objects in the subject field of design history. As Attfield has noted, it is important that popular design that does not conform to good design theory is studied on its own terms and not just as a contrast to elite design. It must be 'interpret[ed] . . . from perspectives beyond the limits set by the "good design" critique'.[75] Gert Selle has made a similar point, calling for a design historical approach that would 'make it possible to understand other people's positions and values. A sort of social-esthetic empathy would be needed in situations in which old, internalized value systems again and again play tricks on us.'[76] There are good examples of industrial design histories of mundane, affordable, commonplace objects—that is democratic design—but it is still necessary to encourage this trend.[77] For instance, little work has been done on the place of non-modernist design—forms inspired by tradition, convention and nostalgia—in the era of modernism. Studying such material whilst avoiding what might be called the 'camp trap',[78] however, requires that it 'is not only included, but also integrated' in historical narratives.[79]

5 The vast majority of material culture does not conform to the narrow principles of good design. The place and role of approaches such as non-modernist design in the age of modernism deserves more attention in design history. Figgjo Fajanse AS, Eidsvoll Vårblomst earthenware service, 1951. Design: Ragnar Grimsrud. Copyright Figgjo AS, Photographer Tom Haga

Attfield's earlier comment indicates a shift of focus from *what* to research in design history to *how* to research design history, which is worth pursuing. As David Raizman and Carma R. Gorman put it: 'Expanding and strengthening the field of design history requires not only judicious selection of the objects to be considered, but also careful attention to the sources and methods used to study them.'[80] There is nothing wrong per se in studying artefacts—be they humble or dazzling. What matters more is the approach; the way in which the objects are engaged and to what purpose. This principle has been brilliantly expressed by Italo Calvino: 'You don't relish a city's seven or seventy-seven marvels, but the answer it gives to your question.'[81] Calvino's inspiring tenet can be read as a caution to historians of material culture not to become fetishists and idolaters.

Fredrik Wildhagen has questioned 'the inclination towards the chic cult object . . . [which] solely indicates a preference amont [sic] a limited number of a MoMA-oriented clique of object-gourmets' and criticized that this connoisseurship nevertheless 'tends to have the major support from writers in the field.'[82] Much has happened in the two decades since Wildhagen aired his frustrations, but his words are still a poignant reminder. Yet precisely because Wildhagen is so critical of the traditional art history of design, pointing to several of its shortcomings in terms of subject matter and methodology and arguing for 'differentiating between a history of design and one of decorative art',[83] it seems somewhat strange that he still chose to treat industrial design and handicraft as interwoven in his 1988 book on Norwegian design in the industrial era, *Norge i form.*[84]

Perhaps more interestingly, though, is that in his quest for a more appropriate theoretical and methodological base for design history, Wildhagen has advocated a departure from an art history of design because of what he describes as 'the need to find a balanced interdisciplinary approach to counteract the art historical approach of an almost unilateral aesthetic evaluation of design, but more than anything to reflect the interdisciplinary character of design itself'.[85] Among the disciplines Wildhagen invites to this quest for a balanced interdisciplinary approach is the history of technology. Nevertheless, even here Wildhagen seems not to have practiced what he preached. In his review of *Norge i form*, Michael Tucker criticized it for providing insufficient 'socio-historical flesh', that is for its *un*balanced interdisciplinarity.[86]

Another advocate of interdisciplinarity, Rainer Wick, deems this strategy 'quite obvious' and proposes design history as 'an intersection of different disciplines, as for instance the history of ideas and ideologies, the history of science and technology, the history of economy and sociology and also of the history of art, as *one* among the others'.[87] More importantly, though, Wick is weary of what he considers to be a common practice—mock interdisciplinarity— and makes demands of a true interdisciplinarity: 'It is not sufficient to take these disciplines into consideration casuistically in order to illustrate or outline one or the other problem or sketch out a "general background"; rather, these disciplines should *systematically* participate in developing a design history that does not want to be squeezed into the corset of a purely art-oriented way of looking at things.'[88] Whether or not design history is in the position to make demands of other disciplines is doubtful, but design historians would be wise to engage with other disciplines.

Interdisciplinarity was also paramount in the editorial policy of the *Journal of Design History* from its very beginning in 1988. The editorial policy presented in the first issue proclaimed:

> The *Journal of Design History* . . . aims to help consolidate design history as a distinct discipline but it will not be narrowly specialist in content or sectarian in tone. The widespread recognition of the cultural significance and economic importance of design will provide a broad base on which to build and the Journal seeks to promote links with other disciplines exploring material culture, such as anthropology, architectural history, business history, cultural studies, design management studies, economic and social history, history of science and technology, and sociology.[89]

More than two decades on, the editors' ambitions have proven sensible and still constitute a sound basis for the history of design.

Much of the debate on establishing a design history proper, distinct from art history, has centered on arguments concerning how to tackle a subject matter made up of industrially manufactured commodities as opposed to works of art. This is not all that surprising, because one might argue that pre-industrial and non-industrial design can be more comfortably—though not completely—explored by other, more established disciplines, such as archaeology and applied art history. It is worth noting, though, that the *Journal of Design History* does not limit its scope to industrial design history. This was heralded from the start in the editorial policy statement that 'the editors seek to encourage contributions on design in pre-industrial periods'[90] and confirmed by the earlier quote from Jeffrey L. Meikle's address on the occasion of the twentieth anniversary of the Design History Society in 1997 regarding the multitude of topics represented in the Journal's first decade.[91] Many sound arguments can be made in favour of this policy, but the vast topical heterogeneity may also at times be overwhelming.

In his proposal for a world history of design, Victor Margolin has argued that a demarcation of the field of study to industrialized societies results in a parochialism ignorant of vast parts of design practice.[92] This is of course true of the field of design history as a whole, but it seems legitimate and reasonable for scholars to make this distinction because industrialization remains an actual and significant demarcation in history, society and culture. A more pressing concern was voiced by Tony Fry, who noted that within industrial design history there is still a problematic bias towards older Western industrialized societies, resulting in a marginalization of problems indigenous to other regions of the industrialized world.[93] This concern is being addressed, however, as design historians from more recently industrialized societies, such as Cuba, Turkey and India, are joining the international research community. Recent biannual conferences organized by the International Committee of Design History and Studies have been important in this development, attracting delegates and topics beyond the usual suspects.[94] With this disclaimer on the centrality of industrial society to the disciplinary discourse in design history, the remainder of this section will discuss some of the more explicit attempts at contributing to the development of the theoretical frameworks and methodological tools—from the *Journal of Design History* and other relevant forums.

Already from the first issue, the *Journal* proved capable of breaking the mould of a conventional art history of design. Tim Putnam, a member of the editorial board of both *Block* and the *Journal of Design History* and a social scientist by training, presented a case study of transformations of the design process at Brown & Sharpe, an American machine-tool manufacturer, in the late nineteenth century.[95] The article is interesting for two reasons: First, because such engineering design was (and still is) highly underrepresented in industrial design history, at least beyond the mythopoeic anecdotes on such heroes as Samuel Colt, Isaac Singer, Henry Ford and others from the history of technology. Second, and more interesting, is Putnam's point regarding the nature of transformations of the design process—that their essential feature was organizational rather than personal.[96] In other words, Putnam argued for a greater attention to studies of design management and process organization rather than the usual musings on individual creative agency. However, Putnam's strong emphasis on structure may seem a bit one-sided, resulting in a rather rigid model of the process.

Since then, the *Journal of Design History* has presented a variety of takes on design history, ranging from articles approaching the history of ideas[97] via studies of economic and political history[98] to those exploring post-colonial,[99] feminist/social[100] and cultural[101] histories as well as the history of technology[102] and business history.[103] Other articles have explored the potential of methodological traditions such as ethnology[104] and psychoanalysis.[105] Unconventional subjects such as the legal matters of designs (intellectual property problems),[106] consumption,[107] propaganda films and television,[108] design journalism,[109] aviation design,[110] participative design processes,[111] eco-design,[112] period furniture,[113] toys,[114] import trading,[115] bicycles,[116] packaging,[117] product photography,[118] computers,[119] artificial limbs[120] and do-it-yourself boat building[121] have been probed. The vast variety of themes and approaches represented here makes it hard to consider this body of research en bloc. But in all their diversity these studies have sought to challenge many of the problematic aspects of conventional design history discussed earlier. It should be clear by now, then, that there is a strong and growing trajectory of industrial design history that has superseded or at least supplemented the tradition dubbed here the *new art history of design*.

Design *History* or *Design* History?

More explicit discussions on the theory and methodology of design history are relatively sparse, but have surfaced from time to time in forums like the *Journal of Design History*, *Design Issues* and *Design Studies*. One of the seminal texts in this respect is Clive Dilnot's two-part essay written for the first volume of *Design Issues* in 1984.[122] On the whole, the essay seems motivated by a desire to relate design history to present-day design practice and education, giving it a strangely instrumental and legitimatizing flair. Only in a note does Dilnot consider the possibility that '[t]here might be considerable value in a study which for once broke with the conventional link of design history to design practice, and inquired instead what possible contributions design history might make to academic issues in general'.[123] Why Dilnot relegates this point to a footnote rather than making it a key issue in his essay is somewhat surprising, considering the topic of the text. The link between design history and design practice is not given. One could just as easily argue that design history is and should be an academic discipline (or at least an academic activity and field) in its own right on par with other histories and that it is not design history's primary concern to inform design practice through the education of designers or otherwise.

Despite this instrumentalist stance, the arguments put forth are well-informed and largely relevant today, more than two and a half decades later. Dilnot's approach is primarily historiographic (at least in Part I), but many important theoretical and methodological issues are also raised (particularly in Part II). The essay's most poignant contribution is the warning against 'the very real possibility of turning the writing of [design] history into the writing of myth' where the author draws on Roland Barthes's influential study of mythology.[124] This critique is linked to his aversion for what he saw as the lingering but long overdue presence of Pevsnerian legitimatizing design history. Given the amount and character of research produced after 1984—some of which was outlined earlier—this latter point may seem somewhat dated today, but this criticism still applies to many of the more popular writings on design history. The same can probably also be said about Dilnot's most fundamental objection against conventional design history: that it has dodged 'methodological inquiry and theoretical self-reflection', resulting in an unsatisfactory dominion of 'self-evident empiricism'.[125]

Another interesting early *Design Issues* article is a 1986 feminist critique by Cheryl Buckley. Drawing on feminist history and feminist art history she called attention to a series of deficiencies and problems in conventional design history, such as the primacy of aesthetic values, the obsession with good design and the great or heroic individual designer, and the prioritization of production (or rather, creation) over consumption and of professional capitalist production over amateur domestic production. Opting for a more progressive design history, Buckley calls for a historiography and methodology that acknowledge the complex social construction of design and its users and meanings.[126] Although Buckley's expressed aim may seem a bit narrow—'to develop a history that does not automatically exclude women'[127]—her objections to conventional design history are sound and her request for a social constructivist history of design is compelling.

Another and more problematic of Buckley's core concerns is to include professional and hobby craft in the subject matter of design history because craft has been a traditionally female arena whereas industrial design has been more of a male domain. Buckley seems to believe these categories are merely terminological constructs that can be disposed of to facilitate a more gender-balanced history. But removing or disregarding actual historical divides—no matter how problematic, undesirable, shifting and complex they might be—can only lead to a distorted image of the past that is highly questionable history. This is not to say that craft history has nothing to do with design history, though—there are many good reasons for the two to maintain and develop mutually beneficial relations. However, as Carma R. Gorman has argued in her criticism of Buckley's programme: '[R]edefining "design" to include "craft" is truly a dangerous move. Such a redefinition can do absolutely nothing to change the fact of past inequities . . . [I]t is foolish to dismiss the way that past practitioners and theorists categorized art, craft, and design, since those categories are an important part of the context and history of production and consumption of objects.'[128]

One of the most heated debates on historiography, theory and methodology was instigated by a 1992 *Design Studies* article by Victor Margolin.[129] Acknowledging the field's considerable development since the 1970s, Margolin stated that 'there is little to show that could gain recognition for design history as a solid field of academic study' and that 'design history has not developed on the basis of a well-understood subject matter or a set of methods and principles to guide research'.[130] To Margolin, the rapidly changing subject matter (design) is a more relevant fulcrum than the approach/methods (history), and, referring to 'the dynamic crossing of intellectual boundaries that are occurring elsewhere',[131] he thus proposes the primacy of a field of inquiry labelled *design studies* where the methodological apparatuses and insights of a wide range of established disciplines, including philosophy, sociology, anthropology, ethnography—*and* history can be used in the study of design.

Although not mentioned by the author, this proposal resembles the developments in science and technology studies (STS)—an interdisciplinary field of study which consolidated around the time Margolin wrote the article and is now well established in academic terms. An important lesson, though, is that the establishment of STS, where philosophers, sociologists, anthropologists and historians work side by side on studies of science and technology in society, has not by any means rendered the discipline of history of technology any less relevant or potent. Hence there is no need to believe that the onset of design studies as a field of study needs to usurp design history or preclude the latter's further disciplinary development. Nevertheless, the virtues of disciplinary autonomy are well worth discussing. But if one were to accept Margolin's claim that design history needs a broader analytic context, then opting for cultural history (widely defined as the historic study of all cultural phenomena) is preferable to design studies, as the former has a greater potential as a framework for developing the theory and methodology of a design *history*.

Not surprisingly, Margolin's article provoked ardent response, particularly from British design historians who did not share Margolin's grim outlook on the merits of design history as an academic discipline. In his reply in *Journal of Design History,* Adrian Forty refuted Margolin's criticism on the grounds that the latter 'has not given credit to the extent that design history has embraced new lines of thought', referring especially to cultural studies and anthropology. In terms of defining the field, Forty did not see design history as a part of design studies, but as a part of history:

> I do not feel the need, as Victor Margolin does, to discover a boundary for design history. To my mind, the main obligation of design history is to write good history—in its ends design history is no different to any other branch of history. . . . Margolin's desire to define a new field of study hardly seems necessary—surely the discipline of history as it has developed over the last century or so already provides a perfectly satisfactory definition of the 'field'. All that is needed is for us to get better at answering the questions that it provokes.[132]

Whereas Forty's identification of design history as a part of history rather than a part of design studies is appealing, the last part of the quote seems to portray the discipline of history as somewhat deceptively harmonic, not mentioning any of the many feuds of modern historiography.

Victor Margolin's response to Forty's reply—published in a 1995 special issue of *Design Issues* together with reprints of Margolin's catalyst essay and Forty's reply as well as six other contributions—clarified Margolin's view on the prime justification of historic studies of design: 'I have proposed "design studies," as a field that can more effectively bring historical research into relation with issues of current practice.'[133] He then goes on to substantiate his argument by claiming that

> There are certainly ample precedents for the relation between historical research and contemporary practice in an academic field. Sociology is a good example. Some scholars concentrate on historical research and focus on issues of interpretation in the work of the preeminent historical figures—Durkheim, Weber, and Parsons, for example. This work is continually brought to bear on contemporary sociological theory as a means of questioning new ways of thought. Such a relation between past and present is immensely helpful and has prevented sociology from becoming too far removed from its own historical

consciousness. Design history is the consciousness of design's past. But without a relation to current practice, what is its purpose?[134]

Two aspects of this argument make it unclear at best, erroneous at worst—depending on conceptual interpretation, what is meant by the terms 'contemporary practice' and 'historical research' and how should they relate to each other? In the case of sociology, it seems fairly clear that contemporary practice refers to the research done by sociologists (except perhaps historical sociology). In the case of design, it is less clear. Is contemporary practice the work carried out by practising designers? Or is it the work carried out by design researchers (e.g. researchers on design methods, process, management and strategy), those in Margolin's proposed field of design studies? Because the former interpretation could be seen as dangerously close to viewing design history as mere cultural backdrop or perhaps just some sort of source book for practising designers, contemporary practice presumably means contemporary design research (commercial and academic?), although the two are not necessarily mutually excluding categories. This interpretation is supported by the analogy with sociology, where contemporary practice seems to mean not social practice but sociological research.[135]

What is meant by historical research, then? In the case of sociology, Margolin is absolutely right in his observation that the discipline's self-reflective historical studies (the historiography of sociology) play an important part in the development of contemporary sociological research. If this is the only type of historical research allowed for in design studies, what remains might be termed a 'history of design ideas', whose principal purpose is to inform contemporary design research practice. This is probably too harsh a reading of Margolin's intentions. Still, his analogy with sociology fails in that he does not mention that one of the principal trends in recent sociology is historical sociology.[136] This can be broadly described as research on all kinds of historical social phenomena, not just reexaminations of Durkheim, Weber and Parsons. When sociologists can find it purposeful to study such topics as Leninist- and Stalinist-era political posters, as Victoria Bonnell has done,[137] and the history of American car design, as David Gartman has done,[138] and if Margolin considers this to be 'historical research . . . brought to bear on contemporary sociological theory', it is hard to envision what kind of design history would *not* establish the prescribed 'relation to current practice'.

The curious point that it is precisely this issue—the relevance of design history to present design practice—that constitutes a common ground for Margolin and Forty is the crux of Jeffrey L. Meikle's contribution to the debate. He is surprised that Forty maintains that quality assessment is the very justification of design history and what makes it relevant to present practice. Such an attitude, says Meikle, 'all but abandons "design history" for "design studies"' and thus devalues Forty's defence of design history's accomplishments:

> Given Forty's stated dedication to 'the discipline of history as it has developed over the past two centuries, [sic]' we might expect to find his position fundamentally different from that of Margolin. In fact, they are quite similar. While defending design historians against the charge that they have accomplished little in twenty years, Forty actually ignores one of their real accomplishments—that is, their rescue of the field from a Pevsnerian concern for tracing an aesthetic evolution of ever more perfect artifacts (and ignoring everything else as, in fact, not really 'design').[139]

Meikle's incredulity at Forty's insistence on quality assessment was enhanced by the fact that a decade earlier Forty had written the widely acclaimed book *Objects of Desire*,[140] which Meikle described as 'one of the first non-Pevsnerian works in the field'.[141] Meikle's answer to the question of what design history is or should be and its relevance to present-day concerns is that which most historians—regardless of empirical affinity—would give: history strives to reveal contingent realities of past society, but nevertheless 'it can indeed illuminate contemporary issues without directly addressing them'.[142]

This reflective outlook on the fundamental characteristics of historical research was substantiated and elaborated by Dennis Doordan, who declared that 'History is the concerns of the present projected onto the past. As the present evolves so, too, do the questions asked of the past. Out of the process of interrogating the past grows not a definitive account of past events but an intelligible rendering of the complexity of human experience.'[143] However

basic and self-evident such reflections are, they nevertheless form an important statement about the historian's ethos and allegiance. This stance also
underlies the critical attitude towards the relations between history and practice: 'to subsume design history within the field of design studies, is to limit
history to a narrowly conceived instrumental role in design practice'.[144] In
short, notions of instrumentality and normativity are extremely deterring to
those whose allegiance to history trumps that to design.

In another reply, Jonathan Woodham accused Margolin of 'misrepresent-
[ing] the academic health and identity of design history' and 'seek[ing] to
colonize design history under the imperial umbrella of design studies'.[145] With
the ambition to restore the honour of the discipline, so to speak, Woodham
provided an updated historiographic account of recent research, drawing attention to the more innovative and refreshing contributions to design history.
Echoing the objections raised by Forty, he concluded that 'Contrary to [Mar-
golin's] suggestions, design historians *have* taken on many of the challenges
posed by other disciplines such as anthropology, cultural studies, or feminist
theory, and there is a growing body of evidence to support this.'[146]

Other debaters expressed more sympathy for Margolin's agenda. Nigel
Whiteley stated that 'In the light of current approaches and preoccupations, it
seems to me inevitable that what was once correctly termed "design history"
should now be more properly called "design studies".'[147] To Whitely, though,
it is precisely the interdisciplinary impulses on recent design history from
fields such as semiology and cultural studies that has resulted in a situation
where history may not always be the dominant organizing method. This paves
the way for a shift to design studies. However, what Whiteley reckons would
be the benefits of such a renaming, apart from moving a few already easily
transgressible disciplinary fences, remains rather elusive.

In his reflections on the initial feud between Margolin and Forty, Alain
Findeli commented that the two were in fact addressing two distinct but related problems. Their highly diverging views on the status and performance of
design history depended on equally diverging views on what part of the term
is to be given primacy—*design* or *history*: 'Consequently, [Forty] is accused
of taking design-as-a-field for granted, whereas [Margolin] could be accused

of taking history-as-a-discipline for granted.'[148] In other words, it can be seen as a debate between *design* historians and design *historians* about pledging allegiances. Findeli's primary concern, though,—spurred by Forty's aforementioned brief and somewhat naive notions of 'the discipline of history as it has developed over the last century or so . . . provid[ing] a perfectly satisfactory definition of the "field"'[149]—is to elaborate on some questions regarding the philosophy of history.

Taking his cue from Michel Foucault's influential but highly disputed *The Archaeology of Knowledge*,[150] Findeli starts out with a short outline of general epistemological and methodological developments in twentieth-century historiography from the flight from Hegelianism via the Annales school and analytic rigour of structuralist history to the archaeological and genealogical methods proposed by Foucault and onwards to the relativism and pluralism of post-structuralist approaches. At issue are the possible modes of historical knowledge, and then where design history could fit in this discussion. Although from a historian's viewpoint this little excursion into general historiography may seem rather cursory, it does expand on and supply a necessary background to Forty's claim that 'the main obligation of design history is to write good history'[151] by inviting reflections on what constitutes *good* history. Findeli joins Forty and Woodham in objecting to Margolin's conviction that the traditional art history template still dominated design history, but, based on his discussion of general historiography, his reply takes on a different character as he speculates: 'Should [Margolin] be willing to extend his view of historical methodology, I wonder whether he would hold on to his diagnosis. But such a rehabilitating of design history through the refinement of research methodologies dissolves the issue of the status of design studies.'[152]

Findeli proposes what he calls 'the polar organic model' as a more nuanced approach to design history based on a fuller understanding of the philosophy of history. This approach should strive to embrace all (or at least as many as possible) of the 'many . . . distinct and equally relevant ways of telling this story' by applying a multitude of organizing structures (in addition to those already commonly practised, he suggested, e.g. design history as the history of technology and materials, as the history of education and of ideas, as the anthropological and economic histories of the material world, as the history of the symbolic function of artefacts and as the history of specific daily practices in connection with design).[153] The purpose of this model is to foster an understanding of design history that reveals its many different trajectories, complexities, pluralisms, multidimensionalities, contradictions, discrepancies, juxtapositions and serialities. This ambition is highly laudable and plausible. Design history as it is practised today—at least in research, perhaps less so in teaching—does approach a vast range of subjects along a great number of organizing structures, although, as Findeli demonstrates, there is a great potential in exploring the less travelled of these and other paths.

Another contribution to the methodological development of design history that takes Foucault as a point of departure comes from Stephen Hayward. His ambition is to put Foucauldian discourse theory to use in design history. Finding Foucault's ideas somewhat too rigid and dismissive of any notion of freedom or creativity in acts of consumption, Hayward calls upon more recent theories of consumption as well as Bourdieu's notion of taste as social distinction in his attempt to modify them to better suit design history.[154]

Although Hayward's adjustment of Foucauldian discourse theory no doubt is essential to its potential application to design history, the most problematic aspect remains unchallenged: how to address and acknowledge the materiality of discursive objects in a satisfactory manner. Because even though Foucault stresses that his discursive artefacts may be buildings and objects just as well as texts, they are rarely recognized beyond their representational and formative functions.[155] The alluring promise of equality of prominence bestowed on objects thus rapidly fades into a bleak flattening out of their material particularities. Discourse analysis may be an appropriate tool if one approaches design history as a history of textual design discourse but is ill equipped to encounter a core concern of most design history: the materiality of objects.

As interesting and important as textual design discourses might be, it is hard to disagree when Jeffrey Meikle states, 'I can't help thinking that the cardinal virtue of design history is its involvement with the material, its concern for the physical stuff.'[156] This remark was meant as a warning not to lose focus on the objects and processes of design in the recent vogue in design history of studying mediation and consumption. Not that these new efforts were not laudable—on the contrary: Meikle sees the search for improved understanding of the use and consumption of design as highly desirable. The problem is simply that 'we have no way of knowing with certainty how and why consumers at a given historical moment responded to particular products', because—as opposed to when studying the production side of design— documentation is normally nonexistent.[157] The danger, then, is that 'we tend too quickly to accept the opinions of designers and promoters about the meanings of their creations to the people who use, inhabit or consume them'.[158] Much of the inspiration for the turn towards consumption studies in design history has come from such disciplines as anthropology, cultural studies and sociology. Invigorating as this may be, Meikle argues that 'social scientists who investigate the consumer side of contemporary design avoid this historian's conundrum'.[159] Echoing Meikle's argument, Regina Lee Blaszczyk reminds us that 'First-person testimonies about the significance of objects in daily life are rare, as few people consciously engage their artifactual vocabularies to write about specific material experiences.'[160] Paul Betts has made a similar point, observing that 'The difficulty of ascertaining why consumers consume certain products and not others, to say nothing of how they understand and use them, is not just the problem of marketing departments. It effectively represents a sobering epistemological limit for all historians of material culture.'[161] The point made by Meikle, Blaszczyk and Betts is as compelling as it is simple; the admirable task of studying past use and consumption is a daunting one, fraught with epistemological and methodological problems.[162]

Material Culture Studies and Design History

As has been mentioned in passing previously, one of the most prominent influences on recent design history has come from a field of study known as material culture studies. If design history's disciplinary status is somewhat unclear and disputable, material culture studies is even more so. In fact, as one of the chief promoters of material cultural studies, Daniel Miller, has stated; 'the subject does not exist as a given discipline . . . and there are many advantages to remaining undisciplined and many disadvantages and constraints imposed by trying to claim disciplinary status'.[163] Thus, there is no point here in trying to define or demarcate this so-called undisciplined discipline. It should suffice to consider it a loosely consolidated field of study focusing on the material aspects of culture. The field has generated a substantial following and has produced a large amount of highly diverse research. Any comprehensive review or discussion is neither possible nor desirable here, though it will be helpful to point to some work within this field that has influenced design history or may do so. In various ways this work can represent the three major strands, or disciplinary origins, of material culture studies: anthropology and ethnography, museology, and archaeology and history of science and technology.

No doubt the first of these three, especially as practised by a group of British anthropologists, has had the most explicit and widespread influence on design history. For the sake of convenience and brevity, this strand will be exemplified by the work of Daniel Miller. The rather uneasy relationship between Miller and design history began in 1987 with the publication of his book *Material Culture and Mass Consumption* in which he dismissed design history as 'a form of pseudo art history, in which the task is to locate great individuals . . . and portray them as the creators of modern mass culture'.[164] This accusation of course did not go unnoticed by design historians, and Miller was invited as keynote speaker at the Design History Society conference in London and Brighton the very same year.[165] The anthropologist's initial provocation proved inspirational rather than insulting to design historians, and his studies of consumption as a creative aspect of culture was met with great interest.

In a review of the book for the *Journal of Design History*, Charles Saumarez Smith described it as 'the best available guide to recent writing and thinking on consumption', but at the same time revealing 'a tendency to intellectual voyeurism, of the anthropologist looking in at the window of other people's activities while never quite participating.' His most fundamental objection to Miller's approach, however, was that 'Objects are seen as actively constituting social relations without a sense of their three-dimensionality, their texture,

their sheer cussedness as the reification of social order.'[166] The apparent paradox in the assertion that material culture studies was unable to satisfactorily
address the materiality of objects only makes the criticism more poignant.[167]
Smith concluded in a reconciliatory manner that 'For the design historian
the lesson would seem to be that the anthropologist's ability to listen to what
people have to say about artefacts is more useful than the social theorist's attempts to abstract them into political or philosophical systems.'[168]

Perhaps not surprisingly, Miller did not share this outlook regarding material culture studies and the attention to the materiality of objects—quite the
contrary:

> What we may regard as unique to our approach is that we remain focused upon the object
> that is being investigated but within a tradition that prevents any simple fetishization
> of material form. Indeed we feel that it is precisely those studies that quickly move the
> focus from object to society in their fear of fetishism and their apparent embarrassment
> at being, as it were, caught gazing at mere objects, that retain the negative consequences
> of the term 'fetishism'. It is for them that Coke is merely a material symbol, banners stand
> in a simple moment of representation or radio becomes mere text to be analyzed.[169]

However, in an earlier, brief historiographic outline for material culture
studies Miller went a long way in acknowledging that the physical materiality of objects had been lost to social anthropologists, and he explained this
partly with the growing gap between social anthropology and archaeology and
partly with the vogue of linguistic analysis: 'Despite the claim of semiotics to
an interest in non-linguistic modes of communication, the emphasis in struc-
turalism and post-structuralism is on "word", "text" and "discourse".'[170] Arjun
Appadurai has proposed a slightly different take on the same problem:

> Even if our own approach to things is conditioned necessarily by the view that things
> have no meaning apart from those that human transactions, attributions, and motiva-
> tions endow them with, the anthropological problem is that this formal truth does not
> illuminate the concrete, historical circulation of things. For that we have to follow the
> things themselves, for their meanings are inscribed in their forms, their uses, their tra-
> jectories. It is only through the analysis of these trajectories that we can interpret the
> human transactions and calculations that enliven things.[171]

Whether or not material culture studies and anthropology succeed in recti-fying the tendency to see things as text is open to debate, but the concern for how the material matters is convincing.

One of the aspects of material culture studies that has made it so alluring to design historians, perhaps especially in Miller's version, is the consistent concern with the use and consumption of things. It should be noted, though, that this alignment of use and consumption is a somewhat unfortunate simpli-fication. As Victor Margolin has argued—referring specifically to Daniel Miller: 'Sociologists and anthropologists have concerned themselves with issues of consumption rather than with issues of use.'[172] Likewise, Judy Attfield has claimed that 'the post-commodity phase is usually ignored as irrelevant to the process of consumption'.[173] Some studies do operate with a broader un-derstanding of consumption, charting the biographies of artefacts way beyond their commodity stage. Even in these studies, however, there is normally a heavy bias towards the *symbolic* use of objects, so that their functional use is still given only limited attention.[174]

As traditional design history has been accused of being obsessed with the production—or rather, the conceptual creation—of things and thus ig-noring their use and consumption, it is highly understandable that this trait of material culture studies has proved fascinating despite its shortcomings. However, the anthropological strand of material culture studies has often focused so strongly on the consumption side that the production side has been left more or less unexplored. One could argue, then, that substituting one bias for another is not all that rewarding, although increased balance in available approaches is a definite improvement. Still, the field of material culture studies has not provided any ready template for research into the relations between the spheres of production and consumption. Even Miller concedes that 'consumption studies have suffered by failing to appreciate the importance of the link to production'.[175] It may seem as though sociologists moving into material culture studies have professed a more symmetrical ap-proach than anthropologists—a textbook example being the case study of the Sony Walkman by Paul du Gay and colleagues where both the production and the consumption of the artefact—as well as the other three sectors of what the authors refer to as the 'cycle of culture', representation, identity and regulation—are given fairly equal consideration. It is of particular interest here that the authors seek to 'emphasize the way in which production and consumption are interrelated and overlap' and stress 'how design is centrally located at this [intermediary] point'.[176] Such an approach would be highly advantageous in design history, where negotiations and mediations between producers/designers and users/consumers provide excellent access to understanding design as material culture.

The impact of material culture studies in general and Daniel Miller's work on design history in particular is personified in Alison J. Clarke, who graduated in design history and went on to earn a PhD in anthropology under the supervision of Miller. She has since moved closer to home in terms of institutional surroundings and research communities more typical of design history.[177] Her work has been published, for example in anthologies edited by Miller,[178] but the cross-fertilization of material culture studies and design history is probably most evident in her 1999 book *Tupperware—The Promise of Plastic in 1950s America*.[179] In terms of a material culture studies approach to design history, the major virtue of the book is that Clarke manages to combine the former's concern for consumption with the latter's insistence on the materiality of the designed object in all its complex relations. The result is a highly inclusive design history encompassing the invention, design, technology, and manufacture, as well as the marketing, retailing, reception, consumption and use of the artefacts in question.

Clarke argues that processes of social and cultural mediation are formative even of seemingly trivial artefacts. Another appealing, but somewhat underdeveloped, approach is how consumers, dealers, distributors, sales managers and product testers are all seen as contributors to the formal product design process.[180] In her conclusion, Clarke makes the very sound claim that 'The "success" of a specific design cannot be traced to one monolithic process but is the result of a multitude of frequently conflicting forces and agents that make up the dynamic between production and consumption.'[181] Nevertheless, the production side of material culture—questions pertaining to design strategies, production technology and manufacturing process—is highly underrepresented and rather compendiously treated. The book is thus a testament to material culture studies' preference for consumption over production.

Another design historian who has taken a particular interest in material culture studies is Judy Attfield. In a review essay on the relationship between material culture studies and design history she sought 'to point out the relation between the decline in confidence in deterministic production models for the interpretation of the history of design with the increase in interest in consumption and material culture as a less rigid framework for the investigation of the relationship between designed objects and those persons and institutions who conceive, produce, sell, buy and use them'.[182] Attfield considered one of the prime virtues of the material culture studies approach to design history to be 'that it does not exclude any artefact or part of the mundane everyday object-world and meant venturing into territories that were once considered beyond the pale'.[183] While lauding material culture studies' efficiency as an antidote to 'the heroic approach' and as a catalyst for consumption studies in design history, she also identified some more problematic aspects of the field's recent proliferation. One of these was the insistence on eluding debates on the field's scope and concerns, making it difficult to survey, assess and employ in a satisfactorily grounded manner. More interesting, however, is that Attfield, echoing the aforementioned criticism by Charles Saumarez Smith, expressed a concern that some strands of material culture studies seem inept at coping with the materiality of objects.[184]

It follows that the ambition to address the physical materiality of artefacts underpins Attfield's 2000 book *Wild Things—The Material Culture of Everyday Life*. Informed by her interest in material culture studies, the book investigates questions of design and identity, the meanings of human–object relations and the social life of things. An introductory statement reads: 'So what I have called here "the material culture of everyday life", acknowledges the physical object in all its materiality and encompasses the work of design, making, distributing, consuming, using, discarding, recycling and so on.'[185] Except for an interesting case study of a reproduction period furniture manufacturer (based on excerpts from the author's doctoral dissertation), however,

Attfield's *Wild Things* rarely considers the pre-commodified stages of arte-facts, thus leaving it open to the previously outlined critique of material culture studies: its insufficient interest in the relations between the spheres of production and consumption. The pertinence of this critique is only enhanced by Attfield's later statement that a key disparity between design history and material culture studies is that in design history, 'work and production are considered as important as the consumption and appropriation of things in analysing material culture'.[186]

It should be clear now that design historians have greeted the anthropo-logical strand of material culture studies with a great deal of interest and enthusiasm and a fair amount of sound criticism. Like most of his colleagues, Victor Margolin has also acknowledged the value of Daniel Miller's research on consumption for design studies, especially his thesis that 'consumption is not a passive act, but a creative project through which people put products to use in ways that were not necessarily intended by those who designed and produced them. Miller has thus broadened the context within which to study products in *contemporary* culture.'[187]

What is most interesting about Margolin's comment is not so much the acknowledgement of Miller's work, but rather the implicit criticism that it has less value for historical studies. This leads to perhaps the most weighty criticism of material culture studies seen from a historian's perspective: the uneasy leap from the usually contemporary scene or concern of social sci-ence to that of history. Typically, Kenneth L. Ames questioned the immediate usefulness of material culture studies to design historians, arguing that its habitual method, ethnography, 'works best when used in the present, that is when scholars can talk to and observe living people.'[188] Reviewing Miller's 1998 edited volume *Material Cultures: Why Some Things Matter*, Ames ob-served that 'The studies in this book rely on historical background to varying degrees but all emphasize the present or very recent past. Historical studies necessarily draw on different forms of data.'[189]

But even when non-historians do engage the past, historians are often re-luctant, worrying about how other fields and disciplines appropriate history. Their attitude towards historical sociology, for instance, has at times been

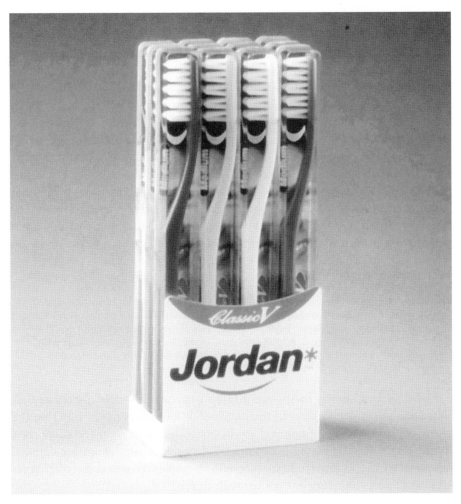

6 Historical studies of consumption and use involve methodological challenges. How can we get at the user experience of products long gone and forgotten? Jordan AS, T-14 toothbrush, 1973. Design: Lars Hjelle. Copyright Norwegian Design Council

rather apprehensive. What happens to historical knowledge when it is used by and represented in other scholarly contexts? Concerned about history's position in the recent reorganization of disciplinary structures in academia, Carolyn Steedman asked: how historical is cultural studies? As she observed, there is no doubt that cultural studies does contain many historical components, but their quality may very well be questionable. She warned against treating history haphazardly, as bits and pieces of readily applicable knowledge, and worried about the status of history's traditional quality assurance standard: the scrutinizing practices of archive research and differentiating source analysis. Furthermore; historians normally acknowledge the impermanence of their research results. Whereas such an acknowledgement does not render the temporariness of their knowledge particularly problematic to historians themselves, '[i]t may matter . . . when text-based historical knowledge is removed from the narrative and cognitive frame of historical practice, and used in another field.'[190] She went on to explain the possible perils:

> It has been observed before what can happen to the written history in these circumstances: it loses its impermanence . . . The historical item (the bit of written history) taken out of its narrative setting in order to explain something else (an event, a development, a structure) is stabilized, made a building block for a different structure of explanation. This has been observed, for the main part, in the use of the written history within sociological explanation. It is probably the case that within British cultural studies . . . history meets the same fate as it has within sociology.[191]

There is the danger, then—according to Steedman—that history suffers abuse and misunderstanding in the hands of other disciplines,[192] and that the historical components of cultural studies become mere props or supporting acts used for legitimatizing purposes: 'Will there be any room for detailed historical work; or are students of cultural studies bound to rely on great schematic and secondary sweeps through time?'[193]

As indicated by the previous mention of museology as the second strand of material culture studies, the concept also refers to the main subject of this discipline—also known as museum studies. One of the protagonists of this field is Susan Pearce. What characterizes this strand of material culture studies is a particular focus on the study of artefacts within the context of museums, critically analysing policies and practices of collecting, curating and exhibiting.[194]

A particularly appealing side to the museum studies approach to the interpretation of objects is its appreciation of and insistence on the multitude of types of meanings that objects may possess or convey. Both the historical, utilitarian, emotional, symbolic and political aspects of objects' meanings are considered legitimate approaches to the study of material culture.[195] Furthermore, the various meanings of things are seen as developing as an interactive process between object and subject.[196] This dynamic understanding of the creation of meaning as a sort of co-production allows for a more active object, but at the same time steers clear of material determinism.

Museum studies is closely linked to museum practice (acquisitive, curatorial and exhibitive) with its hands-on approach to objects. Its greatest potential methodological contribution to design history, then, might perhaps lie in micro-level object analysis, providing an alternative to traditional art historical methods and semiotics. The tendency in discussions on theory and methodology is not to discriminate between widely different types of objects, be they Bronze Age tools, Renaissance paintings or eighteenth-century tombstones. To a design historian this may be both liberating and frustrating—tending perhaps towards the latter because industrial goods seem to be virtually absent. It is important to keep in mind, though, that the objects under scrutiny in design history are often not conventional museum pieces—just as they are not works of art or just signs.[197] Also, museum studies seems prone to the same bias towards the post-objectified phases of artefacts' lives as does consumption studies and thus may be of limited value to design historians trying to understand the complexities of design processes and production systems as integral to material culture.[198]

The third and last of the three strands of material culture studies to be considered here is most decidedly both historical and sensitive to the materiality of artefacts. While being even more resistant to definition and delimitation than consumption studies and museology, it might be loosely described as comprising archaeologists, art historians and historians of science and technology with a particular interest in the object as historical source and the relation between matter and meaning. As evidenced by the titles of three central works in this area, the core concerns are: How can we write *History from Things*?[199] What could we be *Learning from Things*?[200] How can we understand *Things That Talk*?[201] The object as source is the governing idea of this otherwise disparate and interdisciplinary field. As Steven Lubar and W. David Kingery write in their introduction to *History from Things*:

> Historians traditionally use documents rather than artifacts in their effort to understand the past. But the artifact-document dichotomy is to a great extent artificial; documents are a species of artifact . . . By neglecting all but a narrow class of artifacts, those with writing on them, historians have missed opportunities . . . Not only do artifacts present new evidence to support historical arguments; they also suggest new arguments and provide a level of rhetorical support to arguments that mere documents cannot begin to approach. Artifacts, especially when used in conjunction with the sorts of history gleaned from documentary sources, widen our view of history as they increase the evidence for historical interpretations.[202]

This take on material culture studies not only aims to unify artefacts and documents as sources but also aims at a wide coalition of subjects and approaches: 'It is hoped that material culture studies can bring together performance and production, consumers and creators, men and women, diachronic and synchronic, tools and signs, practicality and aesthetics, societies and cultures in a way that enlightens a wide, multidisciplinary audience.'[203]

By insisting on assessing the overall life cycle of artefacts and thus de-emphasizing the conventional production-consumption divide, Lubar, Kingery and others achieve a better distributed set of approaches than those promoted by Daniel Miller, for example, who was discussed earlier. This is most urgently expressed in the contribution by Ruth Oldenziel: 'The static economic dichotomy between production and consumption that underlay many concepts in the history of technology represents the most stubborn taxonomy of all . . . Production and consumption are not separate affairs, but constitute each other.'[204] Sustaining the need to historicize this dynamic relation, Oldenziel and colleagues have elsewhere argued that 'It is at this juncture of mediation [between production and consumption] that social actors and institutions negotiated the mediated design and the appropriation of new products and technologies.'[205] It should be clear, then, that not only are production and

consumption not separate affairs, but—as Kingery points out: 'Design, manufacture, distribution, and use are all activities involving cultural constraints
and social organization.'[206] Another simplistic but resilient dichotomy that is
challenged repeatedly in these essays is the notion of artefact as tool—artefact
as symbol. Criticizing both the old functionalist views and the linguistically
derived semiotics, it is here asserted that any artefact is always both tool and
symbol—and that the relation between the two is complex and dynamic and
subject to changes in time, situations and culture.

7 Even the most tool-like artefact is never *just* a tool—there is always also a symbolic component to it. AS Indre Østfold
Industrier, Norseaxe foldable sporting axe, 1985. Design: John Gulbrandsrød. Copyright Norwegian Design Council

Both *History from Things* and *Learning from Things* resulted from conferences, recognized for their interdisciplinary take on material culture, that were held at the Smithsonian Institution. To design historians, though, their empirical subject matter may be considered too disparate. As Victor Margolin laconically stated: 'These two conferences were important to the field for their focus on methodological issues . . . In neither conference volume, however, was there any mention of design.'[207] Margolin has a point insofar as the Smithsonian volumes are not, and do not purport to be, design history. They do include topics of less than immediate interest to industrial design historians, such as Chinese bronze vessels from around 1000 BC, eighteenth-century English gardens and anthropological metallurgy. Still, Margolin's remark appears unfair because they also include highly relevant and interesting essays with more than a fair mention of design.[208] Thus, one might interpret Margolin's criticism not so much as a claim that the books in question disregard design per se—but that he would have welcomed a greater concern for industrial goods and the industrial design process.

In addition to the contributions already mentioned, the historians of technology in particular made some important contributions—especially on methodological questions—that are of great value to design historians: Robert Friedel 'suggest[ed] that our understanding of history from things also should begin with the materials that go into our artifacts', seeing as 'The material itself conveys messages, metaphorical and otherwise, about the objects and their place in a culture.'[209] More abstract, but equally convincing is Steven Lubar's bid for a political history of machine design.[210] Acknowledging the indirect learning from things in which historians of technology and design engage in—the historians' tacit knowledge, as it were—Joseph Corn lamented that 'Even in an object-centered speciality like the history of technology, being "objective" paradoxically may require suppressing experience with actual objects.'[211] Very different but equally thought-provoking is Michael Brian Schiffer's account of the methodological problems of source research in the study of industrial products and manufacturers belonging to the fringes of the industrial community.[212] Despite their very divergent focuses and approaches, these works are of considerable value to anyone interested in artefacts as sources of knowledge and material culture in general—design historians included.

The more recent volume, *Things That Talk* is just as varied in subject matter and just as intriguing in its examination of the significance of artefacts. As expected, the contributors have quite diverging views on how literally the book title is to be understood. At the one end of the spectrum, the art historian Joseph Koerner acknowledges that objects are 'effective generators of discourse', but refuses any further concessions: 'while I don't believe that the things I write about physically speak to me, there is something satisfying about pretending they do'.[213] The historian of science Peter Galison, on the other hand, seems to go a long way in granting artefacts—in this case the inkblot cards used by psychologists in the Rorschach test—not only a voice of their own but also a highly authoritative one at that: 'Not only did these cards talk; they did so in the virtue of their form and color down to the smallest detail.'[214] Most of the authors, however, take a stand somewhere in between, seeing artefacts as both inarticulate and loquacious, both compliant and defiant. Making things talk—to historians and to historical actors—thus becomes a matter of coaxing, translation, negotiation and networking. One example is Simon Schaffer's demonstration of how different interest groups and the spheres of art, advertisement, industry and science in nineteenth-century Britain strove to make a highly ephemeral and unstable object—soap bubbles—talk correctly and favourably.[215] Despite their at times disturbingly disparate subject matters, these three volumes on thinking about things represent a strand of material culture studies that has a lot to offer design historians in terms of how to approach material artefacts.

As expected, no coherent conclusion has been reached here regarding the merits of material culture studies or its value to design history. When faced with a field of study and subject matter so disparate and comprehensive in terms of theoretical and methodological traditions and empirical foci, such an aspiration would be most overzealous. Yet this chapter has explored some of material culture studies' possibilities and potentials, problems and perils as seen from a design history perspective.

Highlighting the dual role of material objects in design history Raimonda Riccini has proposed that this discipline has the potential to bridge what she sees as a divide between two groups of approaches to the history of material culture: Those considering objects to be the *subject* of historical research (history *of* artefacts) and those considering objects to be *documents* of historical research (history *through* artefacts): 'It is my hypothesis that the history of industrial design represents an opportunity for an integration of these two approaches, an integration in which artifacts would be treated as both *subjects* and as *documents* of research.'[216]

Moving from material culture studies to a cultural history of design, it is befitting to mention an instructive lesson provided by Steven Lubar in *Learning From Things*: 'A technological artifact should be regarded as, to use [Clifford] Geertz' term, a "cultural phenomenon," like any other cultural phenomenon, because it makes for better historical explanation.'[217] Substituting designed/ design for Lubar's technological/technology, if we privilege design—or more commonly in design history; privilege some narrow, culturally constructed niche of design—and do not consider design part of culture, there is a risk of being tossed back to the heroic approach of the Pevsnerian tradition. Because, as Artemis Yagou has argued:

> Designing does not primarily have to do with specifying the formal attributes of an artifact or system, as in the case of conventional art and design historical understanding, but with expressing the cultural content of this artifact or system. In this sense, it may be further argued that the history of design could be conceived not as a history of objects but of ideas.[218]

Whereas in the latter part of her argument Yagou introduces an unnecessary dichotomy—the history of design is best conceived as a history of *both* ideas and objects—her call for an increased emphasis on design as culture is most laudable.

Towards a Cultural History of Design

This chapter began with an assertion that design is not art and that design history should hence not be considered part of or equivalent to art history. However, substituting the wider notion of culture for art results in a completely different situation. It should be quite clear from the previous discussions that design is a thoroughly cultural phenomenon; consequently, design history can be approached as cultural history.

Whereas historians have traditionally flocked to political history and later to social history, cultural history has experienced a considerable upsurge and renewal over the past decades. So much so, in fact, to warrant the epithet 'the new cultural history'.[219] Like the new art history discussed earlier, it is a complex and heterogeneous movement and thus cannot be treated extensively here. A good starting point for an introduction, though, could be one of the most representative and influential works in the field, *The New Cultural History* edited by Lynn Hunt.[220] The 1989 book examines existing models, theories and methodologies for the history of culture and presents examples of new research on a variety of topics.

But what good can come of enlisting industrial design as part of the subject matter for cultural history? As Hunt warns: 'without developing [some] sense of cohesion or interaction between topics, . . . a cultural history defined topically could degenerate into an endless search for new cultural practices to describe'.[221] For design history the benefits consist of a cure for myopia. A cultural history of design help design historians see design as 'any other cultural phenomenon'—that is not giving privilege to the artefacts, actors, institutions and structures studied. As Lubar stated, it simply 'makes for better historical explanation', as a broader outlook facilitates unforeseen contexts, relations and connections.

As an early contribution to the new cultural history, the book can be seen as an attempt to further a sense of cohesion or interaction between topics, and it is thus somewhat cautious and tentative in its form. As Hunt concludes in her introduction: 'For the moment, as this volume shows, the accent in cultural history is on close examination—of texts, of pictures, and of actions—and on open-mindedness to what those examinations will reveal, rather than on elaboration of new master narratives or social theories.'[222] The new cultural history involves critical examinations of Marxism, the Annales school, Michel Foucault's archaeology of knowledge[223] and more recent poststructuralist approaches,[224] but it does not propose a new grand theory. As a theoretically tolerant and topically inclusive field, cultural history thus provides fertile ground for developing new histories of design.

A decade later, Hunt teamed up with sociologist Victoria Bonnell for a reassessment of the new cultural history through their 1999 *Beyond the Cultural Turn*.[225] One of their main general concerns here is to move beyond the old trench warfare between positivism and relativism, acknowledging that culture is neither a mere reflection of more fundamental structures nor entirely symbolic or linguistic: 'The focus on practice, narrative, and embodiment—whether of whole cultures, social groups, or individual selves—is meant to bypass that dilemma and restore a sense of social embeddedness without reducing everything to its social determinants.'[226] Cultural history, then, must not only accept this complexity and the difficult dynamics of historical development but also readily 'emphasize the relational process of identity formation, the conflict between competing narratives, the inherent tension between culture viewed as a system and culture viewed as practice, and the inevitable strain between continuity and transformation'.[227]

On a more particular level, and of principle interest here, is Bonnell and Hunt's recognition of the primacy of material culture as subject matter in recent cultural history. They describe material culture as

> one of the arenas in which culture and social life most obviously and significantly intersect, where culture takes concrete form and those concrete forms make cultural codes more explicit. Work on furniture, guns, or clothing—to name some of the most striking examples—draws our attention to the material ways in which culture becomes part of everyday social experience and therefore becomes susceptible to change.[228]

In other words; Bonnell and Hunt all but declare the cultural history of design to be not only part of but at the very forefront of cultural history.

Perhaps many, or even most, design historians would claim that their work falls under a broader notion of cultural history. Still, design historians rarely make reference to the new cultural history (one exception being Stephen Hayward).[229] Cultural historians studying design, on the other hand, seem to be fewer and farther between. The difference can be hard to define and is probably not all that important either. The pivotal claim for a cultural history of design is that one sees design not as a privileged subject matter but in principle as any other cultural phenomenon.

This historiographical survey concludes with a brief mention of three recent books by cultural historians who in convincing ways have studied industrial design as a cultural phenomenon. First, Jeffrey Meikle's widely acclaimed 1995 book, *American Plastic—A Cultural History*, can be considered a cultural history of design although it has proven pertinent to many fields.[230] A scholar of American studies—itself an interdisciplinary field—Meikle moved into the field of design history with his 1979 book on American interwar industrial design and has recently made another important contribution to the field's survey literature with his 2005 *Design in the USA*.[231]

With its far less conventional approach, *American Plastic* takes a road less travelled. Instead of sorting its subject matter by biographies, professional categories, chronological periods, design styles, industry segments, product types or other traditional classifications, Meikle uses the material—plastic—as an entry point, allowing him to pry open a cross section of all the aforementioned concepts and many more. The book's core concern, though, is to trace the many and complex negotiations through which the many and shifting cultural identities of plastic have been formed and transformed through time and society. As the design, mediation and reception of plastic products are protagonists of these fascinating negotiations, there should be no doubt that *American Plastic* is in full a cultural history of design. Nonetheless, it has a much broader appeal, something that can be illustrated by the fact that the book won the 1996 Dexter Prize from the Society for the History of Technology.

Another cultural history of design that resists easy categorization is the Regina Lee Blaszczyk's 2000 *Imagining Consumers—Design and Innovation from Wedgwood to Corning*.[232] It could just as rightfully be claimed for business history or the history of technology, a trait that only makes it all the more interesting as a cultural history of design.[233] *Imagining Consumers* shares the interest in consumption characteristic of the material culture studies approach discussed earlier. But this book is not so much about consumption patterns and practices, but is more about how manufacturers, by way of what Blaszczyk denotes as intermediaries—for example retailers, wholesal-ers, buyers, salespeople, advertising executives, market researchers, home economists, designers—strove to *imagine* consumers' needs and desires in order to design and develop commercially successful products. Blaszczyk thus proposes a very promising approach to bridging the production–consumption gap: 'Focusing on these fashion brokers as the primary agents of innovation turns the canon of design history inside out and upside down.'[234] In doing so, she is completely in line with the aforementioned proposition to focus on the arenas of negotiations between production and consumption put forward in various wordings by design historians John Heskett, John A. Walker and Grace Lees-Maffei[235] and by historians of technology Ruth Oldenziel and colleagues and Johan Schot and Adri Albert de la Bruheze.[236] In clear agreement with Blaszczyk, although using the term mediators rather that intermediaries,[237] the latter two observe that 'Mediation as a process of mutual articulation and alignment is influenced not only by the work of producers and users but also by the work of mediators and by the existence of institutional loci and arenas for mediation work.'[238]

As a piece of design history, *Imagining Consumers* strongly dissociates itself from the heroic approach:

> In terms of design, this book also departs from the reigning paradigms that emphasize elite objects and dismiss mass-market artifacts. Invented by connoisseurs, the notion of 'good taste' obfuscates the diversity of Americans' material preferences and the messi-ness of the design process . . . For students of consumerism, however, the 'masterpiece' approach is inherently flawed. Its emphasis on high-class definitions of beauty denies the historical significance of commonplace items, the building blocks of popular culture.[239]

Although Blaszczyk's insistence on a design history more attuned to ev-eryday, ordinary, mass-market products and her efforts to examine a more complex and entangled design process are commendable, one might ask how long it is necessary and legitimate to keep on castigating the masterpiece ap-proach. Whereas such work surely still is being produced, the amount of more progressive recent research could indicate that the masterpiece approach can no longer be said to represent the reigning paradigms of design history.[240]

The third and last example of a cultural history of design is Paul Betts's 2004 book *The Authority of Everyday Objects—A Cultural History of West German Design*.[241] In his study of postwar West German industrial design, Betts takes a stand as a cultural historian who has chosen to study industrial design because it is an interesting cultural phenomenon. This apparently self-evident observation is important because this attitude and approach are essential in avoiding the treatment of design as some sort of privileged sphere and escaping the unfortunate situation in which—according to Betts—'design has yet to be fully accepted into mainstream scholarship, not least because it is still seen as a splashy academic newcomer whose achievements are better placed on the coffee table than the scholarly bookshelf'.[242]

The analytical approach makes the book so refreshing—not the subject matter, which is fairly conventional. One of the most obvious omissions is that of vehicles. Of course, demarcations of subject matter must be made, but one might argue that a history of German industrial design devoid of cars, airplanes and trains does seem somewhat skewed. Betts recognizes the limitations of these choices, and clarifies that his study does not pretend to cover the full spectrum of industrial design, but rather deals with a more limited sphere of everyday household objects (and the institutions involved with their negotiations): 'But unlike other design studies, this book is no detailed monograph on any one of these object groups. Of uppermost concern here is why these commonplace wares assumed such heightened cultural significance in the 1950s.'[243] Betts's objective is thus not so much to revise the customary demarcations and categories of traditional design history, but rather to enmesh design in the wider realm of cultural history.

Within its defined scope, two of the book's major arguments are particularly stimulating. The first is an extensive and patent line of reasoning demonstrating that the Nazi period did *not*—as the mythopoeics of much modernist histories would have it—represent a rupture in German modernist design.[244] The second is a comprehensive and well-balanced treatment of the 'unholy' but very popular 1950s design style derogatorily nicknamed *Nierentisch* (kidney table), especially the strategies by which the design elites sought to convince people that these organic, modern forms were not the *correct* modernist design advocated by themselves.[245] As argued earlier, such design, not conforming to the ideals of the modernist design elites, has all too often been ignored in traditional design history.

Pointing out these three books by Meikle, Blaszczyk and Betts rather than other books does imply that they are considered exemplary in some sense. But exemplary does not mean ideal. These books are examples more than exemplars. They are good demonstrations of how cultural histories of design can look, but this is not to say that one should emulate them. What they have in common, and what makes them relevant examples in this discussion, is first of all a broad approach to their subject matter, where design is culture, and design history is cultural history. In different ways they are all very inclusive in terms of the kind of material and questions considered relevant and interesting to a history of design. Furthermore, these books demonstrate the advantages of moving back and forth between things and thoughts, between mind and matter, between the ideal and the real—an approach that makes for good design history.

This historiographical survey has explored how design history has developed over the past decades and has charted some of the major debates and concerns that have shaped the field. As the chapter also outlines some characteristics of what is considered to be good design history, it seems appropriate to ask how this ambition is to be achieved. The next chapter will discuss some theoretical and methodological concepts from an adjacent field of study that have been little explored in design history. These concepts might prove to be a rewarding import that can help lift the shadow of art history further from the discipline of design history.

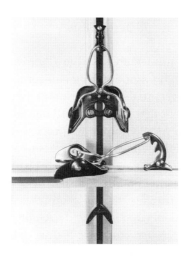

2

Theory and Methodology

The field of study that should be of interest to a design history disengaged from connoisseurship and canonicity could be described as *the seamless web of sociodesign*. This term is a paraphrase of a metaphor well-established in the history of technology: *the seamless web of sociotechnology*. This term was coined as the field moved away from the traditional distinctions between technical, social, economic and political aspects of technological development. The seminal work of Thomas Hughes on sociotechnical systems was highly influential in this respect.[1] In his studies of how electric power networks were built and developed, he found that many of the most prominent actors and problems in the development process were not of a technological nature per se but spanned a vast array of topics and fields, such as law, economics and politics.[2] The point is that technology is not formed in isolation from society—technology and society are formed and transformed simultaneously and in correlation.[3]

Hughes's analysis is not the main issue here, but paraphrasing the metaphor of the seamless web supplies a notion that can serve as a basis for constructing a theoretical and conceptual framework and a methodological repertoire for historical studies of design.[4] The underlying analogy of the paraphrase should be fairly evident. As phenomenon, process and result, design has as little autonomy as technology does. Therefore, one should consider the relation between society and design as a seamless web of sociodesign.

As argued in the previous chapter, design history does not have a very well-defined theoretical framework and methodological apparatus, nor has this seemed to be a particularly prioritized area of inquiry. The many problematic aspects of the heritage from art history have been recognized and questioned, but the field could do with a more thorough debate on these matters. The exploration of alternative, additional and complementary references and sources of inspiration has begun, but few excursions have been made in the direction proposed in this chapter's examination of recent developments in the sociology and history of technology.

As the old notion of design as some sort of applied art becomes increasingly untenable in design practice, design research and design history, it could be argued that design has more in common with technology when considered as a social and cultural phenomenon. Thus, design historians may find that the sociology and history of technology can provide a very appropriate theoretical framework and methodological repertoire for studying design. This chapter discusses some concepts from these adjacent fields that might be of particular value to design history.

History of Technology, SCOT and STS

At the turn of the century, after exhibiting locomotives and scientific instruments side by side with furniture and textiles for several decades, London's South Kensington Museum (which opened in 1857 in the wake of the Great Exhibition of the Works of Industry of all Nations of 1851) was divided and became what are now two separate institutions: the Science Museum and the Victoria and Albert Museum. Without reading too much into the decision, this still seems to be an emblematic event in the separation of the historical representations of the spheres of science and technology on the one hand and design and the decorative arts on the other. John Heskett has observed that the occasional overlap in exhibited objects between the two museums does not mitigate the divide much: 'Wedgwood pottery may be shown at the Science Museum, but in the context of an exhibition on the scientific research of Josiah Wedgwood. Radios have been exhibited at the V and A, but with technical developments being subordinate to aesthetic considerations.'[5] A reunion of the two London museums is most unlikely, but design historians and historians of technology should strive not to perpetuate the division of labour epitomized by the institutional structure of this example.

In a special section on technology and design in a 1997 issue of *Technology and Culture*, the Society for the History of Technology's journal, Barry Katz described the industrial designer as one 'who domesticates new technology and makes it available for human use', and on this basis he argued for tighter bonds between the history of technology and design history: 'This mutual dependency suggests that at the very least the study of design can be deepened by an exposure to the more deeply rooted history of technology, and the study of technology invigorated by new tendencies in the history and theory of design.'[6] There is much to gain from accepting this challenge and exploring the potential of a closer integration and interaction between the history of technology and design history.[7]

To make a crude and certainly unjust generalization, one might say that historians of technology have been occupied predominantly with the content and performance of artefacts (and systems) whereas design historians have traditionally focused on their aesthetics and appearance. Despite the obvious simplification of such a divide, it should be evident that there is a great potential for synergy effects in crossing back and forth. Some historians of technology, such as Thomas Hughes, James Flink and Wiebe Bijker, have already proved the vantages of such cross-fertilization[8] but have by no means exhausted its promise. Much recent design history, by such writers as Jeffrey Meikle, David Gartman and Alison Clarke,[9] has much to contribute to a joint venture, especially by embedding the nuts and bolts in contexts of form, image, identity, ideology and meaning.

8 Design historians are becoming more attentive to the history of technology while historians of technology are showing a greater interest in design history, as there is a considerable overlap between the two disciplines. Tomra Systems ASA, Can-Can reverse vending machine for aluminium beverage cans, 1984. Design: Roy Tandberg. Copyright Tomra Systems ASA

Through its concern for the complexity and multi-dimensionality of technological development, the history of technology has provided good models for understanding design processes beyond the mystique of artistic creation. The major merit of design history is its ability to analyse and critically reflect on the seemingly erratic and less palpable aspects of the material culture. As Dennis Doordan put it, 'Design historians . . . recognize as eloquent what most historians find mute: things. Design history's insight into the eloquence of things is one of its most distinctive contributions to history as a general field of intellectual endeavour.'[10] Just how important design history can be to the history of technology has been neatly pointed out by Henry Petroski: 'Understanding how and why our physical surroundings look and work the way they do provides considerable insight into the nature of technological change and the workings of even the most complex of modern technology.'[11] Of course, design history is not just about the way things look and work, in other words, how technology is given form. The aesthetics, ethics, symbolism, authority and emotivity of artefacts take on a whole new level of meaning and significance when inscribed in ideological, political, social, cultural and consumption contexts.

The merits and challenges of design history was the topic of chapter one, so here the scope will be limited to a brief discussion of how some historians of technology have dealt with industrial design and how this might benefit design history. The aforementioned journal *Technology and Culture* could have served as an arena for this discussion, but the topic is too voluminous to survey briefly.[12] Instead, this chapter will focus on a few central books, and it is only fitting that Thomas Hughes's work makes up the first example.

Hughes's widely acclaimed 1989 book on the history of technology in the United States, *American Genesis*, provides the best entry point.[13] Even if viewed as a history of technology proper, this book is not only highly insightful, convincing and well-composed, but it is also packed with material of great value to design historians, embracing as it does a wide range of topics from invention to scientific practice, engineering, product development, production systems, industrial management, technological systems, economics and politics. However, *American Genesis* has more to offer design historians than this sort of thick complementary insight; it contains elements of more specific design history as well. This is particularly true of the chapter devoted to how European designers, architects and artists envisioned and interpreted American industry and technology in their advocacy of a genuinely modern culture.[14]

The originality in Hughes's treatment of design lies primarily on the contextual level, that he at all incorporates the subject in a project fundamentally about the history of technology. His selection of subject matter within this field, however, is rather conventional, focusing on famous and heroic figures like Peter Behrens, Walter Gropius and Le Corbusier. Much the same can be said of the chapter on technology and culture in his more recent book, *Human-Built World*.[15] Given his stance as a historian of technology, it is also somewhat surprising that he devotes more attention to architecture and art than to industrial design. Furthermore, the material is structured in such a manner that in Hughes's account, design is placed in the category of cultural factors, something that to a design historian appears to counteract a close enough integration of design into his otherwise pervasive sociotechnical systems. In the case of design, it might thus seem as though his web is not quite seamless enough.

Another reputable American historian of technology, Ruth Schwartz Cowan, is the author of the one book from this discipline that probably has had the most profound influence on design history. Her 1983 *More Work for Mother*—a study presenting a fresh approach to the history of household technology and appliances—effectively challenges the conventional technological/social and production/consumption dichotomies and has been a strong source of inspiration, especially for feminist design historians.[16] In a more recent publication, *A Social History of American Technology*, these perspectives are further cultivated and applied to a wider subject matter in a broadly synthetic work. Based on the premise that *Homo faber* (man the maker) is just as appropriate a name for the human species as is *Homo sapiens* (man the wise), Cowan here argues that

The *social* history of technology . . . integrat[es] the history of technology with the rest of human history. It assumes that objects have affected the ways in which people work, govern, cook, transport, communicate: the ways in which they live. It also assumes that the ways in which people live have affected the objects that they invent, manufacture, and use. A social history of technology, in short, assumes a mutual relationship between society and technology: it also assumes that changes in one can, and have, induced changes in the other.[17]

The relevance to design history is so evident and important that it made Victor Margolin comment that 'the overlap between Cowan's social history of technology with material that would be suitable for a history of design' gave hope for a future, 'more broadly constituted history of design'.[18]

A good example of Cowan's approach that is particularly relevant to design history is her account of innovation in nineteenth-century America. The genius individual is certainly acknowledged but not romanticized.[19] Cowan stresses that innovation—both invention, development and diffusion—is fundamentally collaborative (just as design is, one might add). Yes, Cowan introduces Thomas Edison and Alexander Graham Bell, but she also introduces their collaborators, whose resources and services were essential to inventive development—be that technical and scientific skills, mechanical dexterity, draughtsmanship, legal advice, financial counsel. Even those providing food and emotional support are—at least symbolically—acknowledged, plus, of course, those who put up the financial backing and managerial systems.[20] The importance and influence of the light bulb and the telephone—both as technologies and as inventions—are far better understood when viewed as systems rather than as singular phenomena. In other words; both people and objects become more eloquent when considered parts of collectives and systems. By the same token, Cowan's account of the emergence of the American System of Manufacture is appealing because she gives due attention to the economic and political interests not merely as background factors but as integrated elements of the system.[21] However, because of Cowan's focus on large sociotechnical systems and her ambition to cover many subjects over three centuries, her attention to product development and design is limited—although some passages, such as her account of the intricate workings of the military-industrial-academic complex in the development of military and commercial aircraft design after World War II, form notable exceptions.[22]

Whereas Cowan's project is a *social* history of technology, a recent book by Mikael Hård and Andrew Jamison, *Hubris and Hybrids*, proposes a *cultural* history of technology.[23] In terms of geography, time span and topics, this book paints an even broader historical canvas, but its more frequent selection of examples from industrial design and the matching of technological ideas with industrial practice make it highly relevant to design history.

Hård and Jamison call their approach to history 'cultural appropriation', which is described as 'a process by which novelty is brought under human control; it is a matter of re-creating our societies and our selves so that new products and concepts make sense'. This approach is very enticing, much because it allows for more complex narratives than traditional ones—such as those classic narrative strategies Hayden White has dubbed romance and tragedy (the heroic approach and its more recent opposite). By way of cultural appropriation, the authors strive to tell 'dialectical stories of hybridization, of combination, both in terms of practice and identities, institutions and organizations, and discourses and disciplines'.[24]

However, when it comes to design, results of these promises of complexity, hybridization and combination are hard to find. Most of the material related to design is placed in a chapter on artistic appropriation, and design is described as 'popular art'.[25] Designers (and design theoreticians) are discussed alongside painters, photographers and poets and are thus classified as artists. The focus on form and aesthetics as well as heroic figures results in an account that rarely surpasses the master narrative of design history—although the contextualization here is a somewhat different and more interesting one.[26] In this respect, Hård and Jamison's treatment of design resembles that of Thomas Hughes.

Surely, this criticism is somewhat unfair. *Hubris and Hybrids* is not a book on design history, and as it is a very broad and highly synthetic work, it could hardly be expected to provide any exhaustive analysis of a century's development of design. The authors have chosen this format in purposeful opposition to what they consider a tendency among historians of technology 'to write ever more detailed accounts of ever more limited scope'.[27]

The simple fact that *Hubris and Hybrids* is co-authored by a historian and a sociologist can exemplify the increasing interaction and cooperation in recent history and sociology of technology. This tendency is in keeping with developments in the broader parent fields after the so-called cultural/linguistic/historic turn in history and sociology in general, which has led to a blurring of the disciplinary borders. The mutual rapprochement can perhaps be described as a 'nervous romance': historians' interest in sociological theory and methods has given rise to scepticism and enthusiasm in both camps, as has sociologists' engagement with history.[28] Bearing the fundamental differences between history and sociology in mind, there is much to gain from developing the interaction and cooperation already en route and of which Hård and Jamison's work is a good example.

Another example is the thorough theoretical contribution to the history of technology made by Wibe E. Bijker, especially in his 1995 book, *Of Bicycles, Bakelites, and Bulbs*.[29] Typical of most sociologists, Bijker's primary concern seems to be with the formulation of theory, and the book's agenda is thus—as the subtitle reveals—to propose a theory of sociotechnical change. Although this effort is both commendable and highly interesting, another aspect of the book is of interest here. To formulate his theory of sociotechnical change, Bijker analyses three comprehensive case studies from the history of technology: bicycles, Bakelites and bulbs (or rather, fluorescent lighting). Only the first two will be commented on here.

Just how relevant this book is to design historians becomes strikingly evident in the first of the three case studies, which is actually more of a history of design than a history of technology. Here, Bijker meticulously maps and analyses the development of the design of the bicycle from its invention through a myriad of mutations, modifications, marvels and misfits until the conceptual layout and formal configuration stabilized as one that can be recognized in the design of today's bicycles. Through its thick description approach, this account introduces some of the core concepts of Bijker's theory of sociotechnical change, such as the crucial role of a wide variety of what he calls 'relevant social groups' and their attention to different problems and solutions in the development process, and the dismantling of the linear evolutionary model so common in traditional history of technology.[30] This study is thus especially valuable to any design historian interested in typological development.

Bijker continues the construction of the conceptual frame for his theory of sociotechnical change in the second case study, the Bakelite innovation process. Apart from the further theoretical development presented in this chapter, this study is of particular interest to design historians because the author explicitly introduces industrial designers as one of the relevant social groups involved in a process of sociotechnical change alongside, for example users and primary, semi-manufactured and manufactured goods producers.[31] However, and as Bijker readily admits, his treatment of industrial design here is brief and rather limited. He has elsewhere argued that the history of technology would benefit considerably from greater attention to industrial design and that this would render 'the web even more seamless'.[32] But his approach to the topic is refreshing, especially his emphasis on the designers' role in improving manufacturability and the mutual influence between plastic materials and design practice and ideology.[33]

It is no coincidence that this chapter began with an introduction to the notion of the seamless web of sociotechnology and the historian Thomas Hughes's theories on technological systems and hitherto has paused at the sociologist Wiebe E. Bijker's theory of sociotechnical change. Because it was Hughes and Bijker who, together with sociologist Trevor Pinch, edited what could be called the founding text of the theory since known as the social construction of technology (SCOT), *The Social Construction of Technological Systems*, first published in 1987.[34] This point of cohesion is augmented by the fact that the contributors include the historian Ruth Schwartz Cowan, who critically but constructively assessed the relationship between the history and the sociology of technology.[35]

One of the most interesting methodological issues raised in this publication is Pinch and Bijker's concern for 'the asymmetric focus of analysis': the 'preference for successful innovations' in the history of technology 'seems to lead scholars to assume that the success of an artifact is an explanation of its subsequent development'.[36] To counter this bias, Pinch and Bijker believe

9 Design that in some way or another can be described as unsuccessful (e.g. commercially, functionally, aesthetically) is a little explored but potentially rewarding topic. Despite being built in the midst of the 1972 international oil crisis, and governmental funding notwithstanding, this prototype for an electrically powered van never entered series production. Strømmens Værksted, prototype of electrically powered van, 1972. Design: Einar Kjelland-Forsterud (engineering), Terje Meyer and Bjørn A. Larsen (body design). Copyright The Norwegian Museum of Science and Technology

failures must be given as much attention and studied in the same way as successes. The relevance of this claim to design history should be clear, as commercially, functionally, aesthetically or otherwise unsuccessful design is clearly a neglected field of study. A partial exception might be found in the work of Henry Petroski, who has devoted due attention to design failures.[37]

SCOT has been criticized for several reasons, however—most notably it has been accused of more or less replacing technological determinism with social determinism. It has also been deemed inept at dealing with the materiality of artefacts: 'social constructivism denies the obduracy of objects'.[38] Further-more, SCOT's focus on closure and stabilization as key elements in socio-technical change has been criticized for simplifying the role of conflict in the history of technology.[39]

By and large, one might say that SCOT has generated considerable contro-versy and fascination across a range of disciplines, and in design history it has also inspired some very interesting research.[40] SCOT not only functioned as a common arena for historians and sociologists of technology, but it has also been essential in the consolidation of science and technology studies (STS) as a distinct field of study.[41] Besides SCOT, the STS field has generated much theoretical and methodological output that has great potential in terms of im-proving the theoretical and methodological framework of design history. The next section will examine some of these trajectories.[42]

Actor-Network Theory

'The things,' said Ford Prefect quietly, 'are also people.'[43]

Laconically commenting to his less travelled companions, who were marvel-ling at the exotic ensemble of guests and the spectacular interior design of the restaurant at the End of the Universe, the protagonist of Douglas Adams's sci-ence fiction saga *The Hitchhiker's Guide to the Galaxy* quite literally means that *the things are also people*. Albeit in a slightly less verbatim sense, the dismantling of the axiomatic distinction between human and non-human actors is one of the core issues of actor-network theory (ANT). This rather unconventional outlook will require closer attention, but first ANT needs a presentation.

One of the more prevalent critiques of SCOT and other social constitu-tionalist outlooks is that of one-sidedness; that it is overly concerned with the influence of social relations upon technology and underplays the influence of technology upon social relations. Recent STS thinking has tried to overcome this tenacious dichotomy, arguing—as in the words of Donald MacKenzie and Judy Wajcman—that 'it is mistaken to think of technology and society as separate spheres influencing each other: technology and society are mutually constitutive'.[44] ANT can be seen as an attempt to create a theoretical framework better suited to articulate this acknowledgement. The concept was first introduced in the latter half of the 1980s, chiefly by Bruno Latour, Michel Callon and John Law.

According to Law, at the heart of ANT lies the ambition to treat 'entities and materialities as enacted and relational effects' and to 'explore the configuration and reconfiguration of those relations'.[45] Another fundamental aspect is the destabilization of ontological categories. Latour argues that conventional dichotomies such as technology-society and nature-culture must be overcome.[46] The resemblance to the notion of the *seamless web of sociotechnology* and Hughes's term 'sociotechnical systems' is evident. But rather than systems, ANT uses the metaphor of network to highlight the relational aspect between the nodes, or entities. However, it is important to note that in ANT parlance network is not necessarily a tangible entity like telephone networks or sewer systems, nor is it an organizational mode. As Latour defines it: 'Network is a concept, not a thing out there. It is a tool to help describe something, not what is being described . . . [It] is the trace left behind by some moving agent.'[47]

Latour uses the term 'actor-network' to describe how the development and distribution of facts and artefacts happen through negotiations between different interest groups. Facts and artefacts are seen as products of science and technology and scientific theories and technological objects. To a design historian, this would correspond to design ideologies and products. In any case, the point is that facts and artefacts develop as a result of negotiations between the various actors involved applying strategies preconditioned by their different interpretations, agendas, needs and desires. Actors construct these networks through persuasion and enrolment—in short, the accumulation and execution of power. The dynamics often take the form of conflicts, both within the network in question as well as in the relations to other networks

10 All design is part of an actor-network, linked with both people and things—although not always as explicitly as here. Telegrafverkets Hovedverksted for Oslo Telefonanlegg, Riks standard phone booth, 1933. Design: Georg Fredrik Fasting. Copyright The Norwegian Telecom Museum

and elements. According to Latour, it is the extension and momentum of the network that regulate which facts and artefacts prevail. An important aspect though, is that it is not just the facts and artefacts that change in the course of negotiations. The negotiators (actors) also change in such a process, which is characterized by conflicts and transition.

The networks can be large and intricate, and the roles of the various actors highly dissimilar. But who are these actors? Imagining the analysis of a design process, a general, tentative, and far from exhaustive list could look something like this: company management and board, product planners, product management, in-house designers, consultant designers, engineers, technicians, production workers, sales department, marketing department, advertising agency, trade unions, interest groups, media, distribution system, sales channels and a multitude of user groups. The list can no doubt be expanded and modified, depending on the character of the case study, but it can at least indicate the contours of a network's complexity.

The following questions could be asked in consequence of such an outline: Which meanings, attitudes and positions do the various actors have? How do they construct the network? How, where and by what means do the negotiations take place? How and where is power distributed in the network? Which facts and artefacts gain the largest momentum and prevail? Here these questions shall remain open, but it should be clear now that thinking about design in terms of ANT may help structure analysis in a different way and thus provide a fresh view on design processes. Acknowledging Latour's imperative to 'follow the actors!' has the advantage of allowing for multiple vantage points; it can make it possible to study a situation from many angles rather than from the perspective of just one or a few privileged actors.

ANT is a relatively comprehensive and general approach, and its greatest value—at least to design historians—is probably as a sort of mental corrective and conceptual backdrop. Still, in his first extensive formulation of ANT, the 1987 book *Science in Action*, Latour proposed a series of principles and rules of method intended as guidelines for analysis. Some of the most relevant of these deserve mentioning:

'*Rule 1* We study science *in action* and not ready made science or technology; to do so, we either arrive before the facts and machines are blackboxed or we follow the controversies that reopen them.'[48] Put quite simply, this rule prescribes the priority of process over product. A technological product like a computer may be said to be blackboxed when most people know how to operate it without knowing how it actually works. The product is thus taken for granted and is of limited interest as such. But it has not always been that way, and opening the black box reveals the process of how the product was designed, before it was stabilized, conventionalized, and closed. In design history this entails not just the design process as this is conventionally defined, though—but also processes of how meaning and use is formed.

'*Rule 2* To determine the objectivity or subjectivity of a claim, the efficiency or perfection of a mechanism, we do not look for their *intrinsic* qualities but at all the transformations they undergo *later* in the hands of others.'[49] This rule states that a satisfactory understanding of an idea or a product cannot be reached solely by analysing the formulations of the idea or the intentions of the designer and properties of the product—it has to consider how the phenomenon in question is perceived, interpreted and used.

'*Rule 5* We have to be as *undecided* as the various actors we follow as to what technoscience is made of; every time an inside/outside divide is built, we should study the two sides simultaneously and make the list, no matter how long and heterogeneous, of those who do the work.'[50] This rule warns design historians not to give undue priority to certain actors (e.g. professional designers and canonized products). All prejudice and hindsight should be discarded if there is any hope of understanding the actors' attitudes, actions, motives and intentions.

'*First principle* The fate of facts and machines is in later users' hands; their qualities are thus a consequence, not a cause, of a collective action.'[51] This principle calls for a design history more attentive to consumption, appropriation, domestication and use. The meanings of ideas and products are not inherent, but are formed through negotiations carried out in networks.

'*Third principle* We are never confronted with science, technology and society, but with a gamut of weaker and stronger *associations*; thus understanding *what* facts and machines are is the same task as understanding *who* the people are.'[52] This principle insists that the ontological categories of ideologies, artefacts and society are constructions, and not very helpful ones. Any real situation is a network involving all these spheres. Objects and social groups are products of network-building. Both humans and artefacts can be actants in the network.

'*Fifth principle* Irrationality is always an accusation made by someone building a network over someone else who stands in the way; thus, there is no Great Divide between minds, but only shorter and longer networks.'[53] This principle requires design historians to treat all kinds of nonconformist design and ideals analytically on par with their sanctioned counterparts. Any attempt to discredit a design ideology or to ridicule or disqualify a product is a strategic action by an actor with a conflicting agenda. Such disputes should thus be seen as conflicts of interest and power struggles between different networks rather than moral questions or intellectual feuds.

These principles and rules of method may make it easier to bring the ANT perspective into empirical studies. The ANT should not, however, be thought of as a methodological toolkit ready for eclectic exploitation, as undertaking a fully fledged ANT study requires a comprehensive and rather holistic theoretical-methodological approach. In design history ANT is probably better conceived of as a theoretical framework facilitating new and dynamic ways of thinking about design.

ANT is both immensely popular and highly controversial. The eagerness and magnitude with which it has been applied to ever new case studies and transferred to new fields of study has caused even its founders to worry about the development. John Law has pithily described the phenomenon as 'Have theory, will travel.' He argues that what happens to ANT when it is named, described, explained, defined and institutionalized is precisely what happens when a technology is stabilized, conventionalized and closed—it gets blackboxed, and thus imperative and inoffensive, but at the same time impenetrable and intangible.[54] What splendid irony! Much by the same token, in a reassessment of his brainchild, Bruno Latour notoriously stated that 'there are four things that do not work with actor-network theory; the word actor, the word network, the word theory and the hyphen! Four nails in the coffin!'[55] One of the major problems, he claimed, was the constellation of the term

I I An ANT perspective seeks to break down the conventional ontological divides between the natural and the cultural, the human and the non-human, and in stead follow the mediations and translations challenging these categories. Borge Bringsværds Verft, Yngling-class sailboat, 1967. Design: Jan Herman Linge. Copyright Norwegian Design Council

'actor-network', because it 'would remind sociologists of the agency/structure cliché'.[56] The whole point of ANT was precisely to bypass such contradictions: '"Actor" is not here to play the role of agency and "network" to play the role of society. Actor and network—if we want to still use those terms—designates two faces of the same phenomenon, like waves and particles.'[57] Or, as Michel Callon put it; 'The actor network is reducible neither to an actor alone nor to a network.'[58]

John Law sums up the general criticism of ANT as follows: ANT 'has at different times been criticised for its relative lack of interest in major social asymmetries such as gender, its refusal to base its explanations on generally accepted ontological categories, its tendency to a centred managerialism, the flattening character of its network metaphor, and its lack of concern with Otherness'.[59] This is not the place for an exhaustive discussion of the merits of or problems with ANT. However, one of its most controversial aspects deserves some consideration: the notion of non-human actors. Ford Prefect matter-of-factly stated that, in the situation he and his friend were observing, *the things are also people.* Latour and colleagues insist not so much that things *are* people, but that the two—non-humans and humans—nevertheless should not be discriminated between. The actors in ANT can be human or non-human. As might well be understood, it is the latter part of this assertion that some find hard to swallow. Probably the most explicit insistence on non-human agency can be found in Bruno Latour's 1988 article on the sociology of a door-closer. Through a rather elaborate analysis of the basic function of a manual door-closer, known in French as a 'groom', he shows how this mechanical groom takes the place of a human groom in letting people enter before shutting the door behind them, arguing that this is a fundamentally anthropomorphic device. Latour here demonstrates how non-human entities become actants through their design: certain tasks have been delegated to them, and performing these tasks (or not performing them, or performing them badly) makes the non-human actants inhabit the given actor network on a par with human actants. To stick with Latour's case: this line of thought is what makes the sign put up on a door, informing about a dysfunctional door-closer, far more appropriate than the author (of the sign, not the article) might have intended: 'THE GROOM IS ON STRIKE!'[60]

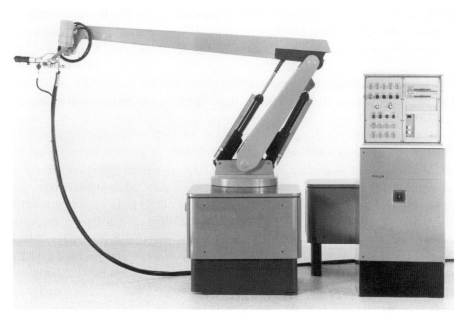

12 ANT invites one to think of artefacts too as actors on par with human ones. Few objects lend themselves better to the idea of non-human actors than robots, but the principle extends to all things. TRALLFA Nils Underhaug A/S, paint-spraying robot, 1973. Design: Ole Molaug, Trygve Slettebøe and Hans Halvorsen. Copyright Norwegian Design Council

Many a scholar has had a hard time accepting the way Latour seeks to give nonhumans a voice.[61] The historian Margaret Jacob, for instance, has described Latour's strategy of letting artefacts speak for themselves—referring especially to the ending of Latour's *Aramis, or The Love of Technology*—as an exercise in 'self-indulging pantheism'.[62] This speaks directly to the major problem of non-human agency—that of will or intentionality. Steven Brown and Rose Capdevila concur that will is a prerequisite for being an agent/actor, and in an attempt to overcome this predicament they have suggested 'a novel way of reading will, one which is entirely devoid of subjective intentions or desires'.[63] It is not clear, however, whether this solves any problems or puts Latour critics at ease.

Andrew Pickering has proposed a similar way out of ANT's intentionality conundrum. By approaching the relationship between mind and matter, between human and nonhuman actants as a temporal and dialectic process of negotiation, where both the human and the non-human are formed and transformed, it becomes possible to think of non-humans delegating tasks to humans without attributing the former with intentionality. Both actions and intentions change over time, Pickering argues, and human intentions are intertwined with non-human responses.[64] It is, in short, a dialectic process of mutual resistance and adaptation.

In his recent book *Reassembling the Social*, Latour defines an actor as someone or something which 'is made to act by many others . . . An "actor" . . . is not the source of an action but the moving target of a vast array of entities swarming toward it.'[65] The actions/tasks performed by human actors have often been delegated to them by others, just as actions/tasks performed by non-human actors have often been delegated to them by designers and others. This is another take on Latour's attempt to dismantle what he sees as an artificial divide between the human and the non-human, the social and the technological/natural. In other words: the supposed intentional will guiding the actions of human actants is no more evident and unproblematic than in the case of non-human actants.

Latour does not present the most scrutinizing analysis of the relation between intentional will and the notion of (nonhuman) actants, but he does, even in his most recent reassessment of ANT confirm his assertion that 'objects too have agency'.[66] The lack of concern for the aspect of intentional will likely stems from maintaining that 'a machine can be studied no more than a human, because what the analyst is faced with are assemblies of human and nonhuman actants where the competences and performances are distributed'.[67] To Latour it is in fact the very 'apparent *incommensurability* of [objects'] modes of action with traditionally conceived social ties' which makes non-human actants so important—their actions are intermittent but crucial in understanding social connections: '[T]he continuity of any course of action will rarely consist of human-to-human connections . . . or of object-object connections, but will probably zigzag from one to the other.'[68]

His interest in action is thus focused on studying settings that include different actants of different kinds. Action is seen as something that takes place in the relations between these different actants, and this view might explain why the quality of intentionality/will seems subordinate to Latour. Because, as he puts it: 'the interesting question . . . is not to decide who is acting . . . but to decide what is acting and how'.[69] The commonsensical notions of intentionality and causality are seen as inhibitions, and Latour maintains that:

> *any thing* that does modify a state of affairs by making a difference is an actor—or, if it has no figuration yet, an actant. Thus, the questions to ask about any agent are simply the following: Does it make a difference in the course of some other agent's action or not? . . . This, of course, does not mean that these participants [the nonhuman actors] 'determine' the action, that baskets 'cause' the fetching of provisions or the hammers 'impose' the hitting of the nail . . . Rather, it means that there might exist many metaphysical shades between full causality and sheer inexistence. In addition to 'determining' and serving as a 'backdrop for human action', things might authorize, allow, afford, encourage, permit, suggest, influence, block, render possible, forbid, and so on.[70]

This chapter is not the place to profess the infallibility or universality of these theories in general and Latour's views on nonhuman agency in particular, but many aspects of these theories may make for new and interesting perspectives on design studies.

In an ANT perspective, then, artefacts may be seen to act in the same way humans do. But, as Sergio Sismondo has observed, this is due to the externalized perspective of ANT whereby the otherwise notable distinction between *actor* and *actant* is downplayed: 'all of the actors of ANT are *actants*, or things made to act'. Sismondo concludes that, despite the fervent rhetoric about non-human actors, most ANT studies tend to concentrate on human actors: 'Humans appear to have richer repertoires of strategies and goals than do non-humans, and so make more interesting subjects of study.'[71]

Thinking of non-humans as actants on a par with human actants poses challenges to many forms of design studies, but it is a fresh and rewarding perspective to keep in mind when analysing design processes, products and their meanings in the writing of a cultural history of design. Historians have often tended to get seduced by the agency of the so-called great human actors, losing sight of the other inhabitants—human as well as non-human—of the actor network. How inept such tendencies are in studies of a complex phenomenon such as industrial design has been succinctly remarked upon by Vilém Flusser:

> [I]ndustrial production, including design, has developed into a complex network that makes use of information from various sources. The mass of information available to a producer goes way beyond the capacity of individual memory . . . Consequently, it has become necessary to act in teams combining human and artificial components; results cannot therefore be attributed to any single author. The design process is organized on an extremely co-operative basis. For this reason, no one person can be held responsible for a product anymore.[72]

This is where the actor-network concept and Latour's insistence on the agency of nonhumans can function as a corrective.

The potential of ANT to design history and design studies is, however, largely unexplored. Mika Pantzar has briefly presented ANT in a design studies context, but there are few who have made anything more of it.[73] Despite its fascinating approach to central issues such as human-artefact relations ANT is even less explored by design historians. It is interesting to note here that Latour refers to Thomas Hughes's work, especially his notion of the seamless web, and states outright that 'There is no difference . . . between history of technology and ANT, except when the social theory is made explicit.'[74] Arguments for a closer relation between the history of technology and design history suggest that there is no reason why ANT should not also be appropriated by design historians.[75] The 2008 Design History Society Annual Conference in Falmouth, *Networks of Design*, featured Bruno Latour as keynote speaker and marked an acute awareness of and growing interest in ANT within design history, and it bodes well for the exploration of ANT and other STS concepts by design historians.

Engaging STS and ANT should be done with care, though, because one of the principal objections STS scholars seem to make against other disciplines' interest in STS in general and ANT in particular is a tendency to consider it a methodological toolkit. For instance, Steve Woolgar has complained that 'the theoretical import, the provocative edge, goes missing, if STS is thought of merely as a set of tools for tackling (historians' or others') predefined problems'.[76] As John Law puts it, ANT is 'better considered as a sensibility to materiality, relationality and process. Whether it is a theory is doubtful.'[77] There is, however, a more practical methodological approach developed in STS that in many ways is based on ANT: an approach conceptualized around the metaphor of script.

Script Analysis

> The designer of the gun had clearly not been instructed to beat about the bush. 'Make it evil,' he'd been told. 'Make it totally clear that this gun has a right end and a wrong end. Make it totally clear to anyone standing at the wrong end that things are going badly for them. If that means sticking all sorts of spikes and prongs and blackened bits all over it then so be it. This is not a gun for hanging over the fireplace or sticking in the umbrella stand, it is a gun for going out and making people miserable with.'[78]

Staring down the barrel of the Kill-O-Zap gun, Douglas Adams' galactic hitch-hiker offers an excellent introduction to understanding what a product's script is.[79]

Whereas ANT is probably best considered a conceptual framework in design history, the affiliated notion of a product script is more of a methodological tool. As discussed earlier, ANT is concerned with how artefacts, or non-humans (as well as human actors), act as mediators, transforming meaning as they form and move through networks. Within this framework, the idea of product script has been developed as an effort to facilitate closer analysis of how products transport and transform meaning. The concept was developed by the Madeleine Akrich, and much of its allure stems from the term's metaphorical character and etymological versatility. Its Latin origin, *scriptum*, means written, and some of today's many derived forms, such as *scripture* and *film script*, should give some hints as to what is meant by a product script.

Akrich uses the term 'script' as a metaphor for the instruction manual she claims is inscribed in an artefact. Any artefact contains a message (the script) from the producer/designer to the user describing the product's intended use and meaning. Douglas Adams's vivid science fiction account of the Kill-O-Zap gun is an exemplary case in point, but the principle applies to more mundane products as well. As Akrich explains in her own, somewhat less sanguine idiom:

> Designers thus define actors with specific tastes, competences, motives, aspirations, political prejudices, and the rest, and they assume that morality, technology, science and economy will evolve in particular ways. A large part of the work of innovators is that of 'inscribing' this vision of (or prediction about) the world in the technical content of the new object. I will call the end product of this work a 'script' or a 'scenario'.[80]

Yet the inscription of meaning in an artefact is not limited to its technical content—which is Akrich's main interest—but is equally the case regarding its design in general.

In a way, introducing script analysis to design history can be seen as formalizing an already existing mode of thought. For example, in 1983, Philippa Goodall observed that 'design *for* use is design *of* use'—which is a more general way of expressing one of the central tenets of the script concept.[81] Script analysis can thus be a highly valuable tool in the quest for better understanding of how a product's utilitarian functions, aesthetic expressions, social meanings and cultural identities are constructed. Moreover, the intentionality of designs has been a fascinating but also troublesome and controversial topic for design historians. One of the potential benefits from introducing Akrich's notion of product script could be as a contribution to a sounder methodological basis for analysis in this field.

The script concept can also be said to reveal design's empowerment to affect behaviour and meaning. As such, it verifies the maxim that design matters, and can thus be of some comfort to those with a vested interest in design. To others, these mechanisms of influence permeating design through scripts may appear less benign—to some even outright terrifying and dangerous. Albeit taken from a work of fiction, the following passage might illustrate this point:

> [O]ne thing is the democratised household design, that is bad enough, there are great enough dangers in the fucking fact that people eventually acquire such fucking good

13 Script analysis can improve the understanding of how meaning (both functional and symbolic) is communicated through design. Jordan AS, Step 1 toothbrush for babies, 2004. Design: Fido Industridesign (Merete Nes, Morten Kildahl and Øyvar Svendsen.) Copyright Norwegian Design Council

taste, and become these fucking monsters that display filthy identity through the plagia-rist design they buy, that alone is fucking scary enough, if you ask me, the fucking design has become an educator now all of a sudden, and the fucking designer cunts talk about morals and love and humanity, and I don't fucking know what kind of smut they're not talking about, and it naturally leads to what is even worse, and that is that the fucking cunt-heads who are trying to be progressive and say that design has expired its function, that it has finished its role, and that they are interested in non-objects, huh? Huh? What-thefuck! NON-OBJECTS! Designers have got a fucking mission, now, all of a sudden, it is people's attitudes that matter to them now all of a sudden, huh, the progressive designer pricks are suddenly supposed to design people's attitudes and people's love for the sur-rounding world, huh? Now it is suddenly time to discard with the educational objects and fucking fifty years too late start talking about ideas and conceptual tasks, fuck, it is so fucking terrifying that I almost start shivering, look Casco, I'm fucking shivering, I'm afraid, that's what I am, I'm fucking afraid of the day when a fucking designer-worldview comes along and creeps into my body, I'm fucking terrified of that, I'm going to kill my-self and my family the day the ideas of fucking fag architects and designers creep under my skin and into my fucking circulatory system, so that I begin to destroy my family with evil taste and fucking design, that is fucking scary, look, I'm shivering, it is fuck-ing scary when the decadent ultra-formalistic fucking ideas of designers and architects begin to spread and sneak out into the public sphere and into people's houses, just like the fucking coffee jug design and the fucking evil fruit dish have, and turn everyone into filthy decadent fucking designerheads, that is too fucking much, it is too fucking dangerous that all should end up with fucking formalistic ideas and fucking formalistic attitudes, I see it happening, everyone has suddenly become so fucking conscious, and everyone is so fucking sure of their own taste, imagine it, it is fucking hell on earth the day everyone is walking around being design- or fucking architect kings in their rot-ten hearts, I see it happening, I see it, it is the most fucking dangerous tendency ever, that everybody suddenly—via that cunt-pompous and cunt-good design—is supposed to be so fucking conscious and self-conscious and self-critical and autonomous and atten-tive and consumption-sceptical and culture industry-sceptical and mass value-sceptical and innovation-sceptical and design-sceptical and zen-like and controversial and home-rebellious, and at the same time, at the same fucking time—via the condescending fucking highbrow fucking faux-self-constituted art-design—everybody is supposed to be so fuck-ing consumption-friendly and non-snobbish-snobbish and cultural industry-indulgent and consumption-indulgent and porn-liberal and amoral and beyond this and that and genre breaking and non-ironic and non-political-political and non-dandy-dandyistic and non-boboistic and so on, and you can go on listing all the fucking positions people are forced into because of the mentality- and behaviour-forming and mentality- and behaviour-expanding fucking design-attitude that it has stolen from the dreary fucking architecture-attitude that it again has stolen from the fucking art-attitude that supposedly originally was intended to mirror and problematize the psycho-world in which it was embedded, but which end up, eventually, with higher and higher rotation speed, on the coffee table of the fucking psycho-head that it originally was supposed to criticise, because the psycho-head all of a sudden has gotten progressionart-like self-critical attitude shoved into his fucking brain via the fucking design, which again sits there thinking it has done a good deed by circulating the in the first place futile criticism, three hundred and sixty fucking degrees and pumped it back into the world as the worst imaginable decadent surplus-nazi mindset the world has ever seen, in the worst possible way design pumps, blind as a bat to what kind of material it deals with, everything it comes by of outdated artistic positions back into the world's fucking asshole with a gigantic OSCAR MIETWOHN-designed enema.[82]

This rampant rage against the (design) machine poured out by one of the shady characters in Matias Faldbakken's first novel from his dystopian trilogy on Scandinavian misanthropy is hardly representative of the common consumer. Nevertheless, looking beyond the obscenities, which incidentally must be said to constitute a prime example of what Tom Wolfe has dubbed 'Fuck Patois',[83] this passage effectively illustrates that the construction of meanings of design and design ideology is not necessarily a smooth operation. No matter how well-intended the designers' inscriptions and programs are, more or less convincing anti-programs are likely to be formed.

The materialization of the designer's more or less informed presumptions/visions/predictions about the relations between the artefact and the human actors surrounding it thus becomes an effort at ordaining the users' understanding of the product's use and meaning. However, there is always the chance that the actors decide not to play the role the designers ascribe to them or that the users misunderstand, ignore, discard or reject the instruction manual and define their roles and the product's use and meaning at odds with the producer's/designer's intentions as conveyed through the script. The script is thus a key to understanding how producers/designers, products and users negotiate and construct a sphere of action and meaning.

It is precisely this attention to what goes on between the sphere of production and the sphere of consumption and use that is so intriguing and promising about script analysis. As discussed earlier, the tendency to focus on either the sphere of production or the sphere of consumption has been criticized in the history of technology and in design history, and requests have been made for approaches that can bridge the two. Bruno Latour has provided a nice image of the insufficiency of studying only one sphere: 'Looking at the mechanism alone is like watching half the court during a

14 Script analysis facilitates studies of how designers configure their users, for example by seeking to anticipate flexible interpretations of their products. HÅG ASA, Capisco saddle seat swivel chair, 1984. Design: Peter Opsvik. Copyright HÅG ASA

tennis game; it appears as so many meaningless moves.'[84] To avoid such a less than satisfactory situation, requires constant movement between designer and user, between the designer's imagined user and the real user (as well as represented users),[85] between intention and interpretation, between what is written into an artefact (inscription) and how it is read (subscription/ de-inscription).[86] In short; mediation and translation should be core concerns, and script analysis can be an appropriate methodological tool in such an approach.[87]

As already mentioned, the concept is based on a series of metaphorical, analogical and etymological modifications of the script theme. The relations to semiotics soon become clear, and because semiotics—due to its embedment in linguistics—has been accused of reducing everything to text and thus being ill equipped to deal with materiality,[88] Akrich and Latour declare that 'semiotics is not limited to signs; the key aspect of the semiotics of machines is its ability to move from signs to things and back'.[89] Providing a guide to our understanding of this system, Akrich and Latour have come up with a vocabulary that explains various connoted terms and how they fit in a script analysis. Some of its most central terms merit a presentation:

> **Script, description, inscription, or transcription:** The aim of the academic written analysis of a setting is to put on paper the text of what the various actors in the settings are doing to one another; the de-scription, usually by the analyst, is the opposite movement of the in-scription by the engineer, inventor, manufacturer, or designer . . .

> **Prescription; proscription; affordances, allowances:** What a device allows or forbids from the actors—humans and nonhuman—that it anticipates; it is the morality of a setting both negative (what it prescribes) and positive (what it permits).

> **Subscription or the opposite, de-inscription:** The reaction of the anticipated actants—human and nonhumans—to what is prescribed or proscribed to them; according to their own antiprograms they either underwrite it or try to extract themselves out of it or adjust their behavior or the setting through some negotiations . . .

> **Re-inscription:** The same thing as inscription but seen as a movement, as a feedback mechanism; it is the redistribution of all the other variables in order for a setting to cope with the contradictory demands of many antiprograms.[90]

Thinking along the lines suggested here provides a tool that connects some of the many and disparate aspects of the complex field of study that is design history. Introducing such a common methodological vocabulary might also make it easier to locate and analyse the intricate relations that make up the seamless web of sociodesign.[91]

A feature of the script concept that is not discussed in Akrich and Latour's vocabulary but that may clarify its value in design history is the suggested distinction between a physical script and a socio-technical script.[92] The physical script is embedded in the artefact's physical form and consists of those properties of the product's physical form and interface that try to tell the user about its intended use. It is this not always particularly successful phenomenon, understood as intrinsic constraints and affordances that Donald Norman discusses in his 1998 book *The Design of Everyday Things*.[93] Although Norman takes on the emotional aspects of design in a more recent book,[94] he is here concerned virtually exclusively with products' utilitarian functions. He can thus be said to be in line with the notion of a physical script but does not relate to the idea of a socio-technical script. To a large extent, the same can also be said about Ian Hutchby, who has discussed the concept of affordances as a what he called a 'remedy' for the relativism he finds in a radical social constitutionalist view on the nature of technology and artefacts. And like Norman, Hutchby has borrowed the concept of affordances from the psychologist James Gibson.[95] In addition to Norman, Tom Fisher has explored the potential of Gibsonian affordances to design studies. Seen in light of Akrich's idea of the script, Fisher makes the important observation that 'affordances cannot simply be "built into" or "read out of" artifacts, but are discovered by users through interaction with them'.[96] Still, although he claims that '[o]ur exploration of the affordances of the material world resolves the objective and cultural aspects of our relationship to materials',[97] Fisher's take on affordances is profoundly linked to the physical object and its perceived material properties, and is it thus less dynamic and versatile than Akrich's notion of the physical and socio-technical script.

The socio-technical script has more to do with the transportation and transformation of a product's symbolic, emotional, social and cultural meanings. Partly, to varying degrees, this is also related to the artefact's physical, formal and aesthetic qualities, but the socio-technical script includes much

more than the artefact itself. It involves all kinds of communication that sur-
rounds and accompanies the product, such as the manufacturer's image,
brand identity, market position, product reputation, user feedback, subcultural appropriation of the product and—probably the most explicit expression
of the socio-technical script—marketing, advertisement and general media
coverage.

It is important, however, that this distinction between, or specification, is
not misread as a simplistic dualism. That would make the concept fall prey to
the same kind of criticism Barry Katz has waged against Peter-Paul Verbeek's
discernment between a product's 'material utility' and its 'social-cultural
utility'. Katz discredits this as 'the old dichotomy between *engineered function* and *designed meaning*', rightly pointing out that '[t]echnology, too, is
laden with referential signification, just as it is unwise to presume that aesthetic categories have no function'.[98] This vital clarification recalls the observation by Mihaly Csikszentmihalyi and Eugene Rochberg-Halton that 'it
is extremely difficult to disentangle the use-related function from the symbolic meanings in even the most practical objects.'[99] This entanglement of
the symbolic and the utilitarian is surely reciprocal, making their assertion
equally valid vice versa; the symbolic meanings cannot be disentangled from
the use-related functions either. Akrich is acutely aware of the problems
caused by the momentum of etymological and ontological conventions and
stresses that 'the links that concern us are necessarily *both* technical and
social'.[100] Thus, the distinction between physical script and socio-technical
script should not be understood as a conceptual dichotomy, but as one
possible—and often rewarding—way of nuancing our conception of how
things act, communicate, and transform meaning. In real life—and hence
in empirical case studies—the physical script and the socio-technical script
will be entangled and reciprocal.

Marit Hubak has made use of script analysis in her study of how the identities
of certain car makes and models were constructed and conveyed through newspaper advertisements. She defines the socio-technical script as '*ideas about or
views of users and attitudes and values connected to cars and motoring*. Thus
marketing is part of the socio-technical script, which is built on the physical
script.'[101] According to Hubak, marketing contains both types of communication,

15 In design culture, mediating a product's use and its meaning cannot easily be told apart. Jonas Øglænd AS, DBS Kombi-series bicycles, 1968. Design: Olav Aanestad. Copyright Cycleurope Norge AS

one direct and one indirect. The physical script is seeking to exercise direct influence over users, as it is promoting the product's physical properties and utilitarian function. The socio-technical script, on the other hand, is seeking to exercise influence by way of indirect attraction. This attraction can be more or less related to utilitarian, symbolic and emotional arguments.[102]

Although advertisement and marketing are important components in an artefact's socio-technical script, it should be stressed that these aspects do not amount to the socio-technical script. The world abounds with products that are no longer manufactured or marketed. Of course, no one knows this better than design historians, as it is normally amongst this inexhaustible motley crew of material culture that we find those artefacts making up our subject matter and sources. These products nevertheless have socio-technical scripts, although they are likely to have changed since first inscribed by manufacturers, designers and marketers. Sticking to cars, a case in point might be the Citroën 2CV launched in 1948. Designed by Pierre Boulanger, Henri Lefèvre, Flaminio Bertoni and Jean Muraret in the late 1930s, this highly unconventional and very popular little car remained in production until 1990. The 2CV was intended as a people's car, and the notorious design specifications demanded that it be 'capable of transporting four people, or two farmers with . . . a bag of potatoes . . . across a ploughed field, without breaking the eggs they carried with them in a basket'.[103] Looking at advertisements from the 1960s and 1970s, the farmer is absent, but the socio-technical script is still geared towards the conventional car consumer, represented for example by the happy nuclear family on a camping trip. In stark contrast to these inscriptions by manufacturers, designers and marketers, the Citroën 2CV became a paramount icon of just about everything opposed to mainstream car culture.

This effectively demonstrates the many elements of uncertainty pertaining to the process of inscription and the power of the users. In the case of the 2CV, it was the users (both actual and represented users) and their constellations of subcultures who transformed the socio-technical script over time. Manufacturers, designers and marketers can react to such subcultural transformation of meaning in different ways. Peter Stanfield has shown how Harley-Davidson has appropriated the historic use—real, represented and fictitious—of its motorcycles in the product development: 'Harley-Davidson . . . has literally *inscribed* the past within the design of its machines.'[104]

Owners, users and consumers contribute to the proliferation and publicity of the product and participate in the formation and transformation of its meaning and identity. It follows that a product should not be regarded as finished when it leaves the factory and is introduced into the market. As Latour put it: 'The fate of facts and machines is in later users' hands.'[105] This is where script analysis can help bridge the gap between the sphere of production and the sphere of consumption: by moving from studying how scripts are constructed and promoted by manufacturers, designers and marketers (inscribed) to how they are read and interpreted by users. Those reading a script can choose to—completely or partially—accept (subscribe) or reject (de-inscribe) it. Or, in cases of illiteracy (i.e. poorly written scripts), the script might be misunderstood or even not detected. As described in the opening quote by Douglas Adams, Ford Prefect most decidedly both understood and subscribed to the menace inscribed in the Kill-O-Zap gun by its designer.

Users thus form their own interpretations of scripts. But as long as the ways in which and circumstances under which the product is used and the meanings formed by/around/through it do not differ too much from those envisioned by the manufacturer/designer/marketer, the script analysis will be an important instrument in understanding the interaction between product and user.[106] The concept is particularly enticing because it brings alive the artefacts studied, and it does so irrespective of whether they are approached from the sphere of production or the sphere of consumption/use. Tracing the transformations through the object as it moves between different actors and arenas can also help undermine the great wall that seems to have been erected between the two spheres.[107]

Domestication

I honestly thought the satellite town would inspire a varied and exciting garden life, says Magnus . . . The problem is that people in Rykkinn are not interested in fruit and plants. They are seemingly only interested in lawn. There is a fundamental difference between people who are interested in fruit and plants and those who are only interested in lawn. In the beginning I believed that the Rykkinn dwellers, who surely have been allotted ample space to cultivate any plants, would show a certain amount of fantasy regarding the use of these flower boxes and gardens. But all along I see the same. Everywhere in Rykkinn there is: crocus and lawn.[108]

Disillusion looms large in Nikolaj Frobenius' novel *Teori og praksis* about the paradise lost of the 1970s satellite town Rykkinn, outside Oslo. The gardening enthusiast and cultural radical Magnus, the protagonist's father, is one of the architects who designed the project. In their appropriation of their new domiciles, his neighbours seem to be struck by what Douglas Coupland has called 'Option paralysis: The tendency, when given unlimited choices, to make none.'[109] However, through their failure (according to Magnus) to properly domesticate their gardens, his fellow Rykkinn dwellers are, in fact, domesticating the architect's ideology by transforming visions of a colourful commune into variations of a conforming community.

Both ANT and script analysis aim at moving back and forth between the sphere of production and the sphere of consumption/use in order to understand the co-production of meaning. The concept discussed here, domestication, was created to pursue this ambition further in the realm of consumption and use. But getting at real practices of consumption and use constitutes a significant methodological challenge to historians. Caroll Pursell wrote of his own field, the history of technology, that it has prioritized 'design over use, production over consumption'.[110] It is no longer controversial to advocate a shift of focus, but that does not mean it is easy to implement. Although great efforts have been poured into this challenge, much due to pragmatic limitations in resources and research methods as well as the availability of empirical evidence, users often remain projected users or represented users. But as recent research has demonstrated, alternative approaches might facilitate such studies. One example may be how Tom McCarthy, in his history of American car culture, has managed to revitalize such an oft-told and well-known story as the conception of style-driven, planned obsolescence in Detroit car design in the latter half of the 1920s by incorporating investigations of the flip side to the new-found mass automobilism; questions pertaining to maintenance, reuse, disposal, scrapping, recycling and so on are integral elements to his narrative.[111] More generally, the social sciences have been at the forefront of consumption studies and might be a valuable source of inspiration. To historians, however, studying use and consumption poses many methodological challenges rendering direct methodology transfer difficult.

Traditionally, consumption has been regarded as a passive function where the consumer/user conforms and adapts to directives issued by producer/designer, caught in the web of materialism under the spell of capitalist society. This simplistic moralism has been challenged at least from the 1970s onward, when Pierre Bourdieu and Jean Baudrillard and others argued that consumption could be seen as symbolic and creative acts.[112] Later positions include Zygmunt Bauman's notion of an aesthetic consumption and Daniel Miller's conception of consumption as identity formation.[113] Common to all these otherwise different outlooks is that they attribute greater competencies and greater responsibilities to the consumer/user. Consumers/users play active roles in forming their lives through creative manipulation of objects, meanings and social systems according to their needs, desires and abilities. In their daily lives people use products by integrating and consuming them. At the same time, people are consumed by the products as they respond to them and engage with their properties, functions and forms. This reciprocal relationship between people and things is what the British sociologist Roger Silverstone and colleagues characterize as the result of a process of domestication.[114]

The metaphorical term 'domestication' is used to describe how people tame the technology and artefacts that surround them. An essential point, though, is that the taming process is characterized by *mutual* change and adaptation. As Knut H. Sørensen puts it: 'Domestication . . . has wider implications than a socialization of technology: it is a *co-production* of the social and the technical.'[115] This is what makes domestication such an apt metaphor, because, as Silverstone straightforwardly asks: 'Wild animals then, wild technologies now: what's the difference?' The point is, though, that '[d]omestication . . . leaves nothing as it is'.[116] Even the most common animal domestication processes, such as house-training a docile puppy, are a question of give and take. Yes, the dog is coaxed or scared into adapting to the owner's rules of conduct, but the owner also has to adapt to the dog's requirements for exercise and nutrition. Much the same can be said of the relation between products/technologies and their consumers/users. Users modify the artefacts so they suit their needs and desires in the best possible way (utilitarian, emotional and symbolic), but at the same time, users' behaviours, feelings, and attitudes are transformed by the products. Artefacts are adapted to patterns of use, but they also create new patterns of use. Such transformations take place in the emotional and symbolic domains as well. Symbolic codes of various kinds are converted into something personal and are associated with questions of identity, emotions and social relations. Domestication is the utilitarian and emotional adaptation to and appropriation of artefacts. Through the process the user adapts to and appropriate the artefact, and makes it meaningful to his or her life. When the product's meaning has been negotiated, constructed and stabilized, it can function as a personal expression for the user.[117]

Domestication is a multidimensional process of negotiation that involves human and non-human actants and is characterized by conflict and collaboration. Abstract space is transformed into concrete place, the house turns into a home, objects become symbols, identity is formed and transformed and social relations are reproduced or destroyed. Users' stories differ in extension and content. Their experiences represent a repertoire of domestication strategies and a catalogue of actions that can be implemented. Domestication is thus neither a harmonious nor a linear process—it is normally conflict-ridden and dynamic. Thus, the concept does not imply a stable consolidation of an artefact's meaning and use. Firstly, one and the same object can be domesticated differently by different users in different societies and cultures. Secondly, what might seem to be a stabilization of an artefact's meaning and the closure of negotiations as its use becomes routine may suddenly be disrupted. Needs and desires might change, external symbolic codes might be internalized or new users might be enrolled. Such situations can lead to a redomestication of the artefact.[118] A typical example would be a student inheriting a chair from her grandparents. As the artefact is transferred from its seemingly stable situation by the fireplace in an old farmhouse to a city studio apartment, from being grandma's crossword puzzle retreat to the student's bedside clothes depot, the chair and its users are tossed into a new round of negotiations, a new process of domestication.

Using the concept of domestication as a prism can provide new insight into what the consumption and use mean. An artefact is never introduced in a sociocultural vacuum. There is no *ding-an-sich* (thing in itself), no ideal, objective object that enters the sphere of consumption and use as a sort of tabula rasa. There are only complex socio-technical situations settings/ entities that contain scripts that are both physical and sociocultural, or *ding-für-mich/dich/uns/euch* (thing for me/you/us/you) as it were.

The concept of domestication can be seen as complementing Akrich's script metaphor. This combination could have great potential for design history in analysing the relation between intention and understanding in the design and use of products. This is precisely in line with Sørensen's recommendation 'to study domestication as a negotiated space of designers' views and users' needs and interests'.[119] Is the artefact being understood and used as intended and inscribed? What is it about the script that ensures this? And what happens if the domestication process takes an unforeseen direction, in other words, when users do not subscribe? In most cases, though, some kind of intermediate position arise, where parts of the script is subscribed to and other parts rejected or misunderstood (de-inscribed), and a process of negotiation commences where both product and user are adapted and transformed until a satisfactory degree of domestication is achieved.

An intriguing illustration of a most mundane example of this phenomenon can be found in a passage from Nicholson Baker's novel *The Mezzanine*— a tribute to the hoards of unsung innovations in commonplace design and technology that tend to elude everyday consciousness but nonetheless profoundly affect people's lives. The book's protagonist ponders why the toilet seats in his office bathroom are horseshoe-shaped as opposed to the complete ovals of those found in his and most other home bathrooms:

> I suppose the gap lessens the problems of low-energy drops of urine falling on the seat when some scofflaw thoughtlessly goes standing up without first lifting the seat. There may be several other reasons for the horseshoe shape, having to do with accessibility, I'm not sure. But I am pleased that someone gave this subject thought, adopting what his company manufactured to deal with the realities of human behavior.[120]

What he in fact is suggesting here is that the horseshoe-shaped toilet seats in corporate bathrooms are the result of a redesign informed by the noncompliance (de-inscription) with some of the basic properties of the original, complete oval design by its users (or rather, a group of lazy, indifferent or inconsiderate users). And like Baker's protagonist, one can take pleasure in the fact that someone has at least made an effort to respond to this most unpleasant instance of users' domestication of an artefact by redesigning it factoring in undesired and desired use. Whether or not it has solved the problem or can even be considered a good attempt at doing so is another question.

In keeping with the Citroën 2CV example, the domestication of three other highly popular people's cars of the postwar era neatly illustrate how use and users matter—how the domestication of a product can be fed back into design and product development. The archetype of the people's car is of course the Volkswagen Type 1, or the Beetle from 1938 to 1946, designed by Ferdinand Porsche and Erwin Komenda. The huge success of this product led other car manufacturers to develop equivalent concepts. Among the more successful were the 1957 Fiat 500, designed by Dante Giacosa, and the 1958 BMC Mini, designed by Alec Issigonis. All were originally developed as quintessential economic and pragmatic people's cars. These scripts were, at least initially, largely subscribed, but both cars underwent drastic domestication processes later in their long production lives in which the products took on new meanings and identities—for example the Beetle as the hippie car and the Mini as the rally car.[121] Various aspects of these negotiated understandings that differed quite radically from the original scripts were then fed back as re-inscriptions into the design of the 1998 VW New Beetle designed by J. Mays and Freeman Thomas, the 2001 BMW New Mini designed by Frank Stephenson and the 2007 Fiat Nuova 500 designed by Frank Stephenson and Roberto Giolito. Of course, these new cars had little or nothing in common with the originals, except for stylistic resemblances. They aspired to be trend icons, not people's cars. In short, the varying subscriptions and de-inscriptions of product scripts—their domestication—can result in re-inscription in new designs. Whereas these examples show a form of domestication that might be deemed collective, cars are also domesticated in more individual ways. The phenomenon known as customizing, in which car owners may spend thousands of work hours and vast sums of money on redesigning and rebuilding ordinary production cars into personalized dream machines is a perfect example of domestication at work.[122] The physical transformation of these artefacts can be quite radical, effectively demonstrating how users matter through their power to de-inscribe and re-inscribe the original design work.

As with script analysis, traces of the basic principles of domestication can be found in earlier design history literature. This is not to say that domestication brings nothing new to the table, only that design historians have long been aware of the fact that the meanings and forms of products are transformed through use. An early example, albeit from architecture, is Philippe Boudon's 1972 study of how the inhabitants of Le Corbusier's row houses at Pessac near

16 Car customizing is a time-honoured and widespread type of domestication of mass-produced artefacts. The photo shows a 1969 Volvo 142 redesigned and rebuilt by its owner Håkan Molin from 1983 to 1986. AB Volvo, Volvo 142, 1966. Design: Jan Wilsgaard. Copyright Håkan Molin

Bordeaux, which were built in the 1920s, radically transformed their homes.[123] As John Walker wrote in 1989 when introducing Boudon's book: '[T]he issue is not only what design does to people, but what people do with design.'[124]

Another good example is found in a 1981 article by Tony Fry: '[V]arious sub-cultures have appropriated the motorbike in order to convert it to an icon of antagonism towards the dominant culture. In technical and visual modification they have redesigned the appearance of the machines to alter their meaning in order to construct significations of opposition amongst an ensemble of such significations.'[125] Fry's example involves a very particular kind of users and a very physical transformation of the products in question—but there is nothing to indicate that the principle should not apply also to more mainstream users of more mundane products and to transformation less dependent on mechanical knowledge and tool equipment. Admittedly, Fry does not use the term 'domestication', but instead he writes about a process of appropriation involving conversion, modification, alteration and construction. As it happens, appropriation and conversion are the first and last—enclosing objectification and incorporation—of the four stages Silverstone and colleagues identified in the process of domestication.[126]

A more recent example of how design history can operate as if it were informed by the concept of domestication, but without reference to it, is Viviana Narotzky's reflections on the continued life of US 1950s cars in Cuba: 'Once the white knights of planned obsolescence, Harley Earl's dream machines have found an undignified eternal youth in the streets of Havana.'[127] In describing how the Cubans go to great lengths in postponing the death of their old US cars, Narotzky effectively shows how—to use Bruno Latour's words—the 'fate of . . . machines is in later users' hands:[128]

> The American *cacharros* require endless tinkering, are held together with chicken wire and mechanical ingenuity. These monumental objects never die in Cuba: they become part of an endless life cycle, a vortex of use, re-use, transformation, appropriation and reconstruction . . . What comes out of this *ronde* are fascinating hybrids. There is nothing further from the Cuban experience of restoration than the Western concept of purity or historical truth. A '58 Dodge may have a Cadillac front grille, a Skoda radiator, a Plymouth fender and a Honda wheel cover.[129]

These old US cars are not only drastically altered and adapted by their Cuban owners, but they are, through their remarkable ubiquitousness in Cuban culture and daily life, in turn certainly altering and adapting their owners as well. This process is what domestication is all about.

Although the ideas behind the concept of domestication thus clearly should appeal to design historians, their explicit references to it are rare. In an article on the cultural transformations of the iconic super-elliptical table designed by Piet Hein and Bruno Mathsson and manufactured by Fritz Hansen beginning in 1968, Gertrud Øllgaard stated that:

> Processes of appropriation have been studied in recent analyses of practices of consumption which stress how consumers re-contextualize commodities by integrating them in their own worlds. These processes leave neither the significance of the object nor the social life and cultural identity of the consumer unaffected . . . Processes of appropriation can include elements of objectification, incorporation and finally conversion of the created into new regimes of value and new processes of objectification.[130]

Why she insists on omitting the term 'domestication' altogether and seems to replace it with appropriation—a term Silverstone and colleagues, as mentioned, use as one of four stages in the process of domestication—is somewhat bewildering,[131] but her very introduction of the concept in a design history context is interesting.[132]

The concept of domestication is a methodological tool devised to analyse how users turn commodities into functional things, meaningful objects and expressive symbols. One of its most attractive qualities is that it follows the artefacts way past the purchase phase and thus facilitates studies not only of consumption but also of use. This feature alone should reveal its potential value to design history. It is, however, a sociological concept, and as such not necessarily all that easy to apply to historical studies. As mentioned earlier, there are many methodological challenges in studying use and consumption that render direct methodology transfer difficult. Like most concepts from the social sciences, domestication is developed from studying contemporary situations and phenomena, where use can be analysed in situ and in real time. Historians are not that fortunate. As discussed previously, Jeffrey Meikle claimed

that 'we have no way of knowing with certainty how and why consumers at a
given historical moment responded to particular products'.[133] He continues:
'How can we know how and why people responded to the products . . . that
surrounded them? How do we know what the results of design mean to the
people who negotiate them, often unselfconsciously, in their daily lives?'[134]
Paul Betts likewise observed that studying 'how [consumers] understand and
use [products] . . . effectively represents a sobering epistemological limit for
all historians of material culture'.[135]

Meikle and Betts are mostly right, albeit perhaps somewhat pessimistic,
because it is possible to achieve some understanding of how users matter
in design history. Getting at the real users in situ, for example by means of
ethnomethodology, will rarely be the solution. Rather, empirical studies of
historic use and consumption are probably better conducted by going after
the imagined users or the represented users.[136] One way of doing so is by focusing on the arenas and actors of mediation, translation and transformation
discussed in this chapter.

So, if one does not want to become a social scientist, but remain a historian—can domestication still be a rewarding concept? The answer is yes, but
the level of abstraction should be raised, as it were. As discussed hitherto, the
concept refers to how concrete products/objects/technologies undergo transformations in the hands of their users. But how about more abstract entities?
Can theories, systems, beliefs and ideas be said to be domesticated in a similar manner? Talking of adoption rather than domestication, such an alignment of the material and the ideological has been advocated in the field of
anthropology. Even though this is a proposal for a cultural biography of things,
Igor Kopytoff promotes equal treatment: 'Biographies of things can . . . show
what anthropologists have so often stressed: that what is significant about
the adoption of alien objects—as of alien ideas—is not the fact that they are
adopted, but the way they are culturally redefined and put to use.'[137] The STS
literature discussed earlier would surely support such a juxtaposition of material and non-material constructs, as it time and again treats facts (scientific
knowledge) and artefacts (technological products/systems) as equal in terms
of theoretical and methodological development.[138] In line with this approach,

Sørensen and colleagues have argued that 'facts may be domesticated in a manner similar to that used with artifacts'.[139] It should thus be possible to talk about not only the domestication of products, media and technologies but also about the domestication of ideas, theories and ideologies.

Of course, when I use a theory/idea (the concept of domestication), adapting and transforming it to better suit my needs and desires (a theoretical framework and methodology geared at the study of transformations occurring in negotiations between design ideologies and their users) that is in itself a process of domestication. I am in fact—to use Roger Silverstone's own words from his recent reassessment of the concept—'domesticating domestication'.[140]

Sørensen has argued that 'the domestication concept could be seen to have a wider potential than its apparent situatedness within the moral economy of the household'.[141] Silverstone has described '[d]omestication as a process of bringing things home—machines and ideas, values and information', thus indicating that the concept can be applied to facts (ideas/ideologies) as well as artefacts (objects/products).[142] Still, talking about the domestication of ideology (or theories, knowledge, beliefs, ideas) is a road less travelled in domestication studies but is not completely without precedents—although these are not always self-proclaimed domestication studies and do not necessarily refer to the concept as it was introduced earlier.

Two such studies from the field of history of technology will be presented, but first a brief remark made by Anna Calvera might indicate the direction of this next part of the chapter. In an article on the challenges of constructing regional narratives in design history, Calvera observes that 'there is a process of adaptation of the ideas and aesthetic references, or technological innovation, coming from abroad and, through feedback, results become subtly different'.[143] Although Calvera, similar to Fry and Øllgaard in the previous examples, does not use the term domestication, she does refer precisely to one aspect of what might be called the domestication of ideology. Her point is that the contents, forms and meanings of ideas/theories/knowledge are transformed by their users—just as with the domestication of products. Though, perhaps, she could have left out the word 'subtly' from the previous passage, as such transformations can be quite striking. What is lacking in Calvera's description to make it domestication proper, however, is that such a process entails not only the adaptation *of* the ideas/aesthetics/technologies but also the adaptation *to* the ideas/aesthetics/technologies. Domestication is relational, dialectic, reciprocal—it is co-production.

Technology does not come alone. As discussed in the introduction of this chapter, Thomas Hughes has eloquently demonstrated this and called attention to the seamless web of sociotechnology. So, when Per Østby studied the domestication of the car in Norwegian society, the car is about as far from an autonomous artefact as can be. Østby's car is a large sociotechnical system where politics, economy, power, morality and ideologies are inseparable from and at least as important elements in the system as the artefact and the physical infrastructure required (e.g. roads, gas stations, traffic lights). This means that when Østby is analysing the domestication of the car (in a country with virtually non-existent car production), he is as much analysing the domestication of *ideas* about the car—or car ideologies.[144] As Sørensen also points out, this study clearly shows that domestication can be a highly rewarding concept not only for understanding transformations taking place when artefacts are being put to use in the realm of the home today but also for understanding transformations taking place when ideas/knowledge/theories/moralities/ideologies are being put to use in the realm of a national community in a historical perspective.[145] In fact, Silverstone makes a point of comparing precisely the home and the nation as complex and contested units but still viable arenas for domestication processes.[146] This leads to an understanding of domestication that should resonate nicely with Calvera's aforementioned call for attention to the adaptation *of* (and *to*) ideas/aesthetics/technologies in the construction of regional (e.g. national) narratives in design history.

The at times confusing use of the terms domestication and appropriation should not be overplayed. Silverstone and colleagues originally defined appropriation as one of four stages in the domestication process, but Silverstone later argued that appropriation is too general a term for that purpose and suggested that commodification take its place as the first phase of domestication.[147] This clarification, alongside the fact that domestication scholars sometimes seem to use the terms domestication and appropriation more or less commensurately,[148] should allow for a joint venture or even a merger between the domestication approach and the appropriation approach.

Mikael Hård and Andrew Jamison have proposed an appropriation approach to studying how ideas of technology, science and modernity have transformed and been transformed through use. Although they prefer the term 'appropriation' to 'domestication', they do refer and relate to parts of the domestication studies discussed earlier, and their approach is very similar to what might be called the domestication of ideology. In the introduction to their 1998 volume *The Intellectual Appropriation of Technology* Hård and Jamison describe the advantages of the appropriation approach as follows:

> The book investigates some of the ways in which visions of technology are shaped by national intellectual traditions . . . [and] suggests that intellectuals tried to ameliorate the incorporation of modern technology by finding a place for it in one or another discursive framework. It is this process that we call intellectual appropriation . . . The goal usually was either to assimilate technology into the existing culture or to adjust culture to the intrinsic demands posed by technology.[149]

Hård and Jamison here point out three central concerns: First, their subject matter is not technology per se, but *visions* of technology. And studying the appropriation of visions is more or less just another term for studying the domestication of ideology. Second, the authors corroborate the validity of national communities as suitable arenas for studying intellectual appropriation (or the domestication of ideology). Third, it becomes clear that transformation is a two-way street. The visions of technology are adapted by mediators to better suit existing conditions, but the mediators and conditions are at the same time reacting and adapting to the ideologies in questions. In their more recent book on the cultural history of science and technology, Hård and Jamison sharpened this dialectical aspect: 'Cultural appropriation is a process by which novelty is brought under human control; it is a matter of re-creating our societies and our selves so that new products and concepts make sense.'[150] On the whole, though, this latter point may seem somewhat undercommunicated in the appropriation approach. The reciprocity of the transformation processes is better explicated by using the term 'domestication'.

Whilst appreciating the ground gained by domestication studies and the similarities between this approach and their own, Hård and Jamison assert that '[a]lthough a cognitive dimension may be found in some of these [domestication] studies, their focus is on habitual action'.[151] In the same volume, though, Aant Elzinga, seems to consider the two terms/approaches more or less synonymous, writing that 'technological change . . . is contingent on diverse socio-cultural patterns and on history . . . We like to speak of this as the appropriation of technology, its domestication.'[152] Another contributor, Catharina Landström, equates the meaning of the terms completely in her claim that 'new technologies were appropriated or domesticated . . . in quite different ways'.[153] Landström then goes a long way in aligning their approach with what is called here the domestication of ideology when she describes the ambition to 'focus less on technology itself than on the ideas and ideologies that surround it'.[154] Moreover, Hård also uses the terms 'domesticate', 'domestication' and 'domesticating' for variation when discussing how the intellectual appropriation of technology takes place.[155] What Hård and Jamison are arguing, then, is not any principal distinction between the two approaches, but rather that appropriation connotes a higher level of reflection among the actors in the transformation processes than does domestication.

This chapter set out by outlining how the history of technology has both contributed to and greatly benefited from the rich theoretical and methodological developments in the field of STS. A very brief and sketchy survey indicated that the way design has been dealt with in histories of technology has at times been cursory and conservative and at other times more refreshing. Arguing that there nevertheless is a great potential in a closer integration and interaction between the history of technology and design history, it follows that design history might also benefit greatly from exploring the theoretical frameworks and methodological insights of the STS field.

Clearly, there are many fundamental differences between the concepts of science, technology and design, and thus, it would be foolish to expect full congruence between science and technology studies and design studies. Still, there are also many and potentially fruitful similarities that deserve greater attention. The processes by which scientific facts/theories and technological artefacts/systems are formed and transformed can be strikingly comparable to how design ideologies and products are formed and transformed. Such an acknowledgement is the best argument for further exploration of a road hitherto less travelled: the potential STS theory and methodology may have to design history.

Translations of STS approaches to design history should be done with caution and respect, though. The dispersion and influence enjoyed by STS recently led Steve Woolgar to ask 'Has STS . . . settled down and moved out to the suburbs?'[156] His answer is that popularity *may* come at a high price, but the spread of STS is also a potential source for reaffirming and even renovating its integrity and provocativity: 'As long as it can continue to identify and recruit new audiences, but at the same time resist its institutionalization and transformation into formulaic suburban life, STS will continue to be a worthy vehicle for "inside out thinking."'[157] So, not only can STS invigorate design history, but design history—as one of the 'new audiences' Woolgar requests— might even return the favour by supplying new testing grounds for the further development of STS.

Another consideration to keep in mind for the historian is that theory and methodology should not be understood too rigidly. Trying to squeeze unruly and at times outright defiant empirical findings into a theoretical straitjacket can only result in poor history. The frameworks and concepts discussed earlier should, then, be interpreted and used in such a way as to avoid the 'Have theory, will travel' syndrome John Law cautioned against.[158]

The ANT is best understood as a general theory, a conceptual framework, and not as a methodological toolkit. Or, as Law puts it, ANT is 'better considered as a sensibility to materiality, relationality and process. Whether it is a theory is doubtful.'[159] Theory or not, to design history, ANT offers a framework that facilitates and informs a dynamic way of thinking about actants and relations.

The script metaphor offers a methodology and a vocabulary for the analysis of how products act as mediators, transporting and transforming meaning. The concept puts the artefacts on center stage and can be used to approach them from the perspective of production, consumption/use, or mediation. Any given setting can be analysed in terms of its prescriptions, proscriptions, transcriptions, inscriptions, subscriptions, de-inscriptions and re-inscriptions. Script analysis can thus provide a great advantage in efforts to bridge the spheres of production and consumption, which is one of the key challenges in design history today.

Through domesticating domestication and transforming the concept from one pertaining to analyses of how media technology is domesticated in the household to analyses of how design ideology is domesticated in other settings of a more versatile nature, an advantageous approach to design history is presented. Various types of design communities domesticate ideologies inherited from their past and those imported from contemporary currents. The concept of domestication becomes valuable when studying such processes by following the actors in their construction, negotiation and mediation of these ideologies. However, the domestication of design ideology does not end with the writings of campaigning designers, enthusiastic journalists, ardent academics and organization men. The mediations between ideology and practice can also be traced in a domestication perspective. As such, the manufacturing industry can be said to represent a second site of domestication, where ideas and ideals undergo new negotiations and transformations in meeting other users, requirements and circumstances.

Design history has a long tradition of appropriating theoretical perspectives and methodological approaches from other disciplines, from the heritage from art history, via the more recent romance with material culture studies to the more eclectic pluralism of today. Proposing, as is done here, yet another source of inspiration, does not eradicate or disqualify others, but rather adds to the theoretical resources and methodological repertoire of design history, making it better equipped to meet the present and future challenges of this intriguing field of study.

Having presented first a historiographical survey, followed by the discussions on theory and methodology put forth here, it is now time to explore some of the epistemological problems at the heart of design history. The third and last chapter seeks to open up the bigger issues concerning terminology, concept formation and categorization, especially those arising when modern design culture is articulated as modernism.

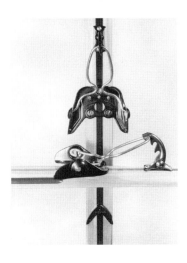

3

Epistemology

The idea of the modern is essential to any study of design since the Renaissance. Terms like 'modern', 'modernity' and 'modernism' are omnipresent and readily used in design history, but at the same time they display a seemingly inherent complexity and ambiguity. Probing their structure and meaning beyond the colloquial and commonsensical thus becomes a fundamental epistemological problem in design history. Discussions of terminology are an important part of the epistemology and meta-theory of any academic discipline. Without venturing into a comprehensive philosophy of modernity, this chapter will engage in some of these discussions, exploring in particular the questions arising when modern design culture is articulated as modernism.[1] A little disclaimer is required here. The issues addressed in this chapter are most significant when the history of design is approached as a history of ideas. They might be of less relevance for empirically close, artefact-based design histories engaging subject matters where the historical dynamics of visual ideology is negligible.

17 Can there be such a thing as a postmodernist airplane, an art deco sewing machine or a futurist rollator? The dynamics of aesthetic ideologies are not always what is most pertinent to design culture. Totenprodukter AS, Topro Troja rollator, 2002. Design: Formel Industridesign AS (Geir Eide, Per Farstad and Nicolay Knudtzon.) Copyright TOPRO AS

In design history there is an abundance of classifying and analytic terms which are often taken for granted. Of these, a surprisingly little explored but yet commonly used is the phenomenon of isms. In much design history litera-ture, the nature of isms seems to be taken for granted and is rarely debated explicitly. As Omar Calabrese has pointed out, terms constructed as tools of classification, like isms generally are, are troublesome in that they often make use of key words designed to unify and connect their subject matter. But to function this way, these denominators have to be extremely simplify-ing and abstract, and thus become obstacles to any rewarding comprehension of history.[2]

The significance of reflexive analysis of terminology has been receiving increased attention in the human and social sciences. Philosophers and so-cial scientists have come to realize that the terms, concepts and categories they use to explain the social world cannot be taken for granted but should themselves be made objects of analysis. This is what Pierre Bourdieu and Loïc Wacquant call 'reflexive sociology'.[3] This reflexivity is also a core component in the proposed concept Margaret R. Somers's terms the 'historical sociol-ogy of concept formation', alongside the 'relationality' and the 'historicity' of concepts:

> A historical sociology of concept formation also requires a relational approach, for what appear to be autonomous concepts defined by a constellation of attributes are better conceived as shifting patterns of relationships that are contingently stabilized in sites . . . [C]oncepts . . . are products of their time and thus change accordingly . . . Understanding how concepts gain and lose their currency and legitimacy is a task that entails recon-structing their making, resonance, and contestedness over time . . . From the perspective of a historical sociology of concept formation, concepts do not have natures or essences; they have histories, networks, and narratives that can be subjected to historical and empirical investigation.[4]

Keeping this in mind and returning to the sphere of design studies, numer-ous questions spring to mind. What is an ism? To find out, one must explore how it is constructed, negotiated, mediated, consolidated and decomposed. How is an ism formed and then transformed? Is there room for negotiations and temporal changes? Isms are often portrayed as discrete entities, but experience still shows evidence of one ism encompassing other isms, overlapping each other or even running parallel to each other. Are isms equivalent, comparable phenomena, or do they operate on different levels? Relations between isms describing systems of beliefs, or epistemes, and those describing aesthetic movements or design styles must also be examined.

To undertake a fundamental critique of the use and misuse of these meta-terms is difficult. Comprehensive analysis of the core issues of design can hardly be achieved without using the terms and language of design discourse. In other words, this chapter sets out to discuss and criticize elements that are indispensable to design history. The task at hand, then, will be to reconstruct these elements of the language of design discourse in order to question and discuss the fundamental terms and notions of interest for further inquiry.

This chapter will discuss some of the aforementioned questions and their relevance to design history. First, a brief historical outline of the fundamental terms 'modern', 'modernity' and 'modernism' is needed. This part is by no means any attempt to conduct a comprehensive investigation of this vast philosophical subject matter, but a brief outline is nevertheless essential as a backdrop for the subsequent discussion. Moreover, a clarification is required of the relation between isms as doctrines or aesthetic ideologies on the one hand and isms as world views or structures of society on the other. The main focus here, then, will be to investigate the nature of isms as tools of classification and analysis, especially in the context of modernism and its etymologically derived isms. From this discussion arises the suggestion that an ism can be understood as a cultural mode defined by negotiations between design ideology and design practice—a notion that will underpin the rest of this study. Having established this understanding of modern isms as articulations of design culture and as decidedly dynamic discources, the chapter will then examine some of the problems and challenges posed by reading isms in the context of historical research. The latter part of this chapter shifts gear, so to speak, assessing the prospects of the concept of paradigms, as developed by Thomas Kuhn and revised by Paul Feyerabend and Margaret Masterman, in framing the dynamics of historical change in design ideology and how it relates to the notion of isms. Concise answers to these questions are of course mere utopia, so this chapter aims rather to suggest a framework for further discussion.

Modern, Modernity, Modernism

Understanding design in the modern world is inconceivable without somehow relating to modernity, modernism and their etymologically derived isms, such as proto-modernism, late modernism, postmodernism and neo-modernism. All these ideologies and modes of thought, and consequently the entire field of study, become tangible only after a closer examination of the stem of these terms—'modern'—even though, in the present context, such an etymological history can only be a rough and very brief outline.

The first known use of the term 'modern' originates from a papal letter from AD 494. The adjective was used to distinguish the new decrees from the old. Even though the meaning of the word has varied and has been used as both a positive and negative description of phenomena, persons and things, the fundamental understanding has always been dominated by the distinction between the new, or the present, and the former, or the past.[5] This understanding of the term prevails to this day, at least in quotidian parlance. For the purpose of this chapter, this understanding of modern is not very helpful because of its time-relative character. It implies that all times were once new or present and, hence, modern. It is more or less synonymous with contemporary. What is modern today will not be tomorrow.

A word derived from the adjective modern, is the noun *modernity*. The latter shows up in the French culture debate of the mid-nineteenth century, and it is often connected to the poet Charles Baudelaire. He made it a keyword in his program for a new aesthetic. The term's time of conception is crucial to its understanding. The developments in technology and science since the Renaissance and the division of labour that followed the Industrial Revolution had resulted in a permanent change in the entire social life and a dissolution of traditional culture. Add to that population growth, urbanization and the rapid development of communication and information infrastructure.

In times like these, some elements of society and culture seem to prevail by means of tradition and conservative forces, while other elements tend to facilitate alterations through upheaval, innovation and instability.[6]

Baudelaire's visions of modernity are complex, and more often than not characterized by equivocations, sometimes even contradictions.[7] According to one of his more enigmatic visions of modernity, the modern aesthetic is dual: On one hand, modern art contains an element of relativity regarding the epoch's fashion and distinguishing features. On the other hand, it contains an eternal, constant element of beauty. Baudelaire considered it the artist's task 'to extract from fashion whatever element it may contain of poetry within history, to distil the eternal from the transitory . . . In short, for any "modernity" to be worthy of one day taking its place as "antiquity", it is necessary for the mysterious beauty which human life accidentally puts into it to be distilled from it.'[8] It is important to note, though, that the concept of novelty underpinning this discussion of modernity is essentially different from what is conceived as the ephemeral novelty of fashion today. Baudelaire's use of the term 'fashion' is broader, describing the aesthetics characterizing the present time. In the quotidian language of today, the novelty of fashion seems to denote a much more frequent and haphazard type of change. It has now also taken on a rather derogatory meaning which does not seem to have biased Baudelaire's use of the term. The novelty of fashion as understood today is an abstract, discontinuous novelty, while the genuinely new and present which is strived for in Baudelaire's modernity always contains tradition—even when it takes the form of negation. With fashion's change for change's sake, one might claim that any substantial value is lost and any wish for true rupture is rendered impossible. Change as formal play seems to abolish the idea of progress which is embedded in the concept of modernity.

Matei Calinescu identifies the existence of two distinct and at times contradictory modernities. The first is modernity as a rationale of society, or a field of experience—characterized by scientific and technological progress, the Industrial Revolution and the enormous social and economic revolts that followed capitalism. The other is modernity as aesthetic concept.[9] Calinescu describes the first type of modernity as bourgeois and characterized by the doctrine of progress, faith in technology and science, pragmatism and the idolization of action and success. The other type of modernity he describes as anti-bourgeois and characterized by radical attitudes, the wish for a rupture with the established order, idealism and a focus on the new role of art and culture. This dual concept of modernity becomes essential when discussing its manifestation in design, but a third related term—'modernism'—is the key conceptual entity, and it requires an introduction.

There is a strong consensus that modernism describes an international tendency implemented in literature, music, theatre, painting and other cultural spheres from the late nineteenth century onwards. The first known use of the term originates from the author Rubén Darío in the early 1890s. And it was within the Hispanic culture that it first took shape of a large, relatively synchronized movement for aesthetic renovation.[10] Modernism in design is, according to Jan Michl, characterized by an 'obligation to be modern'.[11] More generally, modernism can be seen as a constant quest for modernity, or the wish to establish an anti-traditional tradition.

This is what has led many scholars to deem modernism an applicable term in historical analysis. Modernism, as opposed to modern and modernity, describes (although in a bafflingly vague manner) a movement or tendency which, it is often claimed, can be defined as an epoch in history and is thus not impaired by the constantly changing present. Because in modernism, the synonymity between modern and contemporary ceases. But here the consensus ends and the epistemological challenges pick up momentum.

Modernism is a surprisingly comprehensive and thus imprecise term. In architecture, for instance, it is used to describe practices as diverse as Spanish art nouveau and the worldwide suburban brutalism of the 1970s. In design, the ambiguity of modernism might be exemplified by pointing to the correspondence between the two opposed modernities identified by Calinescu and two of the most distinct directions of modernist design: North American styling or streamlining might be said to build on the pragmatic, progress-oriented type of modernity, while Central European functionalism might be said to build on the idealistic, radical type of modernity. Taken to extremes, these two design ideologies might even be labelled kitsch and avant-garde, respectively.

To complicate matters even further, the meaning of the term differs considerably by such variables as geography, languages, and time. The *Modernismus* of 1920s Germany does not have the exact same meaning and content as the modernism of 1960s USA. Acknowledging the polysemic but at the same time seemingly indispensable nature of the term has led Anna Calvera to assert that 'Modernism, Modernist and Modernization are still sacred concepts for Design History, and arguably they are still potent instruments when researching a local reality, but we must also accept that they can change their meaning completely, depending on where and by whom they are used.'[12] Thus, the vagueness of the term notwithstanding, modernism is an important and adequate term, because it itself was an integral part of the items and cultural reality it is used to describe. The term participated in creating the history and was not, like so many other comparable terms, created post facto.[13]

By virtue of its sheer impact on twentieth-century design, the term 'modernism' cannot be done away with. But because of its complexity and comprehensiveness, an adequate theoretical foundation and corresponding methodology is needed to tackle its appearance in situations subject to analysis. Some of the properties and characteristics of modernism will be addressed in the next sections, within the discussion on that intriguing phenomenon called *isms.*

Isms and the Essential Tension of Ideology and Practice

Before any further investigation into the enigma of isms can take place, an important distinction needs to be made. Some of the more comprehensive isms of the twentieth century denote much more than simply a more or less consistent set of aesthetic beliefs or styles. The most prominent ones being modernism and postmodernism. These terms are used in a far more complex and far-reaching manner than, for example cubism or neo-rationalism, and by a far more comprehensive array of academic disciplines than studies of art, architecture and design. They are used extensively in such fields as philosophy, sociology and history, where their meanings are normally constituted by factors of a different or wider nature than within the aesthetic disciplines, although there is, of course, some overlap. But it may seem as though there are two phenomena of quite different scopes that share terminology. To avoid confusion, a closer definition of the two is needed.

When philosophers or historians use the terms 'modernism' or 'postmodernism' they normally do not primarily refer to modes of aesthetic thought or artistic movements. What they have in mind is usually a much wider and profound socio-historical phenomenon—a system of beliefs, a world view, or an episteme. Michel Foucault sees these epistemes as society's structuring conditions, made up of discursive formations that are specific for any given epoch.[14] What is possible to do and think at any given time is at the mercy of these underlying formations and their structure. Foucault compares the premises of eighteenth-century science as an example:

> [T]he naturalists, economists, and grammarians employed the same rules to define the objects proper to their own study, to form their concepts, to build their theories. It is these rules of *formation*, which were never formulated in their own right, but are to be found only in wildly differing theories, concepts, and objects of study, that I have tried to reveal, by isolating, as their specific locus, a level that I have called, somewhat arbitrarily perhaps, archaeological.[15]

Foucault continues: 'what I am attempting to bring to light is the epistemological field, the *episteme* in which knowledge . . . manifests a history . . . of its *conditions of possibility* . . . Such an enterprise is not so much a history . . . as an "archaeology".'[16] So, by conducting an archaeology of science, Foucault contends, people may identify and understand the formations structuring the intellectual and creative achievements of different times and cultures. According to Foucault, the episteme both restricts and affords the discussive and visual possibilities of any given society. The modes and themes of discussion, appreciation, comprehension and thought are governed or facilitated by the episteme in force. Because Foucault's philosophy of history is a highly complex, comprehensive and controversial one, the treatment of it here is deliberately limited to a discussion of his term *episteme* and its usefulness for the argument under consideration here.[17]

The discussion concerns two different types of change that take place on different levels and in different contexts. The first type is the aesthetic-ideological movements or isms that shift relatively frequently and are said to supersede each other, the next seemingly revolutionary and utterly distinct from the prior. The second type is the epistemes—the deep, fundamental sociological structures and more lasting views and modes of thought and comprehension. From here on the term 'isms' will be reserved to denote the first type of phenomena, and the second type will be referred to as 'epistemes'. In the encounter with empirical realities this distinction will probably appear too dualistic and rigid, but at the present stage it might be a helpful conceptualization aid.

Isms first become apprehensible and feasible when they are are reflected against their time's conventions, established rules and dominating debates and when their material manifestations in the form of new art, architecture, and design are viewed in contrast to the existing forms. The epoch's slowly but ever changing episteme both restricts and affords what is possible to say, think, comprehend and do at any given time. This is where the rules that constitute people's actions come into being. Here, the situations in which intentions are embedded arise. This is the background against which every new ism takes shape. Every ism is embedded in and dependent upon the episteme in force, whether it celebrates and explores the episteme's core values or rebels against and negates the same.

As a terminological construct isms far exceed the realm of design—or art, for that matter. Examples may be words like liberalism, radicalism, socialism, conservatism, individualism, constitutionalism, humanitarianism, monarchism, nationalism, communism and capitalism. Robert Palmer and Joel Colton have asserted that all these terms appeared in the English language between the 1820s and the 1840s. The very concept of isms is thus intimately linked with the history of modernity itself. According to Palmer and Colton, '[a]n "ism" . . . can be defined as the conscious espousal of a doctrine in competition with other doctrines'.[18] This definition is very appealing in that it so clearly emphasizes the coexistence and mutual presupposition of isms. On the other hand, as this definition seems to be concerned with the history of ideas in general, it may be too broad for the topic at hand, or perhaps not detailed enough.

Art history, architectural history, design history and all other academic disciplines concerned with aesthetics or ideologies of form in one way or another have no choice but to deal with the phenomenon of isms. Even historians of science and technology have to cope with isms, although in a somewhat different manner. But what are these creations? What do they include or exclude? How are they constructed? How do they develop? And how do people relate to them in historical research?

Colloquially, isms are often seen as theories, say of art, architecture or design. Isms and theories might have some common denominators, but the two terms can hardly be considered synonymous. A scientific theory is normally defined as a logically and/or empirically based set of terms, methods and explanatory systems designed to structure or explain a given phenomenon. Bearing this definition in mind, it seems obvious that an ism cannot be regarded as a theory.

First of all, isms differ very much from each other in terms of to what extent they promote a holistic view, an objective scope, a rational approach, and an empirical foundation. Some pretend to supply the answer to all the problems of the world and promise world peace and happiness for all, and some operate on a more internalistic and subjective level.

Second, isms are, more often than not, based on a compilation of scientific or pseudoscientific and philosophical or pseudo-philosophical fragments collected to act as indisputable facts in support of the ism. Thus, they cannot be said to represent any holistic view or logically based system. Peter Dormer asserted that 'Designers and architects are especially good examples of people who depend upon elaborate justifications and meanings to give both purpose and structure to their work.'[19] Isms may be seen as attempts as just that.

From these inquiries one may deduce that isms are not theories as this term was defined earlier, but rather, as Finn Werne proposes, ideologies.[20] They are more or less consistent sets of beliefs and arguments about what is correct, important and possible at the given time within the given episteme.

Treating isms as ideologies instead of theories also facilitates the analysis by rendering their normative, doctrinaire, and relative nature more evident.

Moreover, isms are dogmatic, evangelistic, and programmatic by nature, and hence a far cry from the alleged objectivity of scientific theories. This is, of course, a too rigid and schematic outline. Even though scientific theories often—at least colloquially—pass for objective systems of logic, much recent research in the field of science and technology studies has convincingly argued that theories or facts can to a considerable degree be considered results of co-construction in the same way artefacts are.[21]

This leads to what is the core of the nature of isms: they are normative. Their normative character is quite obvious. They tend to propose or dictate how art/architecture/design *should* be. Although theories are structural or explanatory—that is they pretend to tell us how things *are*, isms preach the gospel of how things *should* be. This important property poses fundamental challenges for research into the domain of isms that will be revisited later in the chapter.

Erik Nygaard has also pointed out these normative, dogmatic and evangelistic functions within the field of architectural theory, but without abandoning the term *theory*, as this chapter does for the sake of terminological intelligibility. He has, however, tried to diversify and distinguish between different types or levels of theories—identifying a field consisting of manifestoes, architectural theory, and architectural science flanked with architectural criticism and history.[22] This is an important distinction which can help improve the tangibility and level of precision in the history of ideas. But because the construction of design ideologies, just like that of artefacts and scientific theories, is a collective action, they are transformed over time. Isms cannot be comprehended by studying exclusively their origin and what is commonly perceived to be their authors, because their fate really is in the hands of future mediators and users.[23] And to cope with this flexible and dynamic nature of isms, additional theoretical frameworks and methodological tools are needed.

As a prolongation of their normative nature, isms are highly pragmatic, or instrumental. Not only do they suggest how things should be, but they normally also supply the methods with which to achieve the desired state. This instrumentalism gives isms a dualistic character. An ism may be considered a set of properties common to a body of buildings or artefacts—that is a style, a practice of designing. Or, an ism can be considered an ideological superstructure which in turn evokes buildings or artefacts more or less corresponding to the ideology. The most common and rewarding stand to take is somewhere in between these two.[24] An ism can, as shown earlier, be characterized as an ideology, but it cannot consolidate, develop, transform or be preserved without the active participation of the buildings or artefacts in question as well as human actors. Isms are thus taking the form of systems consisting of complex actor networks, and they should be treated as such.

This dualistic character of isms as ideology and isms as style invokes a similar and parallel dualism or controversy in the field of general cultural studies—the often perceived incompatibility of culture seen as a system of symbols and culture seen as practice. William Sewell Jr. has tried to overcome this obstacle by arguing that culture is most fruitfully conceptualized as a dialectic between system and practice and insisting on a necessary tension between the two as the key to understanding cultural transformation and development:

> System and practice are complementary concepts: each presupposes the other. To engage in cultural practice means to utilize existing cultural symbols to accomplish some end. The employment of a symbol can be expected to accomplish a particular goal only because the symbols have more or less determinate meanings—meanings specified by their systematically structured relations to other symbols. Hence practice implies system. But it is equally true that the system has no existence apart from the succession of practices that instantiate, reproduce, or—most interestingly—transform it. Hence system implies practice. System and practice constitute an indissoluble duality or dialectic.[25]

This position again, draws attention to the relation between ideology and practice in design. Sewell's suggestion to emphasize the tense dialectic negotiation between system and practice in order to conceptualize the development and transformation of culture can function as a starting point. Substituting ideology for Sewell's system of symbols, presents an intriguing model for understanding the dualistic character of isms: isms can be seen here as cultural modes. It follows, then, that the culture of design—as experienced and articulated through isms—can be conceptualized as a dialectic between ideology and practice. In other words: Design culture can be understood as a co-production of ideology and practice.

The discrepancy between ideology and practice is an intriguing phenomenon that poses interesting questions not only in terms of design history in general but also regarding the topic at hand: the formation and transformation of isms. (e.g. the role and nature of canon). This fascinating and intricate relation deserves far more attention than what is feasible here. But there is a transitional aspect to this relation—an ism as a style can hardly exist until an ism as an ideology has been proposed and to a certain extent disseminated.

Isms as Dynamic Discourses

A core property of isms is their contemporary connection and historicity. Isms are products of the time, society and episteme in which they arise. An ism is formed as a response or reaction to the existing praxis and governing ideas within the prevalent episteme. In other words, a new ism depends on both contemporary society and history. The episteme in force poses restrictions and affordances on what is possible to think, mean, say and do at any given time, and thus also on the nature of the ism under formation. But this relation is reciprocal—the isms in their turn are part of the ever continuous development of society and episteme.

A striking characteristic of many—if not all—isms is their claim of novelty and revolution. Although arguments, methods and rhetoric differ vastly, an ism arises from the believed need for an abolition, or at least a thorough revision of the old and existing order in favour of a brand new order more in step with present beliefs and ideas. But this claim of novelty often appears to be static. Because of the normative and programmatic nature of isms, they tend to legitimatize the need for revolution, which they proclaim by passing judgement on history and contemporary society in a remarkably prejudiced manner.[26] The old and existing order is seen as a static, monolithic entity and so is—strangely enough—the new envisioned order. But the rhetoric notwithstanding, any new ism is always a change of the existing order and always a change in relation to the existing order.

This is also why revivalist isms like neoclassicism or neo-modernism are never just replicas of the original isms. Any neo-ism arises in a time, society and episteme vastly different from the original and must therefore be of a completely different nature and based on an ideological foundation that may even be in direct conflict with that of the referred ism. The prefix 'neo-' implies historic revival. Neo-modernism is thus based on a revival of or at least a homage to an earlier ism. The pioneers of modernism would never have accepted such a thought. To modernist missionaries neo-modernists would be thoroughbred heretics.

Isms are highly dynamic configurations; they change according to time and space. Like any other social phenomena, they undergo changes and develop constantly from their conception to their eventual passing and through their crusades through different regions and societies. Christianity is not the same in ancient Rome as it in a televangelist's studio. Nor was modernist design the same at the 1939 New York World's Fair, 'Building the World of Tomorrow', as at the 1968 exhibition XIV Triennale di Milano. This transformation takes place through a process of negotiation between all the involved actors. It is also part of the change society at large undergoes restlessly, and it all develops in an intertwined relation to the episteme in force.

In this sense, an ism may resemble a Bakhtinian discourse. Sonya Rose draws upon Mikhail Bakhtin when suggesting that 'discourse is produced in an unending process of recuperation and transformation . . . Yet each recuperation creates something that was not there before: its meanings are the product of a particular conjuncture. Discourses are embedded in contemporaneous networks of meanings and social relationships and have their own histories of transformation.'[27] Although most isms of architecture and design are probably less erratic, periodic and changeable than the moral discourses that are Rose's subject of analysis—such as public apprehension about women's sexual morality—her reflections on the nature of cultural transformation and how it should be analysed are certainly relevant to the topic at hand, indicating the dialectic and dynamic character of any socially embedded cultural phenomenon—such as isms.

But how and where does an ism arise? There is a dogma claiming that art is created in the studio, while isms are created in the galleries. Whether the first part of this assertion is true for fine arts is out of my scope, but it is certainly not true for design. Art has traditionally been seen as relatively autonomous—although this myth has been challenged lately with reference to the artist's relations to markets, conventions, institutions, etc. Design, on the other hand, is far from autonomous—the creative process is entangled by such an array of actors with different agendas as to prevent any notion of autonomous studio creation. But the second part of the assertion—isms are created in the galleries—is interesting if galleries are interpreted in a broad sense to mean the network of social institutions, actors, and mechanisms involved in the sociocultural reception, interpretation, and domestication of art, buildings, and products.

It it only when an array of actors agree on attributing a more or less consistent set of properties and qualities to a group, school or generation that an ism is constituted. In addition to the artists, architects and designers, these actors can be gallery owners, commissionaires, cultural critics, journalists, writers, editors, academics and many others. In some cases, the artists, architects or designers who are assigned to an ism by this powerful actor network flat out refuse to be associated with the ism constructed for them or on their behalf.

After the initial, struggling phase, the new ism is either fought off and marginalized or it is accepted by a sufficiently large community so that it can flourish. In both cases it takes its place in history, either at the junkyard of ideologies and forgotten intentions, or at the centre court of society's ideological entrepreneurs. But since all new isms are so closely tied to the zeitgeist of their own times, they are also doomed to become passé sooner or later. This is rather intriguing considering the fact that in order to succeed, every new ism must insist on its own novel, groundbreaking character at the expense of the existing order's wrong, obsolete arguments. But even the most revolutionary ism eventually loses its provocative abilities and becomes tradition. The most striking example of this paradox is probably the proliferation of functionalism during the interwar years commented on in 1965 by Theodor Adorno in the most severe manner: 'the absolute rejection of style becomes style.'[28]

To explain this transition of an ism from avant-garde to mainstream tendency or forgotten obscurity, Finn Werne uses the terms 'intentional context' and 'extentional context'. By extentional context he refers to a project's relation to the world at large, to the governing episteme of the time. By intentional context he refers to a project's relation to the architect's world of ideas, to his will to novelty. He elaborates: 'The type of intention I speak of here reveals itself through deviation, both in discursive and in visible form, from what is generally accepted at a given time. The extentional reveals itself through the common, the accepted, through use, custom and tradition, while the intentional reveals itself through the special, the novel, the diverging and marginal.'[29] Werne then ties the extensional context to the term 'style' and the intentional to isms. A style refers to a certain part of the extensional context, to an already established ism which serves as legitimizing identity for the project. But the ephemeral character of the avant-garde necessitates a transitional process:

> The ism is thus characterized, more or less, by a number of criteria which are specific for a particular complex of ideas which only *during a relatively limited period* can remain intentional but which subsequently transforms into an extensional context as the ideas win general approval, become what we call general knowledge, or are passed on to history's eternal oblivion of lost and forgotten intentions.[30]

This part of Werne's argument is interesting because it points to a crucial, but little examined property of isms—the inexorable transformation of ideology as it moves through society. Avant-garde isms tend to become conservative styles even when their most prominent and powerful arguments are based on the rejection of such a development. The pioneer revolutionaries of a movement soon enough become the reactionary clergy condemning any development of the isms which exceed or transcend their own original intentions.

The proposition of isms as changing entities is a strong and useful one. It can also be successfully extended to follow the ism's further development. An ism is not consolidated and homogenized once it has lost its avant-garde status and is disseminated as the prevalent ideology. An ism never stops changing. It is therefore of great importance to study how an ism develops after it has passed through the partial transition from intentional to extensional, from avant-garde to *arrière-garde*, from ideology to style. This development should be seen as a reciprocal process of domestication, where the actor network forms and transforms the ism into a culturally significant phenomenon. Society does not consist of a continuous row of avant-garde intentions. Thus,

18 When ideology becomes style: Streamlining was originally inspired by scientific research in aerodynamics, but the formal language rapidly spread to nonmoving and slow-moving objects with nothing to gain from aerodynamic designs. Strømmens Værksted, 'Gullfisken' E-vogn no. 158 tram in Oslo, 1937. Design: Ingvard Müller, Alf Ihlen and Einar Isdahl. Copyright Oslo City Archives

analysing an ism's coming of age, and not exclusively its origin and conception, reveals important, new knowledge that would otherwise be missed.

These questions regarding the construction of categories for analytical purposes—such as isms—are of course not restricted to the realm of design studies. Any historical or existential description and comprehension seems to be structured in such a manner. One can no more conceive of light without darkness than formalism without functionalism. One concept or category overlaps or supplements the other, making any complete or pure identity impossible. This concept of supplementarity, as conceived by Jacques Derrida, has been adopted and developed by Dominick LaCapra, who stresses the importance of acknowledging and highlighting this problem in the writing of history:

> Supplementarity reveals why analytic distinctions necessarily overlap in 'reality', and why it is misleading to take them as dichotomous categories. Analytic or polar opposites always leave a problematic difference or remainder for which they do not fully account . . . Analysis provides clear and distinct ideas which define boundaries and confine ambiguity or overlap to marginal, borderline cases. Insofar as analysis define polar opposites, it constructs ideal types or heuristic fictions.[31]

LaCapra does not suggest an easy answer but points to a precarious problem: how can one conceptualize, describe, analyse and discuss past cultures and societies—in short, write history—without lapsing into static simplifications or unsubstantial fiction? Lloyd S. Kramer has, in his reading of LaCapra, suggested that

> this . . . does not mean that historians can or should abandon all categories or all desire for systematic distinctions, [but] it does suggest that they should give far more attention to the ways in which their categories overlap and contest one another. The problem, of course, is to find a method for writing history that would convey the complexity of overlapping categories without abandoning analytic distinctions and therefore passing into complete obscurity and confusion.[32]

It might be advantageous, then, to challenge the conventional use of analytical categories and develop strategies for uncovering and emphasizing the overlapping, contesting and supplementary character of isms, for example.

It should now be clear that isms are far more complex and dynamic than they are sometimes portrayed. In addition to the issues under discussion here, a major problem is that the varying nature of the different isms makes it difficult, if not impossible, to relate to extensive, holistic isms, like modernism, in the same way as more particular, narrow isms, like neo-rationalism. But awareness of this challenge makes one much better equipped to search for its solution.

Design history, at least in its traditional form, has at times been accused of resembling the writing of myths. This problem can be attributed partly to the mythical character which has been assigned to the phenomenon currently under discussion: isms. The origin of this mythical character of isms can be found in the texts which—together with the canonized works—constitute the primary sources of knowledge on the isms' nature for historical research. As Mikael Hård and Andrew Jamison argue, historians often contribute to the proliferation and reinforcement of myths by not scrutinizing their sources sufficiently—the historian is taken hostage by the sources. In many cases the historian adopts the actors' self-perception as embedded in the sources and passes it on without yielding it enough resistance. The problem here is, of course, that the resulting historical narrative becomes little more than a re-production of the actors' own mythopoeic accounts.[33] This is exactly what has happened in much conventional design history, especially in works chronicling the Great Narrative of Modernism.[34] As Rainer Wick has put it: 'Design history will . . . have to accept the suspicion and the reproach of being unscientific as long as it trusts historical sources blindly without taking the instrument of source-criticism into account.'[35] Of course, much has changed to the better in the historiography of design in the twenty years since Wick issued this warning, but it is still a useful and poignant reminder.

When approaching the phenomenon of an ism, or more precisely the texts embedded in it and the texts describing/explaining/interpreting it, one also immediately comes across the insider/outsider problem. Texts embedded in a given ism are texts that are contemporary with the ism at hand and take part in the construction and consolidation of it, or—if negative in nature—form anti-programs to it. The remarkable preoccupation with ideology reflected by this text production has been explained by Jean Baudrillard as a means of simplification: 'It is the abstract coherence, suturing all contradictions and divisions, that gives ideology its power of fascination.'[36]

The most common examples of such texts are manifestos, magazine and newspaper articles, programmes, exhibition catalogues—all more or less programmatic and evangelistic in form and content. Such texts are most prominent in the initial stages of an ism when architects and designers oppose conventional practice and must seize the pen to express their beliefs. The most famous examples of such texts are probably the early modernist manifestos, which Peter Collins has described as 'pseudo-scientific mumbo-jumbo'[37] (based on the modernists' fascination for science and technology). Finn Werne proposes a paraphrase of Collins to characterize the equally hazy post-modernist writings: 'pseudo-philosophic mumbo-jumbo'[38] (based on the post-modernists' fascination for philosophy).

These texts and their authors are often leading actors in the formation of an ism, and their roles and performances are for the most part vigorously polemic and flamboyant, and their stand in the drama is either that of believer or nonbeliever, avant-garde or *arrière-garde*. Theatrical, religious and military metaphors are utterly suitable here. The debates are often staged much like a play, where the actors act their parts with dramatic gestures and intense pathos. Or they are played out like wars or battles, where military strategists and warriors fight for the cause, strive to defeat their enemy and conquer the world. Also, most isms are surprisingly similar in structure to religions. You will find priests, congregations, scriptures, relics, missionaries, pilgrimages, crusades and the lot in any self-respecting ism.

These actors/missionaries/warriors and texts/relics/weapons are fundamental keys to understanding isms as sociological, cultural, aesthetic, historical and philosophical phenomena. But the aforementioned is extremely important to bear in mind in these interpretations: the embedded texts can be dangerously alluring, deceitful and misleading if read out of context and without proper analytic reflection.

This contemporary believer/nonbeliever dichotomy is one aspect of the insider/outsider problem. Another intriguing aspect of it is found in the texts describing/explaining/interpreting isms historically. Here, the believer/nonbeliever dichotomy fuels heavily biased writings on isms which often take form as chronicles, falsifying or legitimatizing history. The historiography of architecture and design in general and of modernism in particular is saturated with such writings. Believers of modernism, such as Nikolaus Pevsner and Sigfried Giedion, have in elaborate and ingenious ways tried to show and explain the unavoidable victory of modernism, albeit from vastly different origins.[39] Nonbelievers like Charles Jencks and Robert Venturi, on the other hand, have tried fiercely to discredit and dismantle modernism with the same, but oppositely directed, strategy—arguments based on historical necessity, determinism and teleology.[40]

These approaches all share a methodological problem: They seem to be based on a static, contemporary (with the author) notion of the idea they set out to analyse (in this case modernism), and extrapolate backwards in time grasping at fragments of data that can confirm their predetermined views and thus legitimatize or falsify the idea. The unscientific nature and biased outcome of this kind of history has long been common knowledge within the realm of general historiography. Panayotis Tournikiotis has made a timely and intriguing contribution to the transfer of this critique to the field of architectural historiography.[41] His mapping and critique of the long tradition of writing genealogic, projecting, deterministic architectural history is important as a potential corrective in the further development of this field of studies. But though he patently shows how the writing of history is subject to the same transformative processes as any other cultural phenomena, even Tournikiotis regards modernism as a 'relatively immobile object'.[42]

This seems to indicate that there is still a lack of room for or will to a more nuanced and dynamic understanding of modernism, although recent design history has begun exploring this exciting territory. The ism has often been sealed, homogenized and generalized, leaving little room for exploring contradictions, politics, contingencies and efficacies. It has been turned into what Bruno Latour describes as a black box, an impenetrable and unintelligible unit containing but concealing a gamut of controversies once flowing but now closed.[43] To understand the inner workings and dynamics of the ism, the black box has to be reopened and examined. The black-boxing of isms also turns these ideologies into myths. This problem has been raised and debated within the history of ideas, with Quentin Skinner as one of the chief critics.[44] And, as Clive Dilnot has pointed out, it is high time to rid design history of the writing of myths.[45] The danger, of course, as Mikael Hård and Andrew Jamison caution, is that such a catharsis may also result in new myths. Writing alternative histories does not necessarily solve the problem if they make use of the same emplotments and story lines as the traditional mythical narratives.[46]

Thus far, this chapter has investigated the nature of isms as tools of classification and analysis from within. The discussion has centred on the conception of isms as cultural modes characterized by negotiations between design ideology and design practice and on their properties as dynamic discourses. The latter half of this chapter will approach these issues from a different perspective, exploring the prospects of paradigms in framing the dynamics of historical change in design ideology.

Reassessing Paradigms

The history and philosophy of science have long been pondering how science develops and how to explain what is normally called scientific progress. Is science cumulative or sequential? Is absolute truth and knowledge an impossibility or merely a matter of time and effort? One of the most influential contributions to this debate is Thomas Kuhn's provoking book *The Structure of Scientific Revolutions*, first published in 1962.[47] Kuhn's prime motive is to refute the long-standing notion that had dominated the history and philosophy of science, seeing scientific knowledge as accumulative and evolutionary in character. To do so, he introduces two terms intended to better explain the nature of scientific development: 'paradigm' and 'revolution'. The basic idea of the book is that science is formed in paradigms that supersede each other in a revolutionary manner. A paradigm is formed, consolidated, disseminated. Then it is questioned, challenged, and overthrown in favour of a rival candidate in a revolution.

Over the following decades this work has spurred an impressive amount of criticism, praise and revision. It has also inspired many scholars of other disciplines. The next section investigates the relation between these Kuhnian paradigms and the isms so commonly used to classify architecture and design. The relevance and poignancy of such an investigation becomes apparent when one recalls that Kuhn based his theory of paradigms on the classification tradition in art history.[48] The book was, he explains, a direct 'product of . . . my own discovery of the close and persistent parallels between the two enterprises [science and art] that I had been taught to regard as polar'.[49] This is not to say that he considered the histories of art and science as equivalent—in fact, in his metahistorical discussion of their relation he asserts that 'it is only when we take particular care, deploying our subtlest analytic apparatus, that the distinction between artist and scientist and their products seems to evade us. . . . If *careful* analysis makes art and science seem so implausibly alike, that may be due less to their intrinsic similarity than to the failure of the tools we use for close scrutiny.'[50] Kuhn also identified what he saw as one of the fundamental differences between the histories of art and science: 'Unlike art, science destroys its own past',[51] indicating that science was more revolutionary than art. The validity of this claim might certainly be disputed— the point here is simply that Kuhn himself made these connections between science and art, between the history of science and art history. Because the use of isms as a primary system of classification is perhaps the most evident, significant and troublesome aspect of design history's legacy from art history, it certainly will be an interesting exercise to return the favour to Kuhn: Can isms be seen as paradigms? Does design develop through revolutions?

Because of the problems demonstrated by others in transferring Kuhn's theory to the social sciences and the history and sociology of science,[52] and the fundamental differences between the fields of science and design, no easy analogies or synergisms should be expected. It is instructive, for instance, to recall how W. David Kingery has criticized the application of Kuhn's theory of scientific revolutions to the history of technology: 'This model [Kuhn's] has been applied to rapid technological change . . . However, unlike science, which deals with observations and ideas, technology cannot be seen as right or wrong but merely as appropriate for a particular social and cultural environment.'[53] Despite these translational troubles, the topic is well worth exploring because it might shed some light on the mysteries surrounding the nature of the development of design ideology and design practice. The theories proposed in *The Structure of Scientific Revolutions* have been vigorously debated since its publication in 1962. Without reiterating the well-known theories or entering

19 The invention of jet propulsion has been labelled a revolutionary paradigm in the history of (aviation) technology. But although the first passenger jet aircraft, the de Havilland *Comet*, entered commercial service in 1952 propeller propulsion remains suitable, even superior, on certain types of aircraft. Saab AB, Saab 340 turboprop aircraft, 1984. Design: Ulf Edlund and Olle Esping. Copyright Saab AB

this battle, following is a brief presentation of Kuhn's hypothesis and arguments that are of particular relevance for investigating the nature of isms.

A paradigm is the constellation of ideas, values, models, techniques, metaphysical assumptions, symbolic generalizations and so on shared by a research community. It can also be concrete scientific achievements serving as models, examples and references for subsequent research. When scientists share a paradigm and work within a common disciplinary matrix, it brings about coherent, corresponding and accumulative scientific research. When a paradigm gains sufficient momentum and support, it governs all research within its reach, and the research activities become normal science. Those who do not conform to the paradigm are effectively excluded from the scientific community. Stargazers who still insist on geocentricism are not accepted as astrophysicists—much like the designers of traditionalesque objects are not considered serious, professional designers and consequently are excluded from a design community permeated by a modernist ethos.

A striking and appealing aspect of Kuhn's theory, one essential to its understanding, is the persistent stress on the paradigm's dynamic character. It is in a state of continuous transformation and negotiation. But this intra-paradigmatic development is evolutionary and accumulative of nature. Even though a paradigm can be long-lasting, it is unlikely to be everlasting. As time passes, normal science articulates the paradigm in a more and more comprehensive and detailed manner. Thus, the chance of finding anomalies increases drastically. The period of abnormal science in which a paradigm is challenged by one or several alternative theories and subsequently replaced by a new paradigm is, according to Kuhn, characterized by chaos, unconventional methods, violation of laws, fierce rhetoric, generation gap and utter disrespect for traditions and institutions. These characteristics, because of their resemblance to those normally ascribed to political revolutions, led Kuhn to coin his term 'scientific revolution'. Paradigms succeed one another by way of revolutions. This type of development is by definition revolutionary rather than evolutionary, and it is disruptive rather than continuous.

The conversion necessary to recruit disciples and convince the entire profession or the relevant professional subgroup to abandon their tradition of normal science in favour of a new and tentative paradigm is not carried out by logic arguments alone:

> But paradigm debates are not really about relative problem-solving ability, though for good reasons they are usually couched in those terms . . . A decision between alternate ways of practising science is called for, and in the circumstances that decision must be based less on past achievement that on future promise . . . A decision of that kind can only be made on faith.[54]

So, according to Kuhn, a successful paradigm candidate will win the battle not so much based on its problem-solving abilities as on its seductive appeal. Revolutions are thus executed by a negotiation dominated by rhetoric, persuasion and faith. This claim, that revolutions are structured as negotiations between incommensurable disciplinary matrixes and that these negotiations are characterized by emotional/political persuasion rather than logical argument, is one of the most controversial of Kuhn's assertions, and it has led a number of his fellow philosophers of science to accuse him of reducing the nature of science and scientific change to something fundamentally irrational.[55] Whether or not this criticism is appropriate in the field of the history and philosophy of science is beyond the scope of this text, but Kuhn's attention to rhetoric, persuasion and faith as crucial factors in the battle for hegemony is decidedly poignant when considering design history. The art of persuasion demonstrated, for example, by the missionaries of modernism is often so fundamentally emotional and flamboyant in nature that the arguments based on problem-solving abilities are effectively overshadowed.

As already mentioned, there is no general consensus as to whether or not Kuhn's theories are applicable to fields other than natural science.[56] Kuhn acknowledges—albeit somewhat reluctantly—the possible advantages of such a theory transfer. The reason is that he himself has been inspired from other disciplines:

> To the extent that the book portrays scientific development as a succession of tradition-bound periods punctuated by non-cumulative breaks, its thesis are undoubtedly of wide applicability. But they should be, for they are borrowed from other fields. Historians of literature, of music, of the arts, of political development, and many other human activities

have long described their subjects in the same way. Periodization in terms of revolutionary breaks in style, taste, and institutional structure have been among their standard tools.[57]

This, and his explicit declaration that '[art historian Ernst H.] Gombrich's work . . . has been a great source of encouragement to me',[58] shows that an investigation of the appropriateness of Kuhn's theories to design history is warranted, because—as the previous historiographic discussions have shown—this discipline has inherited much of its theories, methods, and terminology from art history. The most prominent example of this is the use of isms as categorizing tools.

Some aspects of Kuhn's conception of paradigms, however, are problematic with respect to its potential application to design history. One of these is the question of which level paradigms operate on. Another is the seemingly assumed exclusivity of one governing paradigm in the periods of normal science. These notions warrant closer investigation.

One of the most articulate critics and refiners of Kuhn's theories is Paul Feyerabend. Like Kuhn, both Feyerabend and his fellow Kuhn dissident Imre Lakatos have been read by sociologists and their theories have been applied to social science.[59] Since the 1975 publication of his book *Against Method*,[60] Feyerabend has been labelled a methodological anarchist or dadaist and an epistemological enfant terrible. His main thesis is that science is mainly an anarchistic enterprise and that a theoretical anarchism is more humanitarian and more likely to encourage progress than a science based on strict methods: *anything goes!* In addition to being analytic, Feyerabend's work is highly normative—he is not only exploring how science is carried out, but he also agitates for how it should be carried out. For the purpose at hand the discussion will be limited to the question mentioned previously, where Feyerabend dissents with Kuhn—namely the unitarian and coherent nature of paradigms.

Feyerabend challenges this assumption by demonstrating through historical examples how the proliferation of theories is beneficial for science. He shows how scientists have, although efforts are commonly being made to avoid this impression, adopted a pluralistic methodology and that this is especially conspicuous in cases of extraordinary achievements:

> Knowledge so conceived is not a series of self-consistent theories that converges towards an ideal view; it is not a gradual approach to the truth. It is rather an ever increasing *ocean of mutually incompatible (and perhaps even incommensurable) alternatives*, each single theory, each fairy tale, each myth that is part of the collection forcing the others into greater articulation and all of them contributing, via this process of competition, to the development of our consciousness.[61]

Feyerabend thus opens up for a modified interpretation of Kuhnian paradigms by suggesting the existence of several, coexisting paradigms. He suggests that the methodological unit to be pursued is constituted by a 'whole set of partly overlapping, factually adequate, but mutually inconsistent theories'.[62] In other words, the existence of a multi-paradigmatic state must be accepted.

Within each disciplinary sub-field defined by each paradigm, the scientific activity can prosper and develop. But each sub-field as defined by each paradigm is more trivial and narrow that the broader field as defined by intuition. Also, the various operational definitions given by each paradigm may be severely discordant with one another. Thus, discussions on fundamental and philosophical basis of the broader field are obscured and hampered.

This situation may be broken up by a revolution, in which precisely these fundamental and philosophical questions are made headliners of the agenda. Such revolutions are most definitely not strictly rational and logical. They are networks of complex structures inhabited by actors with vastly differing and hidden agendas and fought by virtually any means necessary. Feyerabend refers to them as 'power struggles' rather than rational changes.[63]

Although Feyerabend seconds Kuhn's view on the existence, function and characteristics of revolutions, he criticizes Kuhn's developmental pattern *normal science (monism)—revolution (proliferation)—normal science (monism)* by showing that proliferation is not restricted to the periods of crisis and revolution but is always present—both before, during and after revolutions—and is in fact the very crux of the nature of scientific development.[64]

It is not always clear exactly what Kuhn means by the term 'paradigm'. In a later concession to his critics on how the ambivalent and ambiguous use of the term resulted in a state where '[the book] can be too nearly all things to all people',[65] Kuhn himself tried to disentangle the confusion and clarify the situation by admitting to two essentially different uses of it: paradigm as an exemplar and paradigm as a disciplinary matrix.[66] Margaret Masterman, on the other hand, counts at least twenty-two different definitions of paradigm in *The Structure of Scientific Revolutions*.[67] But then she categorizes the definitions and ends up identifying three senses of the term 'paradigm'.

The first sense is the group of definitions that function on a philosophical level. These are called the metaphysical paradigms. This is when a paradigm is defined as a world view, as a set of beliefs, as a metaphysical speculation, as a new way of seeing or as an organizing principle. The second sense is the group of definitions that function on a sociological level. These *sociological paradigms* are when a paradigm is defined as a recognized scientific achievement, as equivalent to a set of political institutions, or as equivalent to an accepted judicial decision or precedent. The third sense is the group of definitions that function on a more pragmatic level. These *artefact paradigms* are when a paradigm is defined as a classic work, as a model, as supplying tools, as instrumentation, or as an analogy, and seem to correspond to Kuhn's understanding of a paradigm as exemplar.[68]

Masterman's differentiation of the Kuhnian paradigms is a crucial step on the way to making the paradigmatic perspective congruous to design history. This assertion results from the previous discussion of isms as highly ambiguous and versatile entities that are used and understood on multiple levels. The implicitness and inconsistency of significations and meanings ascribed to different isms in different contexts complicate a deeper understanding of the phenomenon and thus also hamper a more constructive and valuable epistemological application of these frequently but confusingly used terms. How, then, do these different paradigmatic levels correspond to the different understandings and uses of isms in design?[69]

The metaphysical paradigms correspond to isms describing a world view, a set of beliefs, a metaphysical speculation, a new way of seeing or an organizing principle. Isms of this sort are fairly universal and long-lasting. Examples may be grand epochs of the past, like the Renaissance, or the dominant world view of the twentieth century—modernism. These kinds of isms can be seen as equivalent to what was described earlier as an episteme.[70]

The sociological paradigms correspond to isms describing recognized achievements, sets of institutions, formalities, sets of accepted values, modes or precedents. Isms of this sort can be both ephemeral and enduring in span, both narrow and vast in scope. They may coexist in a multi-paradigmatic state—at times peacefully, at times in conflict. This is where Kuhn pointed to what he saw as a weakness in his own analogy between the historical developments of science and art: '[J]ust because the success of one artistic tradition does not render another wrong or mistaken, art can support, far more readily than science, a number of simultaneous incompatible traditions of schools. For the same reason, when traditions do change, the accompanying controversies are usually resolved far more rapidly in science than in art.'[71] Kuhn thus considers science to be more revolutionary than art, and his view of paradigms in art seems to draw near Feyerabend's multi-paradigmatic model (which concerns science, and not art, though). This clarification is crucial to the potential value of the concept of paradigms to design history. Most isms and movements of twentieth-century design belong on this paradigmatic level—as sociological paradigms. Examples may include art deco, streamlining and deconstructivism.

Describing ideological development and structure in the history of design by introducing the concept of a multi-paradigmatic state has an interesting parallel in John Heskett's recent 'layering theory of design history' where he states that 'in everyday life, in contrast to the theories of academee, the new has never entirely replaced the old, but has instead been layered upon it . . . Design is therefore simultaneously about change, continuity and adaption.'[72] Much in the same vein, Enrico Castelnuovo and Jacques Gubler have argued that 'advanced technology does not do away with the old objects at all. In short the antinomy of the modern and the archaic does not generate conflict, but a process of adaptation.'[73] David Edgerton made a similar point in the history of technology, demonstrating the crucial role of old technologies in today's society.[74]

Although these authors are here concerned primarily with technologies, the same perspective can be applied to the ideological development of design history. Heskett demonstrates how different forms of production that are often linked to different epochs, cultures, societies and design practices in fact 'all still exist in one form or another across the globe, although many have been subject to modification as they continue to evolve'.[75] This is directly analogous to the conceptualization proposed here of ideological development and structure in the history of design as a multi-paradigmatic state. This suggested analogy also concurs with Jean Baudrillard's observation that 'The old sideboard, the car and the tape recorder exist side by side in the one sphere, even though their imaginary modes of existence, just like their technical modes of existence, differ radically.'[76]

Seeking to generalize the same idea, Rainer Wick has warned against what he considered the all too common (as of twenty years ago) practice of considering styles as discrete, consecutive entities, and he asserted that we must acknowledge the 'simultaneousness of the unsimultaneous', that is the fact 'that various layers of historical time—different in duration, speed or acceleration—can temporally overlap'.[77] Similarly, and indicating that this temporal syncretism does in fact apply both to technological and ideological development, Lucila Fernández Uriarte has pointed to 'the parallel existence of different works, technology and cultural periods of historical evolution in the same historic phase'.[78] The complexity of temporal ideology is of course not restricted to the sphere of design, but is prevalent in society at large. As David Lowenthal has observed; 'retrospective nostalgia coexists with impatient modernism.'[79]

Masterman's third paradigmatic level, the artefact paradigms, correspond to isms describing a classic work, a model, an example, a tool box, instrumentation or an analogy. Isms of this sort are highly instrumentalist, pragmatic, and conformist. Isms belong on this paradigmatic level when they are primarily considered as styles or formal expressions. These isms are normally made up of a series of prefigurative exemplars or models functioning as prototypes, as a repertoire or as a reservoir of possibilities. Canonical products/works and their constellations form such isms. One might also consider each canonical product/work to be an artefact paradigm in its own right. This would correspond to Kuhn's notion of a paradigm as a standard example, an exemplar. Studying and learning to understand such exemplars are, according to Kuhn, essential for aspiring members of a professional community (paradigm as disciplinary matrix). His examples refer to how acquiring an arsenal of exemplars from the history of physics (e.g. Galileo's pendulum and the Schrödinger equation) is one of the most fundamental processes whereby students of physics are enrolled in the community of professional physicists.[80] In direct parallel, acquiring an arsenal of exemplars from the history of architecture—by studying canonical works—is one of the most fundamental processes whereby students of architecture are enrolled in the community of professional architects. In

20 The artefact paradigm: The paradigm as a standard example, an exemplar, is often used in training and socializing new members of a discipline. Students of architecture, for instance, are well versed in the canonical works when entering the professional ranks. Restaurant Skansen in Oslo, 1926-1927. Architect: Lars Backer. Copyright Oslo City Archives

the present context, it is interesting to note that Kuhn himself considered this understanding of paradigm as the most relevant parallel to the sphere of art history: 'If the notion of paradigm can be useful to the art historian, it will be pictures not styles that serve as paradigms.'[81] However, it must be stressed that the interpretations of canonical works are also subject to changes according to paradigmatic developments.[82]

Introducing this differential multi-paradigmatic system probably raises more questions than it answers, and there are surely many alternative sound ways of approaching this topic. These reflections are intended as a first step towards a broader conceptual framework for exploring the dynamics of design historical change. In closing, the final section offers some remarks on how the differential multi-paradigmatic system might function as a tool for thought when inquiring into isms as an epistemological phenomenon in particular and structures of ideological developments in design history in general.

Modern Isms

Following the differential paradigmatic system introduced previously one might ask on which paradigmatic-level revolutions occur. Based on the characterizations and distinctions that have been introduced, it is plausible to say that the notion of revolutions in design history belongs to the primary level of metaphysical paradigms. These world views or sets of beliefs can be said to reign relatively sovereign for a longer period, until they are challenged and finally overthrown by rebels. Thus, the classic Kuhnian developmental pattern *normal science (monism)—revolution (proliferation)—normal science (monism)* might seem apt in describing the primary level of metaphysical paradigms, although probably not so regarding the secondary and third levels of sociological and artefact paradigms.

This can be illustrated by borrowing one of Kuhn's favourite examples of a scientific revolution; the shift from Newtonian to Einsteinian physics. Kuhn's claim that this represented a revolution might make sense when considered on an epistemological or metaphysical level, in the same way that relativity theory might be said to have drastically altered the reigning world view. However, for most worldly endeavours, Newtonian physics still makes perfectly good sense—engineers, architects and designers rarely need to supplant Newtonian physics. This suggests that even such a neat example as relativity theory can be said to represent a scientific revolution only when considered at the primary level of metaphysical paradigms and not in the empirical sphere of secondary level of sociological paradigms.

It is customarily and, to a certain extent, rather convincingly argued that modernism represents a metaphysical paradigm resulting from a revolution—although some recent research contributions to the history of early modernist architecture have emphasized continuity over rupture in the analysis of the transitional period from late romanticism to early modernism.[83] One might argue, then—as Mari Hvattum does—that '[t]he much discussed rupture is ... only made possible by a strong continuity in the history of ideas between historicism and modernism'.[84] This ambivalence regarding continuity/rupture might depend, at least in part, on whether one considers modernism as an episteme (metaphysical paradigm, world view) or as an ism (sociological paradigm, design ideology).

Also, modernism still seems to be the reigning primary-level metaphysical paradigm simply because, as Jürgen Habermas has pointed out, the project of modernity has not yet been fulfilled.[85] Andrea Branzi has also argued for the persistence of modernism but asserts that 'the design of today is operating within a modernity that is stripped of enlightenment'.[86] Others, of course, beg to differ: Bruno Latour has argued that the nature-culture dichotomy, which is generally accepted as one of the principle hallmarks of modernity, is no simple matter of fact but largely a matter of faith and, hence, that we have never been modern.[87] When considering changing paradigms in design it is important to bear in mind that a metaphysical paradigm like modernism consists of several domains, of which the artistic/aesthetic/ideological sphere is but one alongside other cultural spheres as well as social, political, economic and technological spheres.[88] Hence, as Habermas argues, negating one or some of these does not automatically turn an ideological movement into a revolution: 'Communication processes need a cultural tradition covering all spheres—cognitive, moral-practical and expressive. A rationalized everyday life, therefore, could hardly be saved from cultural impoverishment through breaking open a single cultural sphere—art—and so providing access to just one of the specialized knowledge complexes. The surrealist revolt would have replaced only one abstraction.'[89] Habermas's example of an ideological movement aspiring to paradigmatic revolution is surrealist art, but most self-proclaimed avant-garde design movements of the last decades could easily take its place, because just like surrealist art, they represent alternative paradigms rather than revolutionary ones—despite the flamboyant rhetoric.

It should be noted that the structural longevity of epistemes makes their characteristics particularly difficult to discern unequivocally in contemporary analysis. These difficulties are only enhanced by the fact that people's identities, thoughts, ideas, and knowledge are afforded and restricted by the very episteme or metaphysical paradigm under investigation.

Nevertheless, the last decades have not lacked for prophecies and assertions of a postmodern revolution. But it is doubtful whether these claims have succeeded in identifying a revolutionary, metaphysical paradigm as defined here. For instance, Charles Jencks claimed that 'Modern Architecture died in St Louis, Missouri on July 15, 1972 at 3.32 p.m. (or thereabouts) when the infamous Pruitt-Igoe scheme, or rather several of its slab blocks were given the final *coup de grâce* by dynamite . . . Boom, boom, boom.'[90] This statement from Jencks's book *The Language of Post-Modern Architecture* refers to the demolition of a housing project planned and constructed in 1950–1954, designed by the firm of Leinweber, Yamasaki & Hellmuth, and it is intended to demonstrate the failure and fall of modernism. It is a punchline of dimensions and it is so marvellously tabloid that even the father of New Journalism, Tom Wolfe, genuflects at Jencks's proclamation of death in his crusade against modernism; *From Bauhaus to Our House*.[91]

Katharine G. Bristol has demonstrated how the Pruitt-Igoe myth is constructed by writers like Jencks, and Peter Blake before him,[92] on a series of highly questionable assumptions regarding the role of architects and architectural design in social housing development and points to a series of other aspects, structures and actors responsible for the demise of this housing project.

By reducing the problems of public housing to a question of autonomous, physical design, Jencks and his co-constructors of the Pruitt-Igoe myth have inflated the power of the architect and architectural design at the expense of the other inhabitants of the actor network in question and thus turned the myth into a weapon in the debate on aesthetic aspects of architectural design.[93] Scholars of postmodernism outside the realm of design and architecture have also criticized Jencks for a lack of academic rigor. Pondering why Jencks is largely considered such an authority on postmodern architecture, Hans Bertens finds it 'tempting to think that this has to do with the fact that his model is eminently accessible—as is his style—while it simultaneously *seems* intellectually respectable'.[94]

It is perhaps unfair to measure Jencks's rhetoric and arguments against stringent demands of academic historical research—the book is a polemic manifest. They do, however, make up an excellent example of the need any emerging ism (in this case postmodernism) has to ridicule and falsify the dominating ideas and practices of the present in order to portray its own ideas as new, revolutionary, seminal and true. By declaring the death of modernism and proclaiming the ascendancy of the new paradigm of postmodernism, Jencks uses an ordering device that is as conventional as it is simplistic. But conceptualizing isms as a 'string of pearls', or a 'family tree' is perhaps the most evident example of his fundamentally modernist affiliation. Because, as John Law has argued; 'the idea that there is a *single* order ... is the dream, or the nightmare, of modernity'.[95] Jencks's act is thus that of a true modernist—because, as Arnfinn Bø-Rygg has pointed out: 'When today—from an allegedly postmodern vantage point—we historicize modernity or declare ourselves to have reached a postmodern state, this is itself a modern impulse.'[96] Or, as Espen Schaanning puts it: 'Whether one tries to disclose the modern project (postmodernity) or refine it (modernity) is all the same as long as the disclosure itself is a modern project.'[97] Similar points have been proposed by others as well: Gianni Vattimo argues that it is precisely the desire to represent something historically new and different that de facto links postmodernism to the basic idea of modernism.[98] Similarly, Matei Calinescu argues convincingly that 'Postmodernism is a face of modernity', alongside modernism.[99]

Acknowledging the problems regarding the advocacy of a postmodern revolution or age, Omar Calabrese has suggested to speak instead of the neobaroque age (*l'età neobarocca*), because the term 'postmodernism' is both too equivocal and too generic to be useful.[100] Contrary to Calabrese, Dick Hebdige asserts that it is precisely the ambiguity of the term that makes it worth exploring: 'the degree of semantic complexity and overload surrounding the term "postmodernism" at the moment signals that a significant number of people with conflicting interests and opinions feel that there is something sufficiently important at stake here to be worth struggling and arguing over.'[101] Whether Calabrese's suggestion solves any problems is highly debatable, but his view on late-modern times as a neobaroque age becomes quite fascinating when paired with Jean Baudrillard's assertion that 'it is the baroque, with its predilection for the allegorical, its new discursive individualism based on redundant forms and tricked-up materials, and its demiurgic formalism, that is the true inaugurating moment of the modern age'. To bring the discussion full circle, to reach fulfilment, as it were: 'The baroque clearly foreshadows on the artistic plane all the themes and myths of our technological civilization, right down to its paroxysmic formalism of detail and movement.'[102] Whatever one chooses to make of these deliberations, it goes to show that any consensus regarding a postmodern paradigm hardly can be said to have materialized.

If postmodernism were to be considered a primary-level, metaphysical paradigm, then the Kuhnian idea of a paradigm as a developmental state following a revolution must be refuted altogether. A different definition substituting for paradigm would then be required, for instance, by returning to the evolutionary theories of Karl Popper or relying on Imre Lakatos's rationalistic ideas of a research programme.[103] However, the term 'evolution' could in itself be troublesome, because it has often been associated with an archaic approach to history where historical development is portrayed as linear, conform, absolutist and deterministic.[104] This has characterized traditions as diverse as traditional moralistic history, positivist history (*wie es eigentlich gewesen*) and the internalist profession histories—where the history of design lines up with those of science, technology and medicine.

Still, in design history there has been a continuous effort at exploring an evolutionary approach eluding the usual pitfalls of determinism and linearity. Philip Steadman offered one of the more elaborate and consistent earlier examples in his 1979 *The Evolution of Designs*.[105] However, even Steadman goes a long way in admitting that this evolutionary approach and biological analogy is not appropriate for the study of *modern* design. Furthermore, this more or less archaeological notion of evolution has other shortcomings as well, one of which has been pointed out by Ian Hodder: 'The evolutionary perspective has emphasized adaptive relationships at different levels of complexity, but it has not encouraged an examination of the particular historical context.'[106] Nevertheless, the interest in the theme of evolution prevails in design history, as reflected in the theme and title of the 2006 Design History Society Annual Conference in Delft, 'Design and Evolution', and in writings attempting to restore an evolutionary approach to design history.[107]

Another problem with Popper's evolutionary approach is that it stands firmly by the representationalist view of science and thus becomes essentially ahistorical.[108] Feyerabend's philosophy of science, on the other hand, denounces representationalism, and can thus provide a better basis for understanding the dynamics of historical change—not only in the history of science but also in design history. This dawning interest in processes intrinsic to the work of Kuhn and Feyerabend has more recently been cultivated extensively within the field of science and technology studies (STS)—as discussed in chapter two.

Whereas postmodernism or other twentieth-century design ideological movements hardly can be considered primary-level, metaphysical paradigms, they can be considered paradigms of secondary-level; sociological paradigms. This requires that an acceptance of Feyerabend's and Masterman's interpretations of Kuhn, which allow for a multi-paradigmatic situation. Seen as a sociological paradigm, an ism is a set of institutions, accepted values and achievements, modes, formalities or precedents. Postmodernism can thus be regarded as a genuine, articulate, adequate, and autonomous paradigm. But it is not *the* new paradigm; it is *a* new, alternative paradigm.

The suggestion here of modernism as a metaphysical paradigm functioning more or less as an episteme for all isms (secondary level, sociological paradigms) of the twentieth century should become more intelligible, and perhaps also more plausible, through some schematic illustrations of the heterogeneous, extensive, and diversified character of modernism as a function of different parameters. Here it is opportune, though, to recall how Dominick LaCapra cautions against treating analytical categories—such as isms—as dichotomous, discrete entities.[109] While keeping in mind that in any empirical analysis, categories presuppose, overlap and supplement each other, in this specific epistemological context it is preferable to emphasize the clarificatory effect of such a highly schematic presentation, despite its obvious shortcomings in terms of unjust simplification.

Considering modernism as a primary-level metaphysical paradigm might allow one to better understand and explore the remarkable transformations of modernism through space and time. First of all, the chronological development of modernism alone should indicate that modernism is a primary-level metaphysical paradigm which is constantly transformed. But the chronological dissection is only one of many possible ways of demonstrating the diversity, complexity and heterogeneity of modernism. Its extensive and inclusive character may also be portrayed as a function of other parameters. For instance, the ideological and political dispersion and divergence clearly show that modernism does not represent any common and homogeneous ground; no shared sets of accepted values and ideas. In other words: modernism, at least when approached in this manner, does not fit the aforementioned definition of a secondary-level sociological paradigm.

Yet another way of displaying the differentiated, comprehensive and inclusive character of modernism is by offering a cross-section of the different movements or segments it encompasses at a given moment in time. This suggests that the primary-level metaphysical paradigm constituted by modernism contains several secondary-level sociological paradigms constituted by the familiar isms of the twentieth century. Modernism as a world view, a metaphysical paradigm or an episteme affords and restricts the isms as a—to paraphrase Feyerabend—whole set of partly overlapping, factually adequate, but mutually inconsistent movements. It follows that each ism of the twentieth century could in general be considered a secondary-level sociological paradigm, which combined form a multi-paradigmatic state. However, this outline is too schematic, and modernism might seem to hover or oscillate somewhere between the primary and the secondary level, featuring some characteristics of a metaphysical paradigm, some of a sociological paradigm.

The terminological and conceptual challenges of studying modernism and modern design are considerable. Yet it is hoped that some of the findings of this initial and tentative inquiry can become helpful guidelines for a design history more sensitive towards its own terminology and reflexive of its own conceptualization principles.

This chapter began with a brief historical outline of the fundamental terms 'modern', 'modernity' and 'modernism', before attempting to clarify the relation between isms as doctrines or aesthetic ideologies on the one hand and isms as world views or structures of society on the other. The distinction between isms and epistemes is crucial to bear in mind but can be difficult to sustain. It becomes increasingly so when the two appear under the same term, as they often do in the case of modernism. This fact most certainly complicates any study of modernism, but it might also be a key to understanding the phenomenon and explaining its comprehensive and prevailing character.

One of the main ambitions of this chapter has been to argue that an ism can be understood as a cultural mode defined by negotiations between design ideology and design practice. After this proposition of modern isms as articulations of design culture, the focus shifted towards a discussion of isms as dynamic discources. Isms are not solid, monolithic blocks. They are constantly formed, transformed and reformed throughout their life spans by way of unceasing negotiations within the actor networks. These processes of domestication show that isms are dynamic, changing phenomena in constant development. If this core property is appreciated, isms are not categorizing straitjackets but instead can become interesting and fruitful objects of study.

The latter half of this chapter sought to approach the issue of isms from a different perspective, exploring the prospects of Kuhnian paradigms in framing the dynamics of historical change in design ideology. The brief reassessment of the Kuhnian notion of paradigms and how this concept might relate to that of isms should by no means be understood as any decisive or exhaustive elucidation, but rather as one possible and tentative way of exploring the many questions raised by the topic at hand.

Introducing the differential paradigmatic system to design history does not by any means solve every epistemological problem posed by isms as a terminological category. But the general view and the analytic tools offered by such a system may render it a valuable contribution to a broader conceptual framework capable of improving the understanding of this complex phenomenon. The presuppositions, presumptions, and tacitness that all to often accompany the use and interpretation of isms bear evidence of the need for enhanced structuring and articulation of this set of problems.

This chapter has sought to explore some basic terms and concepts that are essential to design history. It is meant as an exploratory discussion, and thus deliberately raises more questions than it professes to answer. It clearly leaves a lot to be desired but hopefully can serve as a basis for further deliberation towards a better grounded and more thorough understanding of the epistemological dimensions of design history.

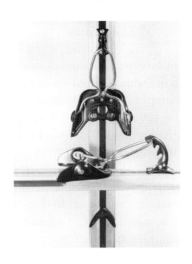

Conclusion

Design history has become a complex and wide-ranging discipline. It now examines design in all its multifariousness, from conception to development, production, mediation and consumption. Its subject matter has expanded so far beyond the myopic attention to 'good design' and 'great designers' that once dominated the discipline that it might perhaps be beneficial to use the term 'design culture'. Guy Julier defines 'Design culture as an object of study . . . that includes both the material and the immaterial aspects of everyday life. On one level it is articulated through images, words, forms and spaces. But at another it engages discourses, actions, beliefs, structures and relationships.'[1] This shift in the focus and practice of design history is grounded and reflected in changes in the theoretical and methodological aspects of the discipline. However, these accompanying theoretical developments have only sparingly and sporadically been subjected to explicit debate. This book is intended as a contribution to such a debate by offering an introduction to some of the defining discourses that have formed the field and that continue to shape design history today.

Chapter one surveyed the historiography of the field. Design history has a brief history in terms of academic grounding. It follows that the discipline's own history, its relation to theory and its development of methods is no done deal but is still very much in formation and should thus be seen as an ongoing discourse. As with all history, the present is made from the past. Understanding what design history is today, then, requires an understanding of what design history has been. A critical discussion of the discipline's own history is therefore essential to its present and future practice. The chapter started out from a critique of the heritage from art history, pointing out some of the problems resulting from this tradition, before discussing the promotion and formation of a design history better suited to deal with a subject matter far beyond the applied arts. The middle section offered an analysis of a debate on the role and place of design history in relation to design practice and design research on the one hand and the broader academic domain of cultural studies and the humanities on the other. The last sections of chapter one assessed the influence on design history from material culture studies before ending up arguing for a cultural history of design.

Chapter two introduced new theoretical frameworks and methodological concepts from the field known as science and technology studies (STS) and discussed their potential to design history. As argued in chapter one, design history does not have a very well-defined theoretical framework and methodological apparatus, nor has this seemed to be a particularly prioritized area of inquiry. The exploration of alternative, additional and complementary references and sources of inspiration has begun, but few excursions have been made in the direction proposed here: recent developments in the sociology and history of technology. Arguing that design has more in common with technology than with art when considered as a social and cultural phenomenon, design historians may find that the sociology and history of technology can provide an appropriate theoretical framework and methodological repertoire for studying design. After an introductory argument for the common ground and common future of the histories of technology and design, chapter two discussed some concepts from STS that might be of particular value to design history, focusing on actor-network theory, script analysis and domestication.

Chapter three discussed selected basic epistemological questions related to historical studies of design. Its main objective was to investigate the rather intangible notion of modern isms as a categorizing concept and analytic tool and to develop an understanding of design ideologies as parts of cultural modes. A brief historical outline of the fundamental terms *modern*, *modernity* and *modernism* was followed by a clarification of the difference between isms as doctrines or aesthetic ideologies on the one hand and isms as world views or structures of society on the other. The main ambition of this chapter was to investigate the nature of isms as tools of classification and analysis, especially in the context of modernism and its etymologically derived isms. From this derived the idea that an ism can be understood as a cultural mode defined by negotiations between design ideology and design practice. Understanding isms as articulations of design culture taps into one of this book's central tenets: that design history has much to benefit from an alignment with cultural history and that its subject matter might prove more inclusive and more manageable if conceived of as design culture.

Talking of design culture may help open up design history and cultivate connections to neighbouring fields and disciplines. Doing so is crucial to the future of design history as a respected member of the academic community. Victor Margolin recently lamented that design history, despite all the ground that has been covered since the 1980s, remains on the margins of the broader field of historical research. He challenged design historians 'to make a persuasive case for the relevance of their knowledge to fora outside of their field'.[2] Drawing attention to the relevance of design culture to those outside the congregation of design researchers and design historians, Ben Highmore has argued that 'What makes design culture such a productive arena for general social and cultural research is that it can supply the objects that demonstrate the thoroughly entangled nature of our interactions in the material world, the way in which bodies, emotions, world trade and aesthetics, for instance, interweave at the most everyday level.'[3] Offering design culture as such an empirical common will have theoretical and methodological implications as well. Bringing new topics, theories and methods to the design historical table is essential to keep the discipline dynamic and vital. Even material and approaches that might at first sight appear less than immediate to design history may on closer inspection prove to be of great value. Pointing to the varied interests in the broader fields of cultural and social sciences over the recent decades in topics spanning from the body to everyday life to science and technology and approaches ranging from intellectual history to feminism to neurobiology and actor-network theory, Highmore proposes 'to see "design culture" (or design studies) as the place where all these topics and approaches could come together, where the entanglements of this range of phenomena can be seen most vividly'.[4] Expecting the entire humanities and social sciences collectively to flock to design culture as their point of empirical convergence, as if it were some sort of academic cornucopia, would be overly optimistic. But if design history is thought of as the history of design culture or as the cultural history of design, then not only will its relevance to the rest of the humanities and social sciences increase, it will also help integrate design history with these disciplines and share their exploration of new topics and methods. This book is intended as one contribution to this endeavour.

Notes

Introduction

1. Don DeLillo, *Underworld* (Scribner, 1997), p. 542.
2. Ben Highmore, 'A Sideboard Manifesto: Design Culture in an Artificial World', in Ben Highmore, ed., *The Design Culture Reader* (Routledge, 2009), p. 4.
3. Bill Brown, 'Thing Theory' in Bill Brown, ed., *Things* (University of Chicago Press, 2004), p. 7.
4. Hazel Conway, ed., *Design History—A Student's Handbook* (Routledge, 1987) and John A. Walker, *Design History and the History of Design* (Pluto, 1989).
5. Quotes are from Lelo company Web site, www.lelo.com, accessed 22 April 2009.
6. Herbert Simon, *The Sciences of the Artificial*, 3rd edn. (MIT Press, 1996), p. 111.
7. Victor Margolin, 'The Product Milieu and Social Action', in Richard Buchanan and Victor Margolin, eds., *Discovering Design: Explorations in Design Studies* (University of Chicago Press, 1995), p. 122.
8. Ludwig Wittgenstein, *Philosophical Investigations,* 3rd edn. (Blackwell, 1967), p. 34e.
9. Henrik Ibsen, 'A Verse Letter' (org. title 'Et rimbrev', written in 1875, translated by John Northam), www.ibsen.net, accessed 24 April 2009.

I Historiography

1. These include Clive Dilnot, 'The State of Design History, Part I', *Design Issues* 1/1, 1984, pp. 3–23; Clive Dilnot, 'The State of Design History, Part II', *Design Issues* 1/2, 1984, pp. 3–20; Enrico Castelnuovo and Jacques Gubler, 'The Mysterious Object—Notes on the Historiography of Design', in Carlo Pirovano, ed., *History of Industrial Design, 3:1919–1990 The Dominion of*

Design (Electa, 1990), pp. 404–413; Victor Margolin, 'Design History or Design Studies: Subject Matter and methods', *Design Studies*, 13/2, pp. 104–16, Jonathan M. Woodham, 'Resisting Colonization: Design History Has Its own Identity', *Design Issues*, 11/1, pp. 22–37; Victor Margolin, 'Design History in the United States, 1977–2000', in Victor Margolin, *The Politics of the Artificial* (University of Chicago Press, 2001), pp. 126–87.

2. Nikolaus Pevsner, *Pioneers of the Modern Movement—from William Morris to Walter Gropius* (Faber & Faber, 1936); Sigfried Giedion, *Mechanization Takes Command—a Contribution to Anonymous History* (Oxford University Press, 1948); Reyner Banham, *Theory and Design in the First Machine Age* (Architectural Press, 1960).

3. For historiographical analyses of their work, see Peter Draper, ed., *Reassessing Nikolaus Pevsner* (Ashgate, 2004); Sokratis Georgiadis, *Sigfried Giedion: An Intellectual Biography* (Edinburgh University Press, 1989); Nigel Whiteley, *Reyner Banham: Historian of the Immediate Future* (MIT Press, 2002); Gillian Naylor, 'Theory and Design: The Banham Factor: The Ninth Reyner Banham Memorial Lecture', *Journal of Design History*, 10/3, pp. 241–52; Vincent Michael, 'Reyner Banham: Signs and Designs in the Time Without Style', *Design Issues*, 18/2, pp. 65–77.

4. Not only was the Design History Society (DHS) founded in Britain (in 1977), but as recently as 2004 about 80 per cent of DHS members were British: Jonathan M. Woodham, 'Local, National and Global: Redrawing the Design Historical Map', *Journal of Design History*, 18/3, p. 258.

5. Walker, *Design History and the History of Design*, pp. 1–2.

6. Reed Benhamou, '*Journal of Design History*, Vol. 1, nos. 1–4.' [Review], *Technology and Culture*, 32/1, p. 136.

7. Margolin, 'Design History in the United States, 1977–2000', in *The Politics of the Artificial* (University of Chicago Press, 2001) pp. 131–33.

8. Articles from the first volumes of *Design Issues* are compiled in Victor Margolin, ed., *Design Discourse: History, Theory, Criticism* (University of Chicago Press, 1989) and Victor Margolin and Richard Buchanan, eds., *The Idea of Design* (MIT Press, 1995).

9. Proceeding from the 1985 conference were published as Mirjam Gelfer-Jørgensen, ed., *Nordisk Funktionalisme 1925–1950* (Det danske Kunstindustrimuseum & Nordisk Forum for Formgivningshistorie, 1986). The *Scandinavian Journal of Design History* was published as an annual from 1991 to 2005. It is currently in a state of hibernation due to funding problems, and no issue has appeared since volume 15 in 2005.

10. The proceedings were published as Anty Pansera, ed., *Tradizione e Modernismo: Design 1918/1940—Atti del convegno* (L'Arca, 1988) and Vanni Pasca and Francesco Trabucco, eds., *Design: Storia e Storiografia* (Progetto Leonardo, 1995).

11. Conway, ed., *Design History* and Walker, *Design History and the History of Design*.

12. Oscar Wilde, *The Picture of Dorian Gray* (1891; repr. Penguin, 1994), p. 6.

13. Walker, *Design History and the History of Design*, p. 17.

14. Jonathan M. Woodham, 'Designing Design History: From Pevsner to Postmodernism', Paper delivered at the Digitisation and Knowledge conference at Auckland University of Technology, April 2001.

15. A selection of articles published in the journal were compiled in Sally Stafford, et al., eds., *The BLOCK Reader in Visual Culture* (Routledge, 1996).

16. Jonathan M. Woodham, *A Dictionary of Modern Design* (Oxford University Press, 2004), p. 51.

17. Among these are John Heskett, 'Modernism and Archaism in Design in the Third Reich', *Block* 3, pp.13–24; Tony Fry, 'Design History: A Debate?', *Block* 5, pp. 14–18; Dick Hebdige, 'Object as Image: The Italian Scooter Cycle', *Block* 5, pp. 44–64; Tony Fry, 'Unpacking the Typewriter', *Block* 7, pp. 36–47; Philippa Goodall, 'Design and Gender', *Block* 9, pp. 50–61.

18. Jonathan Harris, *The New Art History—A Critical Introduction* (Routledge, 2001), pp. 19, 40, 209.

19. Caroline A. Jones, 'Talking Pictures: Clement Greenberg's Pollock', in Lorraine Daston, ed., *Things That Talk—Object Lessons form Art and Science* (Zone Books, 2004), pp. 329–73. Her reference to Latour is from Bruno Latour, *Politics of Nature* (Harvard University Press, 2004).

20. Fran Hannah and Tim Putnam, 'Taking Stock in Design History', *Block* 3, p. 26.

21. Ibid., p. 30.

22. Ibid.

23. Stafford, et al., eds., *The BLOCK Reader in Visual Culture,* p. 131.

24. Ibid.

25. Ibid., p. 132.

26. Heskett, 'Modernism and Archaism in Design in the Third Reich', and Fry, 'Design History: A Debate?',

27. Tomás Maldonado, 'New Developments in Industry and the Training of Designers', *Architects' Yearbook*, 9, p. 176.

28. Castelnuovo and Gubler, 'The Mysterious Object—Notes on the Historiography of Design', p. 408.

29. See e.g. Enrico Castelnuovo, 'For a History of Design', in Carlo Pirovano, ed. in chief, *History of Industrial Design*, 1:*1750–1850 The Age of the Industrial Revolution* (Electa, 1990), pp. 8–11.

30. Some of the reasons for and problems with this tradition are discussed at some length in Walker, *Design History and the History of Design*, pp. 45–63.

31. Hazel Conway, 'Design History Basics', in Conway, ed., *Design History*, p. 9.

32. Jan Michl, 'On Seeing Design as Redesign—An Exploration of a Neglected Problem in Design Education', *Scandinavian Journal of Design History*, 12, pp. 7–23. The quest of attribution, as it is known from art history, thus often becomes futile and uninteresting—a case in point being the first Sony Walkman: In the desire to pinpoint its author, various commentators have attributed it to at least five different persons (including Sony founders Masaru Ibuka and Akio Morita and the general manager of the Sony Tape Recorder Business Division at the time, Kozo Ohsone). The fact that the first Walkman—model no. TPS-L2—was launched in 1979 and hence can hardly be said to be ancient history only strengthens the case against personal attribution as a primary concern in design history: Paul du Gay, et al., *Doing Cultural Studies—The Story of the Sony Walkman* (Sage, 1997), p. 42. As the authors state: 'In

discussing the design of the Walkman, our interest is not with *who* designed it, but with what its design embodies or represents—in other words, with how its very design 'makes meaning'' (p. 62).

33. David Lowenthal, *The Past is a Foreign Country* (Cambridge University Press, 1985), p. 70.

34. Paul Betts, *The Authority of Everyday Objects—A Cultural History of West German Industrial Design* (University of California Press, 2004), esp. chapter one; pp. 23–72.

35. Harris, *The New Art History*, pp. 17 & 194.

36. Ibid., pp. 17 & 194.

37. Giedion, *Mechanization Takes Command*.

38. Jean Baudrillard, *The System of Objects* (1968; repr. Verso, 1996), p. 4.

39. Bernard Rudofsky, *Architecture Without Architects: A Short Introduction to Non-pedigreed Architecture* (Academy Editions, 1964).

40. George Kubler, *The Shape of Time—Remarks on the History of Things* (Yale University Press, 1962), p. 6.

41. Nicos Hadjinicolaou, *Art History and Class Struggle* (Pluto Press, 1978), pp. 35–43.

42. As Cheryl Buckley put it: 'Though many of [the historiographic] methods [used by design historians] are problematic for design history in general, not just a feminist design history, feminist intervention, as in other disciplines, has demarcated the basic ones.': Cheryl Buckley, 'Made in Patriarchy: Toward a Feminist Analysis of Women and Design', *Design Issues*, 3/2, p. 9.

43. Carma R. Gorman, 'Reshaping and Rethinking: Recent Feminist Scholarship on Design and Designers', *Design Issues*, 17/4, p. 74.

44. David Raizman, *History of Modern Design—Graphics and Products Since the Industrial Revolution* (Laurence King, 2003).

45. Mirjam Gelfer-Jørgensen, 'Has Design History Anything to Do with Art History?', *Scandinavian Journal of Design History* 11, p. 17.

46. Ibid., p. 19.

47. Ibid., p. 18.

48. Jeffrey L. Meikle, 'Material Virtues: on the Ideal and the Real in Design History', *Journal of Design History*, 11/3, quote pp. 191–92.

49. Gelfer-Jørgensen, 'Has Design History Anything to Do with Art History?', p. 20.

50. Walker, *Design History and the History of Design*, p. 5.

51. Meikle, 'Material Virtues', pp. 193–94 and Joseph J. Corn, 'Object Lessons/Object Myths? What Historians of Technology Learn from Things', in W. David Kingery, ed., *Learning from Things—Method and Material of Material Culture Studies* (Smithsonian Institution Press, 1996), pp. 46 & 49.

52. The artefact as source has been widely discussed in several of these fields and has resulted in some interesting publications, including Steven Lubar and W. David Kingery, eds., *History from Things—Essays on Material Culture* (Smithsonian Institution Press, 1993); Kingery, ed., *Learning from Things*; Susan M. Pearce, ed., *Interpreting Objects and Collections* (Routledge, 1994); and Daston, ed., *Things That Talk*.

53. Steven Lubar and W. David Kingery, 'Introduction', in Lubar and Kingery, eds., *History from Things*, p. ix.

54. Peter Dormer, *The Meanings of Modern Design* (Thames & Hudson, 1990), p. 10.
55. Fry, 'Design History: A Debate?', p. 14.
56. Ibid. p. 16
57. Ibid. p. 15
58. John Heskett, 'Some Lessons of Design History', in Astrid Skjerven, ed., *Designkompetanse— Utvkling, forskning og undervisning* (Oslo National Academy of the Arts, 2005), p. 12.
59. Gillo Dorfles, 'Introduzione', in Pansera, ed., *Tradizione e Modernismo*, p. 3 (author's translation).
60. Maldonado, 'New Developments in Industry and the Training of Designers', p. 176.
61. As Heskett also points out, this de-contextualized treatment of objects is particularly common in museums. This is also what led Theodor Adorno to declare that 'Museum and mausoleum are connected by more than phonetic association. They testify to the neutralization of culture.' When an object is placed in a museum, especially when put in a showcase or on a pedestal, it is severed from its contexts, it becomes meaningless and dead—like an embalmed body: Theodor Adorno, 'Valéry Proust Museum', in *Prisms* (MIT Press, 1983), p. 175. For a discussion of this problem, see Neil Cummings and Marysia Lewandowska, *The Value of Things* (August/Birkhäuser, 2000).
62. John Heskett, *Industrial Design* (Thames & Hudson, 1980), pp. 7–9.
63. All the more ironic, then, that the book is published as part of a series called 'world of art'.
64. Gert Selle, *Die Geschichte des Design in Deutschland von 1870 bis heute—Entwicklung der industriellen Produktkultur* (DuMont, 1978); Penny Sparke, *Consultant Design—The History and Practice of the Designer in Industry* (Pembridge Press, 1983); Penny Sparke, *An Introduction to Design and Culture in the Twentieth Century* (Allen & Unwin, 1986); Jonathan M. Woodham, *The Industrial Designer and the Public* (Pembridge, 1983); Jonathan M. Woodham, *Twentieth-Century Design* (Oxford University Press, 1997); Tony Fry, *Design History Australia* (Hale & Iremonger, 1988); Paolo Fossati, *Il Design in Italia 1945–1972* (Einaudi, 1972); Anty Pansera, *Storia del Disegno Industriale Italiano* (Laterza, 1993); Jeffrey L. Meikle, *Twentieth Century Limited: Industrial Design in America, 1925–1939* (Temple University Press, 1979); and Jeffrey L. Meikle, *Design in the USA* (Oxford University Press, 2005).
65. John Heskett, 'Industrial Design', in Conway, ed., *Design History*, p. 112.
66. Heskett, 'Industrial Design', p. 125.
67. Ibid. pp. 112–13.
68. Walker, *Design History and the History of Design*, pp. 27, 70 & 174–85.
69. Suzette Worden and Jill Seddon, 'Women Designers in Britain in the 1920s and 1930s: Defining the Professional and Redefining Design', *Journal of Design History*, 8/3, p. 177.
70. Grace Lees-Maffei, 'Studying Advice: Historiography, Methodology, Commentary, Bibliography', *Journal of Design History*, 16/1, 2003, p. 3.
71. Johan Schot and Adri Albert de la Bruheze, 'The Mediated Design of Products, Consumption, and Consumers in the Twentieth Century', in Nelly Oudshoorn and Trevor Pinch, eds., *How Users Matter—The Co-Construction of Users and Technology* (MIT Press, 2003), p. 230.
72. One of many such arenas of mediation and negotiation to be studied is design magazines and the discourses being played out there. See e.g. Kjetil Fallan, 'How an Excavator Got

Aesthetic Pretensions—Negotiating Design in 1960s' Norway', *Journal of Design History*, 20/1, pp. 43–59.

73. Ibid., p. 124; Walker, *Design History and the History of Design*, pp. 33 & 62–3; Conway, 'Design History Basics', p. 9; Rainer Wick, 'Critical observations and General Remarks about Design History', in Pansera, ed., *Tradizione e Modernismo*, pp. 45–6; Fredrik Wildhagen, 'Flodhesten, Gullfisken og Kristine Valdresdatter—Streamlining og designhistorien', in Mirjam Gelfer-Jørgensen, ed., *Nordisk Funktionalisme 1925–1950* (Det danske Kunstindustrimuseum & Nordisk Forum for Formgivningshistorie, 1986), p. 55; Fredrik Wildhagen, 'Towards a Methodology of Design History', in Pansera, ed., *Tradizione e Modernismo*, pp. 18 & appendix; Dormer, *The Meanings of Modern Design*, p. 23; and Woodham, *Twentieth-Century Design*, p. 205.

74. Judy Attfield, 'Fascinating Fitness: the Dangers of Good Design', in Judy Attfield, *Bringing Modernity Home—Writings on Popular Design and Material Culture* (Manchester University Press, 2007), p. 39.

75. Judy Attfield, '"Give 'em Something Dark and Heavy": The Role of Design in the Material Culture of Popular British Furniture, 1939–1965', *Journal of Design History* 9/3, p. 185.

76. Gert Selle, 'There is No Kitsch, There is Only Design!', *Design Issues* 1/1, p. 49.

77. To name but two examples of such monographs: Henry Petroski, *The Pencil—A History of Design and Circumstance* (Knopf, 1989) and Alison J. Clarke, *Tupperware: The Promise of Plastic in 1950s America* (Smithsonian Institution Press, 1999). One could perhaps argue that Tupperware is too iconic and too acknowledged in elite design circles to serve as an example here. Surely, great custodians of elite design such as the New York's Museum of Modern Art and London's Victoria and Albert Museum have gone a long way in canonizing Tupperware. 'However,' as Clarke writes, 'Tupperware's significance as a twentieth-century artifact is better explained by references to the iconic status of the product in popular culture from the 1950s to present day, ranging from sitcoms and cartoon strips to cult magazines and Hollywood films' (pp. 3–4). So, although the cultural elites of MoMA and V&A from time to time 'go slumming' in the shanty town of commonplace plastic utensils, this has by no means disqualified Tupperware as a subject matter for a history of democratic design.

78. Selle, 'There is No Kitsch, There is Only Design!', p. 50.

79. Kjetil Fallan, 'One Must Offer "Something for Everyone"—Designing Crockery for consumer consent in 1950s' Norway', *Journal of Design History*, 22/2, pp. 133–149.

80. David Raizman and Carma R. Gorman, 'Introduction', in David Raizman and Carma R. Gorman, eds., *Objects, Audiences, and Litteratures—Alternative Narratives in the History of Design* (Cambridge Scholars Publishing, 2007), p. x.

81. Italo Calvino, *Le città invisibili* (Einaudi, 1972), p. 44. (The author's translation from: 'D'una città non godi le sette o settantasette meraviglie, ma la risposta che dà a una tua domanda.')

82. Wildhagen, 'Towards a Methodology of Design History', appendix p. 10.

83. Ibid., p. 19.

84. Fredrik Wildhagen, *Norge i Form—Kunsthåndverk og design under industrikulturen* (J.M. Stenersen, 1988).

85. Wildhagen, 'Towards a Methodology of Design History', p. 19.

86. Michael Tucker, 'Norge I Form: Kunsthåndverk og Design under Industrikulturen' [book review], *Journal of Design History* 2(2/3), p. 237.

87. Wick, 'Critical Observations and General Remarks about Design History', p. 45.

88. Ibid.

89. *Journal of Design History*, 1/1, p. U2.

90. Ibid.

91. Meikle, 'Material Virtues', pp. 191–92.

92. Victor Margolin, 'A World History of Design and the History of the World', *Journal of Design History*, 18/3, pp. 235–43.

93. Tony Fry, 'A Geography of Power: Design History and Marginality', *Design Issues*, 6/1, pp. 15–30.

94. For a survey of the geographical distribution of design historical research presented at four of these events and elsewhere and a discussion of problems and possibilities regarding the exploration and expansion of the world atlas of design history, see Jonathan M. Woodham, 'Local, National and Global: Redrawing the Design Historical Map', *Journal of Design History*, 18/3, pp. 257–67.

95. Tim Putnam, 'The Theory of Machine Design in the Second Industrial Age', *Journal of Design History*, 1/1, pp. 25–34.

96. Ibid., p. 29.

97. See e.g. Robin Kinross, 'Herbert Read's "Art and Industry": A History', *Journal of Design History*, 1/1, pp. 35–50, P. Madge, 'An Enquiry into Pevsner's "Enquiry"', pp. 113–26; and Steve Edwards, 'Factory and Fantasy in Andrew Ure', *Journal of Design History*, 14/1, pp. 17–33.

98. See e.g. Paddy Maguire, 'Designs on Reconstruction: British Business, Market Structures and the Role of Design in Post-War Recovery', *Journal of Design History*, 4/1, pp. 15–30; Paddy Maguire, 'Craft Capitalism and the Projection of British Industry in the 1950s and 1960s', *Journal of Design History*, 6/2, pp. 97–113; David Crowley, 'Building the World Anew: Design in Stalinist and Post-Stalinist Poland', *Journal of Design History*, 7/3, pp. 187–203; Guy Julier, 'Barcelona Design, Catalonia's Political Economy, and the New Spain, 1980–1986', *Journal of Design History*, 9/2, pp. 117–27; and Eli Rubin, 'The Form of Socialism without Ornament—Consumption, Ideology, and the Fall and Rise of Modernist Design in the German Democratic Republic', *Journal of Design History*, 19/2, pp. 155–68.

99. See e.g. H. Kumar Vyas, 'The Designer and the Socio-Technology of Small Production', *Journal of Design History*, 4/3, pp. 187–210; H. Alpay Er, 'Development Patterns of Industrial Design in the Third World: A Conceptual Model for Newly Industrialized Countries', *Journal of Design History*, 10/3, pp. 293–307; and Lucila Fernández Uriarte, 'Modernity and Postmodernity from Cuba', *Journal of Design History*, 18/3, pp. 245–55.

100. See e.g. Cheryl Buckley, '"The Noblesse of the Banks": Craft Hierarchies, Gender Divisions, and the Roles of Women Paintresses and Designers in the British Pottery Industry 1890–1939', *Journal of Design History*, 2/4, pp. 257–73; Cheryl Buckley, 'Design, Femininity, and Modernism: Interpreting the Work of Susie Cooper', *Journal of Design History*, 7/4, pp. 277–93; and Worden and Seddon, 'Women Designers in Britain in the 1920s and 1930s', pp. 177–93.

101. See e.g. Peter Stanfield, 'Heritage Design: The Harley-Davidson Motor Company', *Journal of Design History*, 5/2, pp. 141–55; and Jeffrey L. Meikle, 'Into the Fourth Kingdom: Representations of Plastic Materials, 1920–1950', *Journal of Design History*, 5/3, pp. 173–82.
102. See e.g. Louise Purbrick, 'The Dream Machine: Charles Babbage and His Imaginary Computers', *Journal of Design History*, 6/ 1, pp. 9–23 and Gijs Mom, 'Translating Properties into Functions (and Vice Versa): Design, User Culture and the Creation of an American and a European Car (1930–70)', *Journal of Design History*, 21/ 2, pp. 171–81. It might be mentioned here that a special issue on the history of technology was announced for vol. 3 (1990), but this never materialized: *Journal of Design History*, 1(3/4), p. 258.
103. Sally Clarke, 'Managing Design: The Art and Colour Section at General Motors, 1927–1941', *Journal of Design History*, 12/1, pp. 65–79.
104. Gertrud Øllgaard, 'A Super-Elliptical Moment in the Cultural Form of the Table: A Case Study of a Danish Table', *Journal of Design History*, 12/ 2, pp. 143–57 and Pauline Garvey, 'How to Have a 'Good Home'—The Practical Aesthetic and Normativity in Norway', *Journal of Design History*, 16/3, pp. 241–51.
105. Jane Graves, ' "When Things Go Wrong . . . Inside the Inside": A Psychoanalytical History of a Jug', *Journal of Design History*, 12/ 4, pp. 357–67.
106. Otakar Mácel, 'Avant-Garde Design and the Law: Litigation over the Cantilever Chair', *Journal of Design History*, 3(2/3), pp. 125–43. Despite the potentially interesting subject of this article it is severely hampered by the author's disappointingly conventional intention (stated explicitly in the introduction), which was not so much to shed light on the problems of patents and intellectual property as historical phenomena, but mainly to establish the true authorships and attributions of a chair type (was Mart Stam, Marcel Breuer or Ludwig Mies van der Rohe the greater genius?) The article does, however—despite it being seemingly a means more than an end—provide an interesting report of how the legal dispute and the copyright issue pivoted on whether the design in legal terms was to be considered an artistic creation or a technical innovation. Questions regarding copyright legislation are also discussed in Katie Scott, 'Art and Industry—A Contradictory Union: Authors, Rights and Copyrights during the *Consulat*', *Journal of Design History*, 13/1, pp. 1–21.
107. John Benson, 'Working-Class Consumption, Saving, and Investment in England and Wales, 1851–1911', *Journal of Design History*, 9/2, 1996, pp. 87–99, Colin Campbell, 'Consumption and the Rhetorics of Need and Want', *Journal of Design History*, 11/3, pp. 235–46; Victoria Kelley, 'The Equitable Consumer: Shopping at the Co-Op in Manchester', *Journal of Design History*, 11/4, pp. 295–310; Viviana Narotzky, ' "A Different and New Refinement"—Design in Barcelona, 1960–1990', *Journal of Design History*, 13/3, pp. 227–43; and Susie McKellar, ' "Seals of Approval"—Consumer Representation in 1930s' America', *Journal of Design History*, 15/1, pp. 1–13.
108. Jonathan M. Woodham, 'Managing British Design Reform II: The Film "Deadly Lampshade": An Ill-Fated Episode in the Politics of "Good Taste" ', *Journal of Design History*, 9/2, pp. 101–15 and Michelle Jones, 'Design and the Domestic Persuader—Television and the British Broadcasting Corporation's Promotion of Post-war "Good Design" ', *Journal of Design History*, 16/4, pp. 307–18.

109. Jill Seddon, 'The Architect and the "Arch-Pedant": Sadie Speight, Nikolaus Pevsner and "Design Review"', *Journal of Design History*, 20/1, pp. 29–41.

110. Frank Jackson, 'The New Air Age: BOAC and Design Policy 1945–60', *Journal of Design History*, 4/3, pp. 167–85 and Kenneth Agnew, 'The Spitfire: Legend or History? An Argument for a New Research Culture in Design', *Journal of Design History*, 6/2, pp. 121–30.

111. Philip Pacey, '"Anyone Designing Anything?" Non-Professional Designers and the History of Design', *Journal of Design History*, 5/3, pp. 217–25.

112. Pauline Madge, 'Design, Ecology, Technology: A Historiographical Review', *Journal of Design History*, 6/3, pp. 149–66.

113. Attfield, '"Give 'em Something Dark and Heavy"', pp. 185–201.

114. Anthony Burton, 'Design History and the History of Toys: Defining a Discipline for the Bethnal Green Museum of Childhood', *Journal of Design History*, 10/1, pp. 1–21; and Kenneth D. Brown, 'Design in the British Toy Industry Since 1945', *Journal of Design History*, 11/4, pp. 323–33.

115. Kevin Davies, 'Scandinavian Furniture in Britain: Finmar and the UK Market, 1949–1952', *Journal of Design History*, 10/1, pp. 39–52.

116. O. A. van Nierop, A. C. M. Blankendaal, and C. J. Overbeeke, 'The Evolution of the Bicycle: A Dynamic Systems Approach', *Journal of Design History*, 10/3, pp. 253–67.

117. Glenn Porter, 'Cultural Forces and Commercial Constraints: Designing Packaging in the Twentieth-Century United States', *Journal of Design History*, 12/1, pp. 25–43.

118. Catherine Moriarty, 'A Backroom Service?—The Photographic Library of the Council of Industrial Design, 1945–1965', *Journal of Design History*, 13/1, pp. 39–57.

119. Paul Atkinson, 'The (In)Difference Engine—Explaining the Disappearance of Diversity in the Design of the Personal Computer', *Journal of Design History*, 13/1, pp. 59–72 and Paul Atkinson, 'Man in a Briefcase: The Social Construction of the Laptop Computer and the Emergence of a Type Form', *Journal of Design History*, 18/2, pp. 191–205.

120. Mary Guyatt, 'Better Legs: Artificial Limbs for British Veterans of the First World War', *Journal of Design History*, 14/4, pp. 307–25.

121. Andrew Jackson, 'Labour as Leisure—The Mirror Dinghy and DIY Sailors', *Journal of Design History*, 19/1, pp. 57–67.

122. Dilnot, 'The State of Design History, Part I', pp. 3–23 and Dilnot, 'The State of Design History, Part II', pp. 3–20.

123. Ibid., p. 8 (note 32).

124. Ibid., p. 6. Dilnot takes his cue from Roland Barthes, *Mythologies* (Paladin, 1973) esp. the essay 'Myth Today', pp. 109–159. For some interesting recent examples of explicitly mythoclastic design history, see Simon Jackson, 'The "Stump-jumpers": National Identity and the Mythology of Australian Industrial Design in the Period 1930–1975', *Design Issues*, 18/4, pp. 14–23; Simon Jackson, 'Sacred Objects—Australian Design and National Celebrations', *Journal of Design History*, 19/3, pp. 249–55; Per H. Hansen, 'Networks, Narratives, and New Markets: The Rise and Decline of Danish Modern Furniture Design, 1930–1970', *Business History Review*, 80/3, pp. 449–83; and Per H. Hansen, *Da danske møbler blev moderne— Historien om dansk møbeldesigns storhedstid* (Syddansk Universitetsforlag & Aschehoug, 2006).

125. Dilnot, 'The State of Design History, Part II', p. 9.
126. Buckley, 'Made in Patriarchy', pp. 3–14.
127. Ibid., p. 14.
128. Gorman, 'Reshaping and Rethinking', p. 79.
129. Margolin, 'Design History or Design Studies', pp. 104–16.
130. Ibid., pp. 105–106.
131. Ibid., p. 112.
132. Adrian Forty, 'DEBATE: A Reply to Victor Margolin', *Journal of Design History*, 6/2, pp. 131–132.
133. Victor Margolin, 'A Reply to Adrian Forty', *Design Issues*, 11/1, p. 20.
134. Ibid., pp. 20–21.
135. Although sociology and the social sciences in general have a long tradition of a critical normative approach lending an instrumental aspect to research (sociological knowledge should inform social practice). It seems clear that Margolin envisions a similar function for design studies with respect to design practice. Conversely, in history and the humanities, this concept is much more controversial and often disapproved of.
136. This development dates back at least to the 1970s. For a brief introduction, see Victoria E. Bonnell and Lynn Hunt, 'Introduction', in *Beyond the Cultural Turn—New Directions in the Study of Society and Culture* (University of California Press, 1999), pp. 1–32.
137. Victoria E. Bonnell, *Iconography of Power: Soviet Political Posters under Lenin and Stalin* (University of California Press, 1997).
138. David Gartman, *Auto Opium—A Social History of American Automobile Design* (Routledge, 1994). This development has blurred the border between historical sociology and social history.
139. Jeffrey L. Meikle, 'Design History for What?: Reflections on an Elusive Goal', *Design Issues*, 11/1, p. 72.
140. Adrian Forty, *Objects of Desire—Design and Society Since* 1750 (Thames and Hudson, 1986)
141. Meikle, 'Design History for What?', p. 73.
142. Ibid., p. 74.
143. Dennis Doordan, 'On History', *Design Issues*, 11/1, p. 76.
144. Ibid., p. 81.
145. Woodham, 'Resisting Colonization', pp. 22–23.
146. Ibid., p. 36.
147. Nigel Whiteley, 'Design History or Design Studies?', *Design Issues*, 11/1, p. 39.
148. Alain Findeli, 'Design History and Design Studies: Methodological, Epistemological and Pedagogical Inquiry', *Design Issues*, 11/1, p. 46.
149. Forty, 'DEBATE: A Reply to Victor Margolin', p. 132.
150. Michel Foucault, *The Archaeology of Knowledge* (Tavistock Publications, 1972).
151. Forty, 'DEBATE: A Reply to Victor Margolin', p. 132.
152. Findeli, 'Design History and Design Studies', p. 53.
153. Ibid., pp. 62–63.

154. Stephen Hayward, '"Good Design Is Largely a Matter of Common Sense": Questioning the Meaning and Ownership of a Twentieth-Century Orthodoxy', *Journal of Design History*, 11/3, pp. 217–233.

155. In a sense, then, discourse theory can be subjected to the same criticism as semiotics: that it fails to recognize that an object has qualities and functions beyond that as text, sign or symbol.

156. Meikle, 'Material Virtues', p. 198.

157. Ibid., p. 194.

158. Ibid.

159. Ibid., p. 196.

160. Regina Lee Blaszczyk, 'Cinderella Stories—The Glass of Fashion and the Gendered Marketplace', in Roger Horowitz and Arwen Mohun, eds., *His and Hers: Gender, Consumption, and Technology* (University Press of Virginia, 1998), p. 156.

161. Betts, *The Authority of Everyday Objects*, p. 19.

162. Paul Glennie has suggested that documentation of historical consumers' negotiation of the meaning of commodities can be sought in such sources as diaries, correspondence, wills, inventories and personal and household accounts. This may be possible in exceptional cases where the relevant documentation was in fact made and has survived, but in general such evidence would at best be piecemeal and incoherent. These methodological problems concerning the study of—as Meikle put it—'how and why consumers at a given historical moment responded to particular products' is probably why most historical studies of consumption have concentrated on patterns of possessions and practices of purchasing, often drawing on structuralist and quantitative traditions from economic and social history: Paul Glennie, 'Consumption Within Historical Studies', in Daniel Miller, ed., *Acknowledging Consumption* (Routledge, 1995), pp. 164–203. For interesting examples of histories of consumption that seek to pair the studies of consumption practices and gender identities, see Penny Sparke, *As Long as it's Pink—The Sexual Politics of Taste* (Pandora, 1995); Pat Kirkham, ed., *The Gendered Object* (Manchester University Press, 1996); Victoria de Grazia, ed., *The Sex of Things—Gender and Consumption in Historical Perspective* (University of California Press, 1996); and Horowitz and Mohun, eds., *His and Hers*.

163. Daniel Miller, 'Why Some Things Matter', in Daniel Miller, ed., *Material Cultures—Why Some Things Matter* (UCL Press, 1998), p. 4.

164. Daniel Miller, *Material Culture and Mass Consumption* (Blackwell, 1987), p. 142.

165. Woodham, 'Resisting Colonization', p. 33.

166. Charles Saumarez Smith, 'Material Culture and Mass Consumption' [book review], *Journal of Design History*, 1/2, pp. 149–150.

167. Bjørnar Olsen has wielded a similar but more detailed criticism of the inattention to materiality in material studies. In explaining how this inadequacy came about, he draws on e.g. Bruno Latour's notion of the strict ontological divide inherent to the idea of modernity, nature-culture and human-nonhuman, which has 'assigned to things an ambiguous position within the modern constitution. They are located outside the human sphere of power, interests and politics—and still not properly nature. Although prescribed for the non-human

side, material culture ended up with not occupying any of the two positions prescribed by the modern constitution, as either culture or nature.' The inattention to materiality thus results from an intellectual heritage giving absolute primacy to the social. Insisting that artefacts are more than texts, signs, symbols, messages, metaphors and icons, Olsen proposes the actor-network theory (ANT), as conceptualized by Latour, John Law, et al. as a theoretical framework better suited to grasp the materiality of artefact—as 'a regime that cares for the hybrids and those hybrid relations that other systems (be they social or natural) largely have ignored. Thus, it suits material culture, the thing, very well.': Bjørnar Olsen, 'Material Culture after Text: Re-Membering Things', *Norwegian Archaeological Review*, 36/2, pp. 87–104, quotes: pp. 96 & 98. For Latour's discussion of modernity's nature-culture divide, see Bruno Latour, *We Have Never Been Modern* (Harvard University Press, 1993).

168. Smith, 'Material Culture and Mass Consumption' [book review], p. 150.

169. Daniel Miller, 'Why Some Things Matter', p. 9.

170. Daniel Miller, 'Things Ain't What They Used to Be', in Pearce, ed., *Interpreting Objects and Collections,* pp. 13–18, quote: p. 15.

171. Arjun Appadurai, 'Introduction: Commodities and the Politics of Value', in Arjun Appadurai, ed., *The Social Life of Things: Commodities in Cultural Perspective,* (Cambridge University Press, 1986), p. 5.

172. Victor Margolin, 'The Experience of Products', in Margolin, *The Politics of the Artificial,* p. 52.

173. Judy Attfield, *Wild Things—The Material Culture of Everyday Life* (Oxford: Berg, 2000), p. 144.

174. See Arjun Appadurai, ed.), *The Social Life of Things—Commodities in Cultural Perspective* (Cambridge University Press, 1986) and Michael Thompson, *Rubbish Theory—The Creation and Destruction of Value* (Oxford University Press, 1979).

175. Daniel Miller, 'Coca-Cola: A Black Sweet Drink from Trinidad', in Daniel Miller, ed., *Material Cultures,* pp. 169–187, esp. p. 181–184.

176. du Gay, et al., *Doing Cultural Studies,* pp. 52–53.

177. She has held positions in design history at the University of Brighton, the University of Southampton, the Royal College of Art in London, and the University of Applied Arts in Vienna.

178. Alison J. Clarke, 'Window Shopping at Home: Classifieds, Catalogues and New Consumer Skills', in Miller, ed., *Material Cultures,* pp. 73–99 and Alison J. Clarke, 'The Aesthetics of Social Aspiration', in Daniel Miller, ed., *Home Possessions—Material Culture Behind Closed Doors* (Berg, 2001), pp. 23–45.

179. Clarke, *Tupperware.*

180. Ibid., esp. pp. 116–117.

181. Ibid., p. 201.

182. Judy Attfield, 'Beyond the Pale: Reviewing the Relationship between Material Culture and Design History', *Journal of Design History,* 12/4, p. 373.

183. Ibid.

184. Ibid., pp. 373–380. See also Judy Attfield, 'Material Culture in the Social World' [book review], *Journal of Design History,* 15/1, pp. 65–66.

185. Attfield, *Wild Things,* p. 3.
186. Judy Attfield, 'Material Culture in the Social World' [book review], p. 66. An example of her work that succeeds better in investigating the relations between the spheres of production and consumption is Judy Attfield, ed., *Utility Reassessed—The Role of Ethics in the Practice of Design* (Manchester University Press, 1999).
187. Margolin, 'Design History or Design Studies', p. 115 (emphasis added).
188. Kenneth L. Ames, 'Material Cultures: Why Some Things Matter' [book review], *Journal of Design History,* 13/1, p. 75.
189. Ibid.
190. Carolyn Steedman, 'Culture, Cultural Studies and the Historians', in Simon During, ed., *The Cultural Studies Reader* (Routledge, 1993), p. 48.
191. Ibid.
192. It is tempting, here, to suggest an example from one of the seminal works in material culture studies of what to a historian seems like a rather distorted understanding of history: The anthropologist Mary Douglas and the economist Baron Isherwood operated with a time concept they called 'ethnographic present', which they defined as 'a special tense that aims to concentrate past, present, and future into a continuous present', and that is based on the premise that 'Whatever is important about the past is assumed to be making itself felt here and now.': Mary Douglas and Baron Isherwood, *The World of Goods—Towards an Anthropology of Consumption* (Allen Lane, 1979), p. 23.
193. Steedman, 'Culture, Cultural Studies and the Historians', p. 55.
194. See e.g. Susan M. Pearce, ed., *Museum Studies in Material Culture* (Leicester University Press, 1989).
195. Susan M. Pearce, 'Introduction', in Pearce, ed., *Interpreting Objects and Collections,* pp. 4–5.
196. Susan M. Pearce, 'Objects as Meaning; or Narrating the Past', in Pearce, ed., *Interpreting Objects and Collections,* pp. 26–27.
197. Nevertheless, museology may occasionally have the potential to transgress these categories in invigorating ways. A case in point, where a simple distortion or partial inversion of a classical value such as authenticity proved both fertile and original, was the 1990 British Museum exhibition 'Fakes?' The project presented forged artefacts not as atrocity propaganda but out of genuine interest in their functions and meanings for makers and customers: Mark Jones, 'Why Fakes?', in Pearce, ed., *Interpreting Objects and Collections,* pp. 92–97.
198. See e.g Susan M. Pearce, 'Thinking about Things', in Pearce, ed., *Interpreting Objects and Collections,* pp. 125–132. The model proposed by Ray Batchelor based on a case study of a 1910 AEG electric kettle seems more appropriate to design history. This invokes the relevance of studying not only the innovative technology and design the product represents but also the conditions of the miners in the nickel mines, the roles of the sheet-metal dealer and the AEG workers, the distribution systems, the marketing strategies and the patterns and experiences of use: Ray Batchelor, 'Not Looking at Kettles', in Pearce, ed., *Interpreting Objects and Collections,* pp. 139–143.
199. Lubar and Kingery, eds., *History from Things.*
200. Kingery, ed., *Learning from Things.*

201. Daston, ed., *Things That Talk*.
202. Lubar and Kingery, eds., *History from Things*, p. ix
203. W. David Kingery, 'Introduction', in Kingery, ed., *Learning from Things*, p. 15.
204. Ruth Oldenziel, 'Object/ions—Technology, Culture, and Gender', in Kingery, ed., *Learning from Things*, pp. 60–62.
205. Ruth Oldenziel, Adri Albert de la Bruhèze, and Onno de Wit, 'Europe's Mediation Junction: Technology and Consumer Society in the 20th Century', *History and Technology*, 21/1, p. 107.
206. W. David Kingery, 'Technological Systems and Some Implications with Regard to Continuity and Change', in Lubar and Kingery, eds., *History from Things*, p. 227.
207. Margolin, 'Design History in the United States, 1977–2000', p. 154.
208. The editors of *History from Things* state that 'nine [of seventeen] essays address the design of the artifact, seven essays address the use of the artefact, and eight essays address the perceptions of the artifact. In five essays the artifact manufacture is of concern': Lubar and Kingery, eds., *History from Things*, p. xvi.
209. Robert Friedel, 'Some Matters of Substance', in Lubar and Kingery, eds., *History from Things*, p. 42.
210. Steven Lubar, 'Machine Politics: The Political Construction of Technological Artifacts', in Lubar and Kingery, eds., *History from Things*, pp. 197–214.
211. Corn, 'Object Lessons/Object Myths?', p. 47.
212. Michael Brian Schiffer, 'Pathways to the Present—In Search of Shirt-Pocket Radios with Subminiature Tubes', in Kingery, ed.) *Learning from Things*, pp. 81–88.
213. Joseph Leo Koerner, 'Bosch's Equipment', in Daston, ed., *Things That Talk*, p. 45.
214. Peter Galison, 'Image of Self', in Daston, ed., *Things That Talk*, p. 271.
215. Simon Schaffer, 'A Science Whose Business Is Bursting: Soap Bubbles as Commodities in Classical Physics', in Daston, ed., *Things That Talk*, pp. 147–192.
216. Raimonda Riccini, 'History from Things: Notes on the History of Industrial Design', *Design Issues*, 14/3, p. 56.
217. Steven Lubar, 'Learning from Technological Things', in Kingery, ed., *Learning from Things*, p. 32.
218. Artemis Yagou, 'Rethinking Design History from an Evolutionary Perspective: Background and Implications', *The Design Journal*, 8/3, p. 53.
219. Sometimes known as the 'linguistic turn', especially in the humanities. For a brief introduction, see e.g. Georg G. Iggers, *Historiography in the Twentieth Century—From Scientific Objectivity to the Postmodern Challenge* (Wesleyan University Press, 1997), pp. 118–133.
220. Lynn Hunt, ed., *The New Cultural History* (University of California Press, 1989).
221. Lynn Hunt, 'Introduction', in *The New Cultural History*, p. 9.
222. Ibid., p. 22.
223. As Hunt writes: 'Although historians have been intrigued by Foucault's trenchant criticisms, they have not taken his method—or anti-method—as a model for their practice.': Ibid., p. 8.
224. There is, for example, an important critique of the all too often simplistic black-and-white dichotomy posed between positivism and relativism: Lloyd S. Kramer, 'Literature, Criticism,

and Historical Imagination: The Literary Challenge of Hayden White and Dominick La-
Capra', in Hunt, ed., *The New Cultural History*, p. 124. See also Dominick LaCapra, *History
& Criticism* (Cornell University Press, 1985), p. 140.

225. Bonnell and Hunt, eds., *Beyond the Cultural Turn*.
226. Bonnell and Hunt, 'Introduction', p. 26.
227. Ibid.
228. Ibid., p. 11.
229. Hayward, '"Good Design Is Largely a Matter of Common Sense"', p. 217.
230. Jeffrey L. Meikle, *American Plastic—A Cultural History* (Rutgers University Press, 1995).
231. Meikle, *Twentieth Century Limited* and Meikle, *Design in the USA*.
232. Regina Lee Blaszczyk, *Imagining Consumers—Design and Innovation from Wedgwood to
Corning* (Johns Hopkins University Press, 2000).
233. Two years before the publication of Blaszczyk's book, Raimonda Riccini deplored that 'the
history of industrial design has, for a long time been able to ignore business history, just
as the history of enterprise has been able to avoid a real confrontation with the history
of products.' One might agree or disagree with this claim—Riccini mentions some well-
known earlier exceptions concerning such emblematic companies as Wedgwood, Thonet
and AEG—but Blaszczyk's book should be particularly welcomed by those who are inclined
to agree: Riccini, 'History from Things', p. 43. The author's attempt at combining design
history with business history can be seen in: Kjetil Fallan, 'The *Realpolitik* of the Artificial—
Strategic Design at Figgjo Fajanse Facing International Free Trade in the 1960s', *Enterprise
and Society*, 10/3, pp. 559–89.
234. Blaszczyk, *Imagining Consumers*, p. 12.
235. Heskett, 'Industrial Design', pp. 112–113; Walker, *Design History and the History of Design*,
pp. 27, 70, & 174–185; and Lees-Maffei, 'Studying Advice', p. 3.
236. Oldenziel, de la Bruhèze and de Wit, 'Europe's Mediation Junction', pp. 107–139 and Schot
and de la Bruheze, op.cit.
237. The way these two terms are used by Blaszczyk and Schot and de la Bruheze makes them
virtually interchangeable, which is fairly unproblematic in this context. Bruno Latour, on
the other hand, uses both terms and distinctly separates their meaning. He reserves the
term *intermediary* to designate something that conveys meaning without altering it in any
way, whereas a mediator transforms the meaning on its way from one place to another:
Bruno Latour, *Reassembling the Social—An Introduction to Actor-Network-Theory* (Oxford University Press, 2005), p. 39.
238. Schot and Albert de la Bruheze, 'The Mediated Design of Products, Consumption, and Consumers in the Twentieth Century'. The authors do not distinguish between the terms *intermediary* and *mediator*—they even refer to Blaszczyk's concept of *fashion intermediaries*
as a prime example of what they are proposing: for studies of mediators. (See note 13,
pp. 234 & 290).
239. Blaszczyk, *Imagining Consumers*, p. 273.
240. Penny Sparke demurs to another side to Blaszczyk's approach. While recognizing it as 'an
important and timely book' and lauding its interdisciplinary accomplishments, Sparke asserts that 'it fails to link stylistic change with other significant historical shifts outlined

here, such as that from gentility to domesticity, or from women as housewives to women as consumers.': Penny Sparke, 'Imagining Consumers—Design and Innovation from Wedgwood to Corning. By Regina Lee Blaszczyk' [book review], *Technology and Culture*, 42/2, p. 346.

241. Betts, *The Authority of Everyday Objects*.
242. Ibid., p. 3.
243. Ibid., p. 2.
244. Ibid., pp. 23–72. This part of the book expands on earlier work on the same topic by Betts and by John Heskett: Paul Betts, 'The Bauhaus and National Socialism—a Dark Chapter of Modernism', in Jeannine Fiedler and Peter Feierabend, eds., *Bauhaus* (Könemann, 1999), pp. 34–41; John Heskett, 'Design in Inter-War Germany', in Wendy Kaplan, ed., *Designing Modernity—The Arts of Reform and Persuasion 1885–1945* (Thames and Hudson, 1995); and Heskett, 'Modernism and Archaism in Design in the Third Reich', pp. 13–24.
245. Betts, *The Authority of Everyday Objects*, pp. 109–138.

2 Theory and Methodology

1. The phrase "the seamless web of sociotechnology" is often attributed to Hughes, but to the author's knowledge he has never used this exact wording. He has, however, written that 'the web is seamless', and that he believes 'encompassing systems should be labelled sociotechnical systems rather than technological systems.': Thomas P. Hughes, 'Edison and Electric Light', in Donald MacKenzie and Judy Wajcman, eds., *The Social Shaping of Technology*, 2nd edn. (Open University Press, 1999), p. 58 and Thomas P. Hughes, *Networks of Power: Electrification in Western Society, 1880–1930* (John Hopkins University Press, 1983), p. 465. Hughes's theory of the seamless web is most explicitly expressed in: Thomas P. Hughes, 'The Seamless Web: Technology, Science, Etcetera, Etcetera', *Social Studies of Science*, 16/2, pp. 281–92.
2. Hughes, *Networks of Power*.
3. For a more concise presentation of Hughes's theoretical perspectives on technological development, see Thomas P. Hughes, 'The Evolution of Large Technological Systems', in Wiebe E. Bijker, Thomas P. Hughes, and Trevor J. Pinch, eds., *The Social Construction of Technological Systems—New Directions in the Sociology and History of Technology* (MIT Press, 1987), pp. 51–82.
4. It is interesting to note here that Tomás Maldonado has criticized Hughes and other historians of technology contributing to the sociotechnical systems approach for focusing too uniformly on technological macro systems that are 'simultaneously *excellent* and *very poor* examples' for exploring the relationship between society and technology. Excellent, Maldonado states, 'because their connection with society is so evident', but poor 'precisely because their probative obviousness prevents less evident, but no less important, aspects of the society-technology relationship from emerging in the overall assessment.' One might agree or disagree, but his observation is a challenge to be kept in mind by design historians,

whose subject matter is rarely macro systems: Tomás Maldonado, 'Taking Eyeglasses Seriously', *Design Issues,* 17/4, p. 34

5. Heskett, 'Industrial Design', p. 126.
6. Barry M. Katz, 'Technology and Design: A New Agenda', *Technology and Culture,* 38/2, p. 453.
7. This conviction formed the basis for a session entitled 'Our Common Past? Conversations between History of Technology and Design History', which the author organized for the 2006 Annual Meeting of the Society for the History of Technology in Las Vegas, October 12–15. Panelists were Barry M. Katz, Penny Sparke, Per Østby and Kjetil Fallan. Hans-Joachim Braun chaired the session, and Martina Hessler acted as commentator.
8. See e.g. Thomas P. Hughes, *American Genesis—A Century of Invention and Technological Enthusiasm, 1870–1970* (Viking, 1989); Thomas P. Hughes, *Human-Built World—How to Think about Technology and Culture* (University of Chicago Press, 2004); James J. Flink, *The Automobile Age* (MIT Press, 1988); and Wiebe E. Bijker, *Of Bicycles, Bakelites, and Bulbs—Toward a Theory of Sociotechnical Change* (MIT Press, 1995).
9. Meikle, *American Plastic;* Gartman, *Auto Opium;* and Clarke, *Tupperware.*
10. Doordan, 'On History', p. 78.
11. Henry Petroski, *The Evolution of Useful Things* (Vintage Books, 1994), p. 31.
12. A few relatively recent examples indicate this potential: Eugene Levy studied a commercially unsuccessful project where Edison Electric Institute hired Henry Dreyfuss and Associates to design power pylons in 1966: Eugene Levy, 'The Aesthetics of Power: High-Voltage Transmission Systems and the American Landscape', *Technology and Culture,* 38/3, pp. 575–607. Ronald Kline and Trevor Pinch showed how users influenced early car design through their interpretations, modifications and feedback: Ronald Kline and Trevor Pinch, 'Users as Agents of Technological Change: The Social Construction of the Automobile in the Rural United States', *Technology and Culture,* 37/4, pp. 763–95. Rudi Volti analysed the relationships between car design and geography, economy and politics: Rudi Volti, 'A Century of Automobility', *Technology and Culture,* 37/4, pp. 663–785. Michael Brian Schiffer introduced the concept of the 'cultural imperative' to better understand the complexity of the often esoteric process from idea to commodity in product development: Michael Brian Schiffer, 'Cultural Imperatives and Product Development: The Case of the Shirt-Pocket Radio', *Technology and Culture,* 34/1, pp. 98–113. Shelly Nickles explored how consumers' needs and values were interpreted and fed into the design of refrigerators in 1930s America: Shelly Nickles, '"Preserving Women": Refrigerator Design as Social Process in the 1930s', *Technology and Culture,* 43/4, pp. 693–727. Finally, Boel Berner discussed the organization of engineering design offices in early twentieth-century Sweden: Boel Berner, 'Rationalizing Technical Work: Visions and Realities of the "Systematic Drawing Office" in Sweden, 1890–1940', *Technology and Culture,* 48/1, pp. 20–42. For a historiographic analysis of the first decades of *Technology and Culture,* see John M. Staudenmaier, *Technology's Storytellers: Reweaving the Human Fabric* (MIT Press, 1985).
13. Hughes, *American Genesis.*
14. Ibid., pp. 295–352.
15. Hughes, *Human-Built World,* pp. 111–52.

16. Ruth Schwartz Cowan, *More Work for Mother—The Ironies of Household Technology from the Open Hearth to the Microwave* (Basic Books, 1983).

17. Ruth Schwartz Cowan, *A Social History of American Technology* (Oxford University Press, 1997), p. 3.

18. Margolin, 'Design History in the United States, 1977–2000', p. 157.

19. In an observation later in the book, Cowan points to the origins of a very interesting intellectual paradox regarding the personality cult and hero worship surrounding great inventors: 'Students of intellectual history will know that there is a common pattern in the history of ideas: when ideas are very powerful, they are sometimes adopted even by opposing sides in the same debate. Thus in the decades before and after the Civil War, some advocates of industrialization adopted some ideas of their Romantic opponents. We can see this pattern developing, for example, in the ways in which Americans began talking about inventors. Several successful inventors—Whitney, Fulton, Morse, Edison, and Bell—had literally became national celebrities, almost on par with such political celebrities as Washington, Jefferson, and Lincoln. Poems applauding their achievements were published in newspapers; streets, towns, and babies were named after them. A surprising number of people talked and wrote about inventors using the language, and the concepts, of Romanticism.': Cowan, *A Social History of American Technology*, pp. 209–10.

20. Ibid., pp. 119–47.

21. Ibid., pp. 78–82.

22. Ibid., pp. 256–65.

23. Hård and Jamison, *Hubris and Hybrids*.

24. Ibid., p. 4. For White's theory of narrative strategies in the writing of history, see Hayden White, *The Content of the Form: Narrative Discourse and Historical Representation* (Johns Hopkins University Press, 1987).

25. Hård and Jamison, *Hubris and Hybrids*, p. 147.

26. Ibid., pp. 145–67.

27. Ibid., p. 293.

28. This development dates back at least to the 1970s. As Victoria E. Bonnell and Lynn Hunt pointed out: 'Although the cultural turn has swept through the precincts of both historians and historical sociologists, practitioners of these disciplines have not always moved in the same direction; nor has the relationship between these disciplines always been comfortable.': Bonnell and Hunt, 'Introduction', p. 5. For a survey of this development, see e.g. Terrence McDonald, 'What We Talk about When We Talk about History: The Conversations of History and Sociology', in *The Historic Turn in the Human Sciences* (University of Michigan Press, 1996), pp. 91–118.

29. Bijker, *Of Bicycles, Bakelites, and Bulbs*.

30. Ibid., pp. 19–100.

31. Ibid., pp. 179–88.

32. Wiebe E. Bijker, 'The Social Construction of Bakelite: Toward a Theory of Invention', in Bijker, Hughes, and Pinch, eds., *The Social Construction of Technological Systems*, p. 179.

33. Bijker here largely takes his cue from Meikle, *Twentieth Century Limited*.

34. Bijker, Hughes, and Pinch, eds., *The Social Construction of Technological Systems*. The SCOT programme was laid out by Pinch and Bijker three years earlier in Trevor Pinch and Wiebe Bijker, 'The Social Construction of Facts and Artefacts: or How the Sociology of Science and the Sociology of Technology Might Benefit Each Other', *Social Studies of Science*, 14/3, pp. 399–441.

35. Ruth Schwartz Cowan, 'The Consumption Junction: A Proposal for Research Strategies in the Sociology of Technology', in Bijker, Hughes and Pinch, eds.,*The Social Construction of Technological Systems*, pp. 261–80.

36. Trevor J. Pinch and Wiebe E. Bijker, 'The Social Construction of Facts and Artifacts: Or How the Sociology of Science and the Sociology of Technology Might Benefit Each Other', in Bijker, Hughes, and Pinch, eds., *The Social Construction of Technological Systems*, p. 22.

37. Henry Petroski, *To Engineer Is Human—The Role of Failure in Successful Design* (St. Martin's Press, 1985) and Petroski, *The Evolution of Useful Things*.

38. Madeleine Akrich, 'The De-scription of Technological Objects', in Wiebe E. Bijker and John Law, eds., *Shaping Technology/Building Society—Studies in Sociotechnical Change* (MIT Press, 1992), p. 206.

39. Mikael Hård, 'Beyond Harmony and Consensus: A Social Conflict Approach to Technology', *Science, Technology and Human Values*, 18/4, pp. 408–32.

40. See e.g. Purbrick, 'The Dream Machine', pp. 9–23; van Nierop, Blankendaal and Overbeeke, 'The Evolution of the Bicycle', pp. 253–67; Atkinson, 'The (In)Difference Engine', pp. 59–72; Arwen P. Mohun, 'Designed for Thrills and Safety: Amusement Parks and the Commodification of Risk, 1880–1929', *Journal of Design History*, 14/ 4, pp. 291–306; Douglas N. Lantry, 'Dress for Egress: The Smithsonian National Air and Space Museum's Apollo Spacesuit Collection', *Journal of Design History*, 14/4, pp. 343–59; Atkinson, 'Man in a Briefcase', pp. 191–205; Paul Atkinson, 'The Best Laid Plans of Mice and Men: The Computer Mouse in the History of Computing', *Design Issues*, 23/3, pp. 46–61; and Paul Atkinson, 'A Bitter Pill to Swallow: The Rise and Fall of the Tablet Computer', *Design Issues*, 24/4, pp. 3–25. The potential of SCOT as it relates to design history is also mentioned in Raimonda Riccini, 'Innovation as a Field of Historical Knowledge for Industrial Design', *Design Issues*, 17/4, p. 30 and Riccini, 'History From Things', p. 54.

41. For introductions to the STS field of research, see e.g. Sheila Jasanoff, Gerald E. Markle, James C. Petersen, and Trevor Pinch, eds., *Handbook of Science and Technology Studies* (Sage, 1995); Edward J. Hackett, Olga Amsterdamska, Michael Lynch, and Judy Wajeman, eds., *The Handbook of Science and Technology Studies* (MIT Press, 2008); and Sergio Sismondo, *An Introduction to Science and Technology Studies* (Blackwell, 2004).

42. A group of STS scholars put together a 2004 special issue of *Design Issues* on STS and design studies that contains valuable perspectives on the social complexity of design; unfortunately it lacks any discussion of their applicability to historical research: Edward Woodhouse and Jason W. Patton, 'Design by Society: Science and Technology Studies and the Social Shaping of Design', *Design Issues*, 20/3, pp. 1–12. The same must be said of a recent follow-up article: Jack Ingram, Elizabeth Shove, and Matthew Watson, 'Products and Practices: Selected Concepts from Science and Technology Studies and from Social Theories of Consumption and Practice', *Design Issues*, 23/2, pp. 3–16.

43. Douglas Adams, *The Restaurant at the End of the Universe: The Hitchhiker's Guide to the Galaxy 2* (Pan Books, 1980), p. 83.

44. Donald MacKenzie and Judy Wajcman, 'Introductory Essay: The Social Shaping of Technology', in MacKenzie and Wajcman, eds., *The Social Shaping of Technology*, p. 23.

45. John Law, *After Method—Mess in Social Science Research* (Routledge, 2004), p. 157.

46. Bruno Latour, *Science in Action* (Harvard University Press, 1987) and Latour, *We Have Never Been Modern*.

47. Latour, *Reassembling the Social*, pp. 131–32.

48. Latour, *Science in Action*, p. 258.

49. Ibid.

50. Ibid.

51. Ibid., p. 259.

52. Ibid.

53. Ibid.

54. John Law, 'After ANT: Complexity, Naming and Topology', in John Law and John Hassard, eds., *Actor Network Theory and After* (Blackwell, 1999), p. 8.

55. Bruno Latour, 'On Recalling ANT', in Law and Hassard, eds., *Actor Network Theory and After*, p. 15. Latour later, in a quite humorous manner, made a U-turn regarding the appropriateness of the term: 'I was ready to drop this label [actor-network theory] for more elaborate ones like 'sociology of translation', 'actant-rhyzome ontology', 'sociology of innovation', and so on, until someone pointed out to me that the acronym A.N.T. was perfectly fit for a blind, myopic, workaholic, trail-sniffing, and collective traveller. An ant writing for other ants, this fits my project very well!': Latour, *Reassembling the Social*, p. 9.

56. Bruno Latour, 'On recalling ANT', p. 16.

57. Ibid. pp. 18–19.

58. Michel Callon, 'Society in the Making: The Study of Technology as a Tool for Sociological Analysis', in Bijker, Hughes and Pinch, eds., *The Social Construction of Technological Systems*, p. 93.

59. Law, *After Method*, p. 157.

60. Bruno Latour (under the pseudonym Jim Johnson), 'Mixing Humans and Nonhumans Together: The Sociology of a Door-Closer', *Social Problems*, 35/3, pp. 298–310.

61. One of the most vehement critics of Latour's work in general is David Bloor, protagonist of the so-called Edinburgh School of the field known as sociology of scientific knowledge and the strong programme approach: David Bloor, 'Anti-Latour', in *Studies in History and Philosophy of Science*, 30/1, pp. 81–112. Bruno Latour retorted with equal vigour in 'For Bloor and Beyond—A Reply to David Bloor's "Anti-Latour"', *Studies in History and Philosophy of Science*, 30/1, pp. 113–29.

62. Margaret C. Jacob, 'Science Studies after Social Construction—The Turn toward the Comparative and the Global', in Bonnell and Hunt, eds., *Beyond the Cultural Turn*, p. 106. Her reference is to Bruno Latour, *Aramis, or The Love of Technology* (Harvard University Press, 1996), p. 293, and the following passage from Latour's renarration of Aramis' (the failed Parisian guided-transportation system) speech from beyond the grave: 'You loved me

provided that I did not exist as a whole . . . Then people grew frantic on my account. They had meetings about me again. I had to exist as a line . . . so that the Budget Office would support me.'

63. Steven D. Brown and Rose Capdevila, 'Perpetuum Mobile: Substance, Force and the Sociology of Translation', in Law and Hassard, eds., *Actor Network Theory and After*, pp. 26–50.

64. Andrew Pickering, *The Mangle of Practice—Time, Agency, and Science* (University of Chicago Press, 1995), pp. 6–23.

65. Latour, *Reassembling the Social*, p. 46.

66. Ibid., p. 63.

67. Madeleine Akrich and Bruno Latour, 'A Summary of a Convenient Vocabulary for the Semiotics of Human and Nonhuman Assemblies', in Bijker and Law, eds., *Shaping Technology/Building Society*, p. 259.

68. Latour, *Reassembling the Social*, pp. 74–5.

69. Ibid., p. 60.

70. Ibid., pp. 71–2.

71. Sismondo, *An Introduction to Science and Technology Studies*, p. 72.

72. Vilém Flusser, 'The Ethics of Industrial Design?', in *The Shape of Things—A Philosophy of Design* (Reaktion, 1999), p. 67.

73. Mika Pantzar, 'Domestication of Everyday Life Technology: Dynamic Views on the Social Histories of Artifacts', *Design Issues*, 13/3, pp. 61–2. In recent architectural research there has been some interest in ANT. For a discussion of its relevance, see Kjetil Fallan, 'Architecture in Action—Traveling with Actor-Network Theory in the Land of Architectural Research', *Architectural Theory Review*, 13/1, pp. 80–96.

74. Latour, *Reassembling the Social*, p. 81 (note 101).

75. One of the rare examples of a design historical study—although written by a business historian—that does contain reference to ANT, more precisely Latour's *Reassembling the Social*, is Hansen, 'Networks, Narratives, and New Markets', p. 452 (note 13).

76. Steve Woolgar, 'What Happened to Provocation in Science and Technology Studies?', *History and Technology*, 20/4, p. 345.

77. Law, *After Method*, p. 157.

78. Adams, *The Restaurant at the End of the Universe*, p. 134.

79. An earlier and shorter version of this and the following section was originally published as Kjetil Fallan, 'De-scribing Design: Appropriating Script Analysis to Design History', *Design Issues*, 24/4, pp. 61–75.

80. Akrich, 'The De-scription of Technological Objects', p. 208. Another contributor to the same publication, W. Bernard Carlson, made a somewhat similar point—although perhaps with a less terse conjunction between artefact and meaning than Akrich's script metaphor allows for—when he argued that 'inventors invent both artifacts and frames of meanings that guide how they manufacture and market their creations . . . [I]ndividuals must make assumptions about who will use a technology and the meanings users might assign to it. These assumptions constitute a frame of meaning inventors and entrepreneurs use to guide their efforts at designing, manufacturing, and marketing their technological artifacts': W. Bernard Carlson,

'Artifacts and Frames of Meaning: Thomas A. Edison, His Managers, and the Cultural Construction of Motion Pictures', in Bijker and Law, eds., *Shaping Technology/Building Society*, pp. 176–77.

81. Goodall, 'Design and Gender', p. 58.
82. Matias Faldbakken (under the pseudonym Abo Rasul), *The Cocka Hola Company—Skandinavisk misantropi* (Cappelen, 2001), pp. 292–95 (author's translation).
83. Tom Wolfe, *I am Charlotte Simmons* (Farrar, Straus, Giroux, 2004), p. 38.
84. Bruno Latour, 'Where Are the Missing Masses? The Sociology of a Few Mundane Artefacts', in Bijker and Law, eds., *Shaping Technology/Building Society*, p. 247.
85. John Schot and Albert de la Bruheze, 'The Mediated Design of Products, Consumption, and Consumers in the Twentieth Century', p. 235 and Madeleine Akrich, 'User Representations: Practices, Methods and Sociology', in Arie Rip, Thomas J. Misa, and Johan Schot, eds., *Managing Technology in Society. The Approach of Constructive Technology Assessment* (Pinter Publishers, 1995), pp. 167–84.
86. Akrich, 'The De-scription of Technological Objects', p. 208.
87. For a case study following such an approach see Kjetil Fallan, 'Form, Function, Fiction: Translations of Technology and Design in Product Development', *History and Technology*, 24/1, pp. 61–87.
88. For instance, Mihaly Csikszentmihalyi and Eugene Rochberg-Halton have asserted that 'most accounts of how things signify tend to ignore the active contribution of the thing itself to the meaning process.': Mihaly Csikszentmihalyi and Eugene Rochberg-Halton, *The Meaning of Things—Domestic Symbols and the Self* (Cambridge University Press, 1981), p. 43.
89. Akrich and Latour, 'A Summary of a Convenient Vocabulary for the Semiotics of Human and Nonhuman Assemblies', p. 259.
90. Ibid., pp. 259–62.
91. Wiebe E. Bijker and John Law, 'What Next? Technology, Theory, and Method', in Bijker and Law, eds., *Shaping Technology/Building Society*, p. 202.
92. Marit Hubak, 'The Car as a Cultural Statement', in Merete Lie and Knut H. Sørensen, eds., *Making Technology Our Own?—Domesticating Technology into Everyday Life* (Scandinavian University Press, 1996), p. 175.
93. Donald A. Norman, *The Design of Everyday Things* (MIT Press, 1998). See esp. pp. 81–104.
94. Donald A. Norman, *Emotional Design—Why We Love (or Hate) Everyday Things* (Basic Books, 2004).
95. Ian Hutchby, 'Technologies, Texts and Affordances', *Sociology*, 35/2, 2001, pp. 441–56.
96. Tom H. Fisher, 'What We Touch, Touches Us: Materials, Affects, and Affordances', *Design Issues*, 20/4, p. 26.
97. Ibid., p. 31.
98. Barry M. Katz, 'Intelligent Design', *Technology and Culture*, 47/2, p. 388. His reference is to Peter-Paul Verbeek, *What Things Do—Philosophical Reflections on Technology, Agency, and Design* (Pennsylvania State University Press, 2005).

99. Csikszentmihalyi and Rochberg-Halton, *The Meaning of Things,* pp. 20–21.
100. Akrich, 'The De-scription of Technological Objects', p. 206.
101. Hubak, 'The Car as a Cultural Statement', p. 175.
102. Ibid., pp. 175–176.
103. Penny Sparke, *A Century of Car Design* (Mitchell Beazley, 2002), pp. 102–5.
104. Stanfield, 'Heritage Design', p. 154, (emphasis added).
105. Latour, *Science in Action,* p. 259.
106. Akrich, 'The De-scription of Technological Objects', p. 216.
107. A useful and inspiring survey of more general strategies for historians aiming at tearing down the wall or bridging the gap between the spheres of production and consumption can be found in Sally Clarke, 'Consumer Negotiations', *Business and Economic History,* 26/1, pp. 101–22.
108. Nikolaj Frobenius, *Teori og praksis* (Gyldendal, 2004), pp. 64–5 (author's translation).
109. Douglas Coupland, *Generation X* (St. Martin's Press, 1991), p. 139.
110. Carroll Pursell, 'Seeing the Invisible: New Perspectives in the History of Technology', *ICON,* 1, p. 9.
111. Tom McCarthy, *Auto Mania: Cars, Consumers, and the Environment* (Yale University Press, 2007), pp. 77–98.
112. Pierre Bourdieu, *Distinction: A Social Critique of the Judgement of Taste* (1979; repr. Routledge & Kegan Paul, 1984); Baudrillard, *The System of Objects*; Jean Baudrillard, *The Consumer Society* (1970; repr. Sage, 1998); and Jean Baudrillard, *For a Critique of the Political Economy of the Sign* (1972; repr. Telos, 1981).
113. Zygmunt Bauman, 'Broken Lives—Broken Strategies', in *Life in Fragments: Essays in Postmodern Morality* (Blackwell, 1995), pp. 72–104; Miller, *Material Culture and Mass Consumption*; and Daniel Miller, 'The Myths of Consumption', in *Acknowledging Consumption,* pp. 20–35.
114. Roger Silverstone, Eric Hirch, and David Morley, 'Information and Communication Technologies and the Moral Economy of the Household', in Roger Silverstone and Eric Hirsch, eds., *Consuming Technologies. Media and Information in Domestic Spaces* (Routledge, 1992), pp. 15–31. For survey and critical discussion of the concept, see Thomas Berker, Maren Hartmann, Yves Punie, and Katie J. Ward, eds., *Domestication of Media and Technology* (Open University Press, 2006).
115. Knut H. Sørensen, 'Domestication: The Enactment of Technology', in Berker, Hartmann, Punie, and Ward, eds., *Domestication of Media and Technology,* p. 46, (emphasis added).
116. Roger Silverstone, 'Domesticating Domestication. Reflections on the Life of a Concept', in Berker, Hartmann, Punie, and Ward, eds., *Domestication of Media and Technology,* p. 231.
117. Merete Lie and Knut H. Sørensen, 'Making Technology Our Own?', in *Making Technology Our Own?,* pp. 8–17.
118. Knut H. Sørensen, *Technology in Use. Two Essays on the Domestication of Artefacts,* STS Working Paper 2/94 (University of Trondheim, 1994), pp. 6–7.
119. Sørensen, 'Domestication: The Enactment of Technology', p. 46.

120. Nicholson Baker, *The Mezzanine* (1988; repr. Granta, 1998), p. 74. For a brief account of how this particular work of fiction might stimulate design historians, see Meikle, 'Material Virtues', pp. 197–99.

121. For an account of the multifaceted domestications or cultural appropriations of the VW Beetle, see Phil Patton, *Bug—The Strange Mutations of the World's Most Famous Automobile* (Simon & Schuster, 2003).

122. Remaining uncharted territory in design history, in the mid-1960s, Tom Wolfe celebrated car customizing as the primordial art form of US youth culture: Tom Wolfe, *The Kandy-Kolored Tangerine-Flake Streamline Baby* (1965; repr. Bantam Books, 1999), pp. 75–104.

123. Philippe Boudon, *Lived-In Architecture—Le Corbusier's Pessac Revisited* (Lund Humphries, 1972).

124. Walker, *Design History and the History of Design,* p. 183.

125. Fry, 'Design History: A Debate?', p. 17.

126. Silverstone, Hirch, and Morley, 'Information and Communication Technologies and the Moral Economy of the Household', pp. 15–31.

127. Viviana Narotzky, 'Our Cars in Havana', in Peter Wollen and Joe Kerr, eds., *Autopia: Cars and Culture* (Reaktion Books, 2002), p. 174.

128. Latour, *Science in Action,* p. 259.

129. Narotzky, 'Our Cars in Havana', p. 174.

130. Øllgaard, 'A Super-Elliptical Moment in the Cultural Form of the Table', pp. 144. (See notes 4 and 5 p. 155 for references to Silverstone et al.)

131. It should be mentioned that Silverstone et al. admit that from the 'perspective [of anthropology] appropriation stands for the whole process of consumption as well as for that moment at which an object crosses the threshold between the formal and the moral economies.': Silverstone, Hirch, and Morley, 'Information and Communication Technologies and the Moral Economy of the Household', p. 22.

132. Penny Sparke has, in a study of how aluminium kitchen utensils were domesticated in early twentieth-century USA, used the *term* domestication to signify a dynamic process of reciprocal transformation in a manner very close to that indicated by the *concept* domestication as developed by Silverstone et al. However, she makes no mention of the concept and does not refer to any of its literature, and her use of the term must thus be said to be of a more generic kind: Penny Sparke, 'Cookware to Cocktail Shakers: The Domestication of Aluminum in the United States, 1900–1939', in Sarah Nicols, ed., *Aluminum by Design* (Carnegie Museum of Art/Abrams, 2000), pp. 112–39.

133. Meikle, 'Material Virtues', p. 194.

134. Ibid., p. 195.

135. Betts, *The Authority of Everyday Objects,* p. 19.

136. A good example can be found in a recent cultural history of the Piaggio Vespa scooter where the users are eminently present, e.g. through the owner's clubs. In a design and domestication perspective, it is particularly interesting the way in which the intricate relationship and communication between the users/clubs and the manufacturer are analysed: Thomas

Brandt, *Frie hjerter og små motorer. Kulturell produksjon, formidling og bruk av den italienske Vespa-scooteren, 1946–1969*, doctoral dissertation (Norwegian University of Science and Technology, 2006).

137. Igor Kopytoff, 'The Cultural Biography of Things: Commoditization as Process', in Appadurai, ed., *The Social Life of Things*, p. 67.

138. See e.g. Pinch and Bijker, 'The Social Construction of Facts and Artifacts', pp. 17–50 and Latour, *Science in Action*. The latter even introduces the term *technoscience* to surpass the conventional conceptual divide between the two (pp. 174–75).

139. See e.g. Knut H. Sørensen, Margrethe Aune, and Morten Hatling, 'Against Linearity—On the Cultural Appropriation of Science and Technology', in Meinolf Dierkes and Claudia von Grote, eds., *Between Understanding and Trust—The Public, Science and Technology* (Harwood Academic, 2000) pp. 240–41.

140. Silverstone, 'Domesticating Domestication', pp. 229–48.

141. Sørensen, 'Domestication: The Enactment of Technology', p. 46.

142. Silverstone, 'Domesticating Domestication', p. 233.

143. Anna Calvera, 'Local, Regional, National, Global and Feedback: Several Issues to Be Faced with Constructing Regional Narratives', *Journal of Design History*, 18/4, p. 380.

144. Per Østby, *Flukten fra Detroit: Bilens integrasjon i det norske samfunnet*, doctoral dissertation/STS rapport no. 24 (Universitetet i Trondheim, 1995) see p. 64 for explicit references to the concept of domestication as coined by Silverstone et al. For an English excerpt of this study, see Per Østby, 'Escape from Detroit—The Norwegian Conquest of an Alien Artifact', in Knut H. Sørensen, ed., *The Car and its Environments—The Past, Present and Future of the Motorcar in Europe*, Proceedings from the COST A4 (Vol. 2) Workshop in Trondheim, Norway—May 6–8 1993 (Commission of the European Communities, Directorate General XII, 1994), pp. 33–68.

145. Sørensen, 'Domestication: The Enactment of Technology', pp. 47–50.

146. Silverstone, 'Domesticating Domestication', pp. 241–242.

147. Ibid., pp. 233–234.

148. See e.g. Sørensen, Aune, and Hatling, 'Against Linearity', pp. 237–257. Regarding the commensurability of the terms, Sørensen et al. here stress that the 'process of appropriation is not a simple integration of technology into a cultural setting. To domesticate an artifact is to negotiate its meaning and practice in a dynamic, interactive manner. This negotiation implies that technology and social relations are transformed. To use the concept of domestication as an analytical tool is to emphasize that the cultural appropriation of an artifact is a multidimensional process.' (p. 140).

149. Mikael Hård and Andrew Jamison, 'Conceptual Framework: Technology Debates as Appropriation Process', in Mikael Hård and Andrew Jamison, eds., *The Intellectual Appropriation of Technology—Discourses on Modernity, 1900–1939* (MIT Press, 1998), pp. 12 & 15.

150. Hård and Jamison, *Hubris and Hybrids*, p. 4.

151. Mikael Hård and Andrew Jamison, 'Conceptual Framework', p. 15. Their reference is to Lie and Sørensen, eds., *Making Technology Our Own?*

152. Aant Elzinga, 'Theoretical Perspectives: Culture as Resource for Technological Change', in Hård and Jamison, eds., *The Intellectual Appropriation of Technology*, p. 31.
153. Catharina Landström, 'National Strategies: The Gendered Appropriation of Household Technology', in Hård and Jamison, eds., *The Intellectual Appropriation of Technology*, p. 163.
154. Ibid., p. 164.
155. Mikael Hård, 'German Regulation: The Integration of Modern Technology into National Culture', in Hård and Jamison, eds., *The Intellectual Appropriation of Technology*, pp. 45, 54, & 66.
156. Woolgar, 'What Happened to Provocation in Science and Technology Studies?', p. 340.
157. Ibid., p. 347.
158. Law, 'After ANT', p. 8.
159. Law, *After Method*, p. 157.

3 Epistemology

1. Excerpts of an early version of this chapter were published as Kjetil Fallan, 'Modernism or Modern *ISMS*?—Notes on an Epistemological Problem in Design History' *Nordic Journal of Architectural Research*, 17/4, pp. 81–92.
2. Omar Calabrese, *L'età neobarocca* (Laterza, 1987), pp. 4–5.
3. Pierre Bourdieu and Loïc J. D. Wacquant, *An Invitation to Reflexive Sociology* (Polity Press, 1992).
4. Margaret R. Somers, 'The Privatization of Citizenship—How to Unthink a Knowledge Culture', in Bonnell and Hunt, eds., *Beyond the Cultural Turn*, pp. 133–35.
5. Tore Eriksen, 'Modernitet', in Knut Ove Eliassen and Thomas Brandt, eds. *Maskinkultur—Utsnitt fra fabrikkens tidsalder* (NTNU/Fabrikken, 2001), pp. 60–1.
6. Arnfinn Bø-Rygg, *Modernisme, antimodernisme, postmodernisme—Kritiske streiftog i samtidens kunst og kunstteori* (Stavanger University College, 1995), p. 78.
7. For a concise and intelligible introduction to Baudelaire's many visions of modernity, see Marshall Berman, *All That Is Solid Melts Into Air—The Experience of Modernity* (Verso, 1983), pp. 131–171.
8. Charles Baudelaire, 'The Painter of Modern Life', [1863] in Charles Baudelaire, *The Painter of Modern Life and Other Essays* (Phaidon, 1964), pp. 12–13.
9. Matei Calinescu, *Five Faces of Modernity* (Duke University Press, 1987), p. 41.
10. Ibid., p. 69.
11. Jan Michl, 'Is There a Duty to Be Modern?', in Anty Pansera, ed., *Tradizione e Modernismo: Design 1918/ 1940—Atti del convegno* (L'Arca, 1988), p. 4.
12. Calvera, 'Local, Regional, National, Global and Feedback', pp. 376–77.
13. Bø-Rygg, *Modernisme, antimodernisme, postmodernisme*, p. 77.
14. Foucault, *The Archaeology of Knowledge*, pp. 147–49, 193–94.
15. Michel Foucault, *The Order of Things—An Archaeology of the Human Sciences* (1st English ed.; repr. Routledge, 1989), p. xii, (emphasis added).

16. Ibid., pp. xxiii–xxiv, (emphasis added).
17. For a discussion of Foucault's disputed inspiration of and influence on historians see e.g. Jan Goldstein, ed., *Foucault and Writing of History* (Blackwell, 1994); Allan Megill, 'The Reception of Foucault by Historians', *Journal of the History of Ideas,* 48/1, pp. 117–141; and Patricia O'Brien, 'Michel Foucault's History of Culture', in Hunt, ed., *The New Cultural History,* pp. 25–46. In a round of polemic 'Foucault-bashing', Marshall Berman accused Foucault's ideas of being overly structuralist, rigid and totalitarian: 'Foucault's totalities swallow up every facet of modern life. He develops these themes with obsessive relentlessness and, indeed, with sadistic flourishes, clamping his ideas down on his readers like iron bars, twisting each dialectic into our flesh like a new turn of the screw.': Berman, *All That Is Solid Melts Into Air,* p. 35.
18. Robert R. Palmer and Joel Colton, *A History of the Modern World,* 8th edn. (McGraw-Hill, 1995), p. 464.
19. Dormer, *The Meanings of Modern Design,* p. 106.
20. Finn Werne, *Arkitekturens ismer* (Arkitektur Förlag, 1998), p. 124.
21. See e.g. Michel Callon, John Law, and Arie Rip, eds., *Mapping the Dynamics of Science and Technology—Sociology of Science in the Real World* (Macmillan, 1986) and Peter Galison, *How Experiments End* (University of Chicago Press, 1987). For an assessment of the troublesome relativistic implications of extreme versions of the social constructivist approach, see e.g. Jacob, 'Science Studies after Social Construction', pp. 95–120.
22. Erik Nygaard, 'Arkitekturteorien—mellem manifester og videnskab', *Nordic Journal of Architectural Research,* 15/3, p. 41.
23. Latour, *Science in Action,* p. 29.
24. In fact, to escape the somewhat tainted reputation of the word 'style', Nicos Hadjinicolaou suggested replacing it with the term 'visual ideology': Hadjinicolaou, *Art History and Class Struggle,* p. 104.
25. William Sewell Jr., 'The Concept(s) of Culture', in Bonnell and Hunt, eds., *Beyond the Cultural Turn,* p. 47.
26. The remarkable degree to which this process resembles any sort of sociocultural youth quake (e.g. beatniks, hippies, punks) in that it is generational is described in David Pye, *The Nature and Aesthetics of Design* (Barrie & Jenkins, 1978), p. 134.
27. Sonya O. Rose, 'Cultural Analysis and Moral Discourses—Episodes, Continuities, and Transformations', in Bonnell and Hunt, eds., *Beyond the Cultural Turn,* pp. 228–229.
28. Theodor Adorno, 'Functionalism Today', essay presented to the Deutscher Werkbund conference in 1965. in Neil Leach, ed., *Rethinking Architecture* (Routledge, 1997), p. 10.
29. Werne, *Arkitekturens ismer,* p. 27 (author's translation).
30. Ibid., p. 28 (author's translation).
31. Dominick LaCapra, *Rethinking Intellectual History—Texts, Contexts, Language* (Cornell University Press, 1983), p. 152.
32. Kramer, 'Literature, Criticism, and Historical Imagination', p. 113.
33. Hård and Jamison, *Hubris and Hybrids,* pp. 205–206 & 294–307.
34. Sometimes this mythopoeia is further enhanced by social and personal relations between actors and historians. For instance, the British design historian Jonathan M. Woodham has

shown how '[s]uch close-knit inter-relationships of campaigners, critics and historians have done much to perpetuate a very partial view of British design between the wars.': Jonathan M. Woodham, 'British modernism between the wars: an historical "Léger de main"?', in Pansera, ed., *Tradizione e Modernismo*, p. 8.

35. Wick, 'Critical Observations and General Remarks about Design History', p. 44.
36. Baudrillard, *For a Critique of the Political Economy of the Sign*, p. 101.
37. Peter Collins, *Changing Ideals in Modern Architecture: 1750–1950* (Faber and Faber, 1965), p. 293.
38. Werne, *Arkitekturens ismer*, pp. 24–25.
39. Nikolaus Pevsner, *Pioneers of the Modern Movement—From William Morris to Walter Gropius* (Faber & Faber, 1936) and Sigfried Giedion, *Space, Time and Architecture: The Growth of a New Tradition* (Oxford University Press, 1949).
40. Charles A. Jencks, *The Language of Post-Modern Architecture* (Academy Editions, 1977) and Robert Venturi, *Complexity and Contradiction in Architecture* (Museum of Modern Art, 1966).
41. Panayotis Tournikiotis, *The Historiography of Modern Architecture* (MIT Press, 1999).
42. Ibid., p. 221.
43. Latour, *Science in Action*, p. 131.
44. Quentin Skinner, 'Meaning and Understanding in the History of Ideas', in James Tully, ed., *Meaning and Context: Quentin Skinner and His Critics* (Princeton University Press, 1988), pp. 29–67.
45. Dilnot, 'The State of Design History, Part II', pp. 3–20, esp. pp. 6–7.
46. Hård and Jamison, *Hubris and Hybrids*, pp. 294–307.
47. Thomas Kuhn, *The Structure of Scientific Revolutions* (University of Chicago Press, 1962)
48. Thomas Kuhn, *The Structure of Scientific Revolutions*, 2nd edn. (University of Chicago Press, 1970), p. 208.
49. Thomas S. Kuhn, 'Comment on the Relations of Science and Art', in *The Essential Tension—Selected Studies in Scientific Tradition and Change* (University of Chicago Press, 1977), p. 340.
50. Ibid., p. 341.
51. Ibid., p. 345.
52. See e.g. George Ritzer, *Toward an Integrated Sociological Paradigm: The Search for an Exemplar and an Image of the Subject Matter* (Allyn and Bacon, 1981); Barry Barnes, *T. S. Kuhn and Social Science* (Columbia University Press, 1982); Pinch and Bijker, 'The Social Construction of Facts and Artifacts', pp. 24–25; and Donald MacKenzie, 'Missile Accuracy: A Case Study in the Social Processes of Technological Change', in Bijker, Hughes and Pinch, eds., *The Social Construction of Technological Systems*, p. 209. However, relativist readings of Kuhn were also an influential step on the way towards general theories of social construction. For one example, see Barry Barnes, 'Thomas Kuhn', in Quentin Skinner, ed., *The Return of Grand Theory in the Human Sciences* (Cambridge University Press, 1985), pp. 83–100.
53. Kingery, 'Technological Systems and Some Implications with Regard to Continuity and Change', p. 225.

54. Kuhn, *The Structure of Scientific Revolutions,* pp. 157–158.
55. Frederick Suppe, 'The Search for Philosophic Understanding of Scientific Theories', in Frederick Suppe, ed., *The Structure of Scientific Theories* (University of Illinois Press, 1977), p. 150.
56. For a brief account of the controversial character of Kuhn's work, even within the sociology of science, see Joyce Appleby, Lynn Hunt, and Margaret Jacob, *Telling the Truth About History* (Norton, 1994), pp. 163–166.
57. Kuhn, *The Structure of Scientific Revolutions,* p. 208.
58. Kuhn, 'Comment on the Relations of Science and Art', pp. 340–341.
59. Richard Biernacki, 'Method and Metaphor After the New Cultural History', in Bonnell and Hunt, eds., *Beyond the Cultural Turn,* pp. 62–84.
60. Paul Feyerabend, *Against Method—Outline of an anarchistic theory of knowledge* (NLB, 1975).
61. Feyerabend, *Against Method,* p. 30.
62. Ibid., p. 39.
63. Ibid., p. 199.
64. Paul Feyerabend, 'Consolations for the Specialist', in Imre Lakatos and Alan Musgrave, eds., *Criticism and the Growth of Knowledge* (Cambridge University Press, 1970), pp. 207–208.
65. Thomas Kuhn, 'Second Thoughts on Paradigms', in Suppe, ed., *The Structure of Scientific Theories,* p. 459.
66. Kuhn, *The Structure of Scientific Revolutions,* pp. 182–187 [postscript] and Kuhn, 'Second Thoughts on Paradigms', pp. 459–482. For a discussion and critique of Kuhn's reformulations, see: Frederick Suppe, 'Exemplars, Theories and Disciplinary Matrixes', in *The Structure of Scientific Theories,* pp. 483–499.
67. Margaret Masterman, 'The Nature of a Paradigm', in Lakatos and Musgrave, eds., *Criticism and the Growth of Knowledge,* pp. 61–65.
68. Ibid., p. 65 and Kuhn, 'Second Thoughts on Paradigms', p. 471.
69. The use of the term *isms* here should not be taken literally—any term describing an ideological or aesthetic movement in architecture or design is included even if it does not end with the prescribed suffix—hence, art deco, Scandinavian design, streamlining, and their likes are all isms in this regard.
70. See e.g. Foucault, *The Order of Things.*
71. Kuhn, 'Comment on the Relations of Science and Art', p. 348.
72. Heskett, 'Some Lessons of Design History', p. 13.
73. Castelnuovo and Gubler, 'The Mysterious Object', p. 411.
74. David Edgerton, *The Shock of the Old—Technology and Global History Since 1900* (Oxford University Press, 2007).
75. Heskett, 'Some Lessons of Design History', p. 13.
76. Baudrillard, *The System of Objects,* p. 118.
77. Wick, 'Critical Observations and General remarks about Design History', p. 46.
78. Uriarte, 'Modernity and Postmodernity from Cuba', p. 246.
79. Lowenthal, *The Past Is a Foreign Country,* p. 35.

80. Kuhn, 'Second Thoughts on Paradigms', pp. 471 & 477.
81. Kuhn, 'Comment on the Relations of Science and Art', p. 351.
82. Juan Pablo Bonta, *Architecture and its Interpretation—A Study of Expressive Systems in Architecture* (Lund Humphries, 1979), pp. 131–174.
83. See e.g. Anders V. Munch, *Den stilløse stil: Adolf Loos* (Kunstakademiets Arkitekskoles Forlag, 2002) and Mari Lending, *Omkring 1900—Kontinuiteter i norsk arkitekturtenkning* (Pax, 2008). In a sense, though, this is nothing new—already in his 1960 *Theory and Design in the First Machine Age* Reyner Banham demonstrated how classical ideals regarding composition, plan and aesthetic principles prevailed also in the modern architecture of the 1920s: Tournikiotis, *The Historiography of Modern Architecture*, pp. 145–146. Only a few years later, and much in the same vein, Peter Collins traced the sources of the ideas of twentieth-century architecture to much older origins: Collins, *Changing Ideals in Modern Architecture*.
84. Mari Hvattum, 'Historisme og modernisme i moderne arkitekturhistorieskriving', *Nordic Journal of Architectural Research,* 19/1, 2006, p. 89. (author's translation.)
85. Jürgen Habermas, 'Modernity—An Incomplete Project', in Hal Foster, ed., *The Anti-Aesthetic—Essays on Post-Modern Culture* (Bay Press, 1983), pp. 3–15.
86. Andrea Branzi, *Learning From Milan—Design and the Second Modernity* (MIT Press, 1988), p. 46.
87. Latour, *We Have Never Been Modern.*
88. The notion of postmodernism as a revolutionary paradigm is therefore just as problematic in the history of technology as it is in art history and design history, because, as Andrew Murphie and John Potts have observed, '[t]here is an overlapping of techniques and concerns into the "postmodern" period that often goes unremarked.': Andrew Murphie and John Potts, *Culture & Technology* (Palgrave Macmillan, 2003), p. 62.
89. Habermas, 'Modernity—An Incomplete Project', p. 11.
90. Jencks, *The Language of Post-Modern Architecture*, p. 9.
91. Tom Wolfe, *From Bauhaus to Our House* (Farrar, Straus & Giroux, 1981), pp. 63–64.
92. Peter Blake, *Form Follows Fiasco—Why Modern Architecture Hasn't Worked* (Little, Brown & Co., 1974), pp. 154–155.
93. Katharine G. Bristol, 'The Pruitt-Igoe Myth', in Keith L. Eggener, ed., *American Architectural History—A Contemporary Reader* (Routledge, 2004), pp. 352–364.
94. Hans Bertens, *The Idea of the Postmodern—A History* (Routledge, 1995), p. 57, (emphasis added).
95. John Law, *Organizing Modernity* (Blackwell, 1994), p. 2.
96. Arnfinn Bø-Rygg, 'What Modernism Was—Art, Progress and the Avant-garde', in Mari Hvattum and Christian Hermansen, eds., *Tracing Modernity—Manifestations of the Modern in Architecture and the City* (Routledge, 2004), p. 23.
97. Espen Schaanning, *Modernitetens oppløsning: Sentrale skikkelser i etterkrigstidens idéhistorie* (Spartacus, 2000), p. 15 (author's translation).
98. Gianni Vattimo, *La fine della modernità* (Garzanti, 1985), p. 12–15.
99. Calinescu, *Five Faces of Modernity,* p. 265–312.

100. Calabrese, *L'età neobarocca,* pp. 14–17. This topic is further explored in Mario Perniola, *Enigmi—il momento egizio nella società e nell'arte* (Edizioni Costa & Nolan, 1990), pp. 103–123.
101. Dick Hebdige, *Hiding in the Light—On Images and Things* (Routledge, 1988), p. 182.
102. Baudrillard, *The System of Objects,* p. 113.
103. See e.g. Karl Popper, *The Logic of Scientific Discovery* (Hutchinson, 1959); Karl Popper, *Objective Knowledge—An Evolutionary Approach* (Clarendon Press, 1972); and Imre Lakatos, 'The History of Science and its Rational Reconstruction', in Imre Lakatos, *Philosophical Papers,* eds. John Worrall and Gregory Currie (Cambridge University Press, 1978).
104. For a critical survey of such historiographic traditions, see e.g. Appleby, Hunt, and Jacob, *Telling the Truth About History,* pp. 15–125.
105. Philip Steadman, *The Evolution of Designs: Biological Analogy in Architecture and the Applied Arts* (Cambridge University Press, 1979). It may be interesting to note that the concluding chapter of the book appeared in the first issue of Design Research Society's journal *Design Studies*: Philip Steadman, 'The History and Science of the Artificial', *Design Studies,* 1/1, pp. 49–58.
106. Ian Hodder, 'Theoretical Archaeology: A Reactionary View', in Pearce, ed., *Interpreting Objects and Collections,* p. 51.
107. See e.g. Yagou, 'Rethinking Design History From an Evolutionary Perspective', pp. 50–60 and van Nierop, Blankendaal and Overbeeke, 'The Evolution of the Bicycle', pp. 253–267.
108. Rune Nydal, *I vitenskapens tid—Introduksjon til vitenskapsfilosofi etter Kuhn* (Spartacus, 2002), p. 142.
109. LaCapra, *Rethinking Intellectual History,* p. 152.

Conclusion

1. Guy Julier, *The Culture of Design,* 2nd edn. (Sage, 2008), p. 7.
2. Victor Margolin, 'Design in History', *Design Issues,* 25/2, p. 104
3. Highmore, 'A Sideboard Manifesto', p. 2.
4. Ibid.

Bibliography

Adams, D., *The Restaurant at the End of the Universe: The Hitch Hiker's Guide to the Galaxy 2*, London: Pan Books, 1980.

Adorno, T., 'Functionalism Today', essay presented to the Deutscher Werkbund conference in 1965, in N. Leach, ed., *Rethinking Architecture*, London: Routledge, 1997.

Adorno, T., 'Valéry Proust Museum', in *Prisms*, Cambridge, Mass.: MIT Press, 1983.

Agnew, K., 'The Spitfire: Legend or History? An Argument for a New Research Culture in Design', *Journal of Design History*, 6/2 (1993), pp. 121–30.

Akrich, M., 'The De-scription of Technological Objects', in W. E. Bijker and J. Law, eds., *Shaping Technology/Building Society—Studies in Sociotechnical Change*, Cambridge, Mass.: MIT Press, 1992.

Akrich, M., 'User Representations: Practices, Methods and Sociology', in A. Rip, T. J. Misa, and J. Schot, eds., *Managing Technology in Society. The Approach of Constructive Technology Assessment*, London: Pinter Publishers, 1995.

Akrich, M., and Latour, B., 'A Summary of a Convenient Vocabulary for the Semiotics of Human and Nonhuman Assemblies', in W. E. Bijker and J. Law, eds., *Shaping Technology/Building Society—Studies in Sociotechnical Change*, Cambridge, Mass.: MIT Press, 1992.

Ames, K. L., 'Material Cultures: Why Some Things Matter' [book review], *Journal of Design History*, 13/1 (2000), pp. 74–75.

Appadurai, A., ed., *The Social Life of Things—Commodities in Cultural Perspective*, Cambridge: Cambridge University Press, 1986.

Appleby, J., Hunt, L., and Jacob, M., *Telling the Truth About History*, New York: Norton, 1994.

Atkinson, P., 'The Best Laid Plans of Mice and Men: The Computer Mouse in the History of Computing', *Design Issues*, 23/3 (2007), pp. 46–61.

Atkinson, P., 'A Bitter Pill to Swallow: The Rise and Fall of the Tablet Computer', *Design Issues*, 24/4 (2008), pp. 3–25.

Atkinson, P., 'The (In)Difference Engine—Explaining the Disappearance of Diversity in the Design of the Personal Computer', *Journal of Design History*, 13/1 (2000), pp. 59–72.

Atkinson, P., 'Man in a Briefcase: The Social Construction of the Laptop Computer and the Emergence of a Type Form', *Journal of Design History*, 18/2 (2005), pp. 191–205.

Attfield, J., 'Beyond the Pale: Reviewing the Relationship between Material Culture and Design History', *Journal of Design History*, 12/4 (1999), pp. 373–80.

Attfield, J., *Bringing Modernity Home—Writings on Popular Design and Material Culture*, Manchester: Manchester University Press, 2007.

Attfield, J., '"Give 'em something dark and heavy": The Role of Design in the Material Culture of Popular British Furniture, 1939–1965', *Journal of Design History*, 9/3 (1996), pp. 185–201.

Attfield, J., 'Material Culture in the Social World' [book review], *Journal of Design History* 15/1 (2002), pp. 65–6.

Attfield, J., ed., *Utility Reassessed—The Role of Ethics in the Practice of Design*, Manchester: Manchester University Press, 1999.

Attfield, J., *Wild Things—The Material Culture of Everyday Life*, Oxford: Berg, 2000.

Baker, N., *The Mezzanine*, London: Granta, 1998 [1988].

Banham, R., *Theory and Design in the First Machine Age*, London: Architectural Press, 1960.

Barnes, B., *T. S. Kuhn and Social Science*, New York: Columbia University Press, 1982.

Barnes, B., 'Thomas Kuhn', in Q. Skinner, ed., *The Return of Grand Theory in the Human Sciences*, Cambridge: Cambridge University Press, 1985.

Barthes, R., *Mythologies*, London: Paladin, 1973.

Batchelor, R., 'Not Looking at Kettles', in S. M. Pearce, ed., *Interpreting Objects and Collections*, London: Routledge, 1994.

Baudelaire, C., *The Painter of Modern Life and Other Essays*, London: Phaidon, 1964.

Baudrillard, J., *The Consumer Society*, London: Sage, 1998 [1970].

Baudrillard, J., *For a Critique of the Political Economy of the Sign*, St. Louis: Telos, 1981 [1972].

Baudrillard, J., *The System of Objects*, London: Verso, 1996 [1968].

Bauman, Z., 'Broken Lives—Broken Strategies', in *Life in Fragments: Essays in Postmodern Morality*, Oxford: Blackwell, 1995.

Benhamou, R., '*Journal of Design History*, Vol. 1, nos. 1–4' [review], *Technology and Culture*, 32/1 (1991), p. 136.

Benson, J., 'Working-Class Consumption, Saving, and Investment in England and Wales, 1851–1911', *Journal of Design History*, 9/2 (1996), pp. 87–99.

Berker, T., Hartmann, M., Punie, Y. and Ward, K. J., eds., *Domestication of Media and Technology*, Maidenhead: Open University Press, 2006.

Berman, M., *All That Is Solid Melts Into Air—The Experience of Modernity*, London: Verso, 1983.

Berner, B., 'Rationalizing Technical Work: Visions and Realities of the "Systematic Drawing Office" in Sweden, 1890–1940', *Technology and Culture*, 48/1 (2007), pp. 20–42.

Bertens, H., *The Idea of the Postmodern—A History*, London: Routledge, 1995.

Betts, P., *The Authority of Everyday Objects—A Cultural History of West German Industrial Design*, Berkeley: University of California Press, 2004.

Betts, P., 'The Bauhaus and National Social-ism—a Dark Chapter of Modernism', in J. Fiedler and P. Feierabend, eds., *Bauhaus*, Cologne: Könemann, 1999.

Biernacki, R., 'Method and Metaphor After the New Cultural History', in V. E. Bonnell and L. Hunt, eds., *Beyond the Cultural Turn—New Directions in the Study of Society and Culture*, Berkeley: University of California Press, 1999.

Bijker, W. E., *Of Bicycles, Bakelites, and Bulbs—Toward a Theory of Sociotechnical Change*, Cambridge, Mass.: MIT Press, 1995.

Bijker, W. E., 'The Social Construction of Ba-kelite: Toward a Theory of Invention', in W. E. Bijker, T. P. Hughes, and T. J. Pinch, eds., *The Social Construction of Technological Systems—New Directions in the Sociology and History of Technology*, Cambridge, Mass.: MIT Press, 1987.

Bijker, W. E., and Law, J., 'What Next? Technology, Theory, and Method', in W. E. Bijker and J. Law, eds., *Shaping Technology/Building Society—Studies in Sociotechnical Change*, Cambridge, Mass.: MIT Press, 1992.

Bijker, W. E., Hughes, T. P., and Pinch, T. J., eds., *The Social Construction of Technological Systems—New Directions in the Sociology and History of Technology*, Cambridge, Mass.: MIT Press, 1987.

Bijker, W. E., and Law, J., eds., *Shaping Technology/Building Society—Studies in Sociotechnical Change*, Cambridge, Mass.: MIT Press, 1992.

Blake, P., *Form Follows Fiasco—Why Modern Architecture Hasn't Worked*, Boston: Little, Brown & Co., 1974.

Blaszczyk, R. L., 'Cinderella Stories—The Glass of Fashion and the Gendered Marketplace', in R. Horowitz and A. Mohun, eds., *His and Hers: Gender, Consumption, and Technology*, Charlottesville: University Press of Virginia, 1998.

Blaszczyk, R. L., *Imagining Consumers—Design and Innovation from Wedgwood to Corning*, Baltimore: Johns Hopkins University Press, 2000.

Bloor, D., 'Anti-Latour', *Studies In History and Philosophy of Science*, 30/1 (1999), pp. 81–112.

Bonnell, V. E., *Iconography of Power: Soviet Political Posters under Lenin and Stalin*, Berkeley: University of California Press, 1997.

Bonnell, V. E., and Hunt, L., eds., *Beyond the Cultural Turn—New Directions in the Study of Society and Culture*, Berkeley: University of California Press, 1999.

Bonta, J. P., *Architecture and its Interpretation—A Study of Expressive Systems in Architecture*, London: Lund Humphries, 1979.

Bø-Rygg, A., *Modernisme, antimodernisme, postmodernisme—Kritiske streiftog i samtidens kunst og kunstteori*, Stavanger: Stavanger University College, 1995.

Bø-Rygg, A., 'What Modernism Was—Art, Progress and the Avant-garde', in M. Hvattum and C. Hermansen, eds., *Tracing Modernity—Manifestations of the Modern in Architecture and the City*, London: Routledge, 2004.

Boudon, P., *Lived-In Architecture—Le Corbusier's Pessac Revisited*, London: Lund Humphries, 1972.

Bourdieu, P., *Distinction: A Social Critique of the Judgement of Taste*, London: Routledge & Kegan Paul, 1984 [1979].

Bourdieu, P., and Wacquant, L. J. D., *An Invitation to Reflexive Sociology*, Cambridge: Polity Press, 1992.

Brandt, T., 'Frie hjerter og små motorer. Kulturell produksjon, formidling og bruk av den italienske Vespa-scooteren, 1946–1969', doctoral dissertation, Trondheim: Norwegian University of Science and Technology, 2006.

Branzi, A., *Learning from Milan—Design and the Second Modernity,* Cambridge, Mass.: MIT Press, 1988.

Bristol, K. G., 'The Pruitt-Igoe Myth', in K. L. Eggener, ed., *American Architectural History—A Contemporary Reader,* London: Routledge, 2004.

Brown, B., 'Thing Theory', in B. Brown, ed., *Things,* Chicago: University of Chicago Press, 2004.

Brown, K. D., 'Design in the British Toy Industry Since 1945', *Journal of Design History,* 11/4 (1998), pp. 323–33.

Brown, S. D., and Capdevila, R., 'Perpetuum Mobile: Substance, Force and the Sociology of Translation', in J. Law and J. Hassard, eds., *Actor Network Theory and After,* Oxford: Blackwell, 1999.

Buckley, C., 'Design, Femininity, and Modernism: Interpreting the Work of Susie Cooper', *Journal of Design History,* 7/4 (1994), pp. 277–293.

Buckley, C., 'Made in Patriarchy: Toward a Feminist Analysis of Women and Design', *Design Issues,* 3/2 (1986), pp. 3–14.

Buckley, C., '"The Noblesse of the Banks": Craft Hierarchies, Gender Divisions, and the Roles of Women Paintresses and Designers in the British Pottery Industry 1890–1939' *Journal of Design History,* 2/4 (1989), pp. 257–73.

Burton, A., 'Design History and the History of Toys: Defining a Discipline for the Bethnal Green Museum of Childhood', *Journal of Design History,* 10/1 (1997), pp. 1–21.

Calinescu, M., *Five Faces of Modernity,* Durham, NC: Duke University Press, 1987.

Callon, M., 'Society in the Making: The Study of Technology as a Tool for Sociological Analysis', in W. E. Bijker, T. P. Hughes and T. J. Pinch, eds., *The Social Construction of Technological Systems—New Directions in the Sociology and History of Technology,* Cambridge, Mass.: MIT Press, 1987.

Callon, M., Law, J. and Rip, A., eds., *Mapping the Dynamics of Science and Technology—Sociology of Science in the Real World,* Basingstoke: Macmillan, 1986.

Calvera, A., 'Local, Regional, National, Global and Feedback: Several Issues to Be Faced with Constructing Regional Narratives', *Journal of Design History,* 18/4 (2005), pp. 371–83.

Calvino, I., *Le città invisibili,* Turin: Einaudi, 1972.

Campbell, C., 'Consumption and the Rhetorics of Need and Want', *Journal of Design History,* 11/3 (1998), pp. 235–46.

Calabrese, O., *L'età neobarocca,* Bari: Laterza, 1987.

Carlson, W. B., 'Artifacts and Frames of Meaning: Thomas A. Edison, His Managers, and the Cultural Construction of Motion Pictures', in W. E. Bijker and J. Law, eds., *Shaping Technology/Building Society—Studies in Sociotechnical Change,* Cambridge, Mass.: MIT Press, 1992.

Castelnuovo, E., 'For a History of Design', in C. Pirovano, ed. in chief, *History of Industrial Design, 1:1750–1850 The Age of the Industrial Revolution,* Milan: Electa, 1990.

Castelnuovo, E., and Gubler, J., 'The Mysterious Object—Notes on the Historiography of Design', in C. Pirovano, ed. in chief, *History of Industrial Design, 3:1919–1990 The Dominion of Design,* Milan: Electa, 1990.

Clarke, A. J., 'The Aesthetics of Social Aspiration', in D. Miller, ed., *Home Possessions—Material Culture Behind Closed Doors,* Oxford: Berg, 2001.

Clarke, A. J., *Tupperware: The Promise of Plastic in 1950s America,* Washington, D.C.: Smithsonian Institution Press, 1999.

Clarke, A. J., 'Window Shopping at Home: Classifieds, Catalogues and New Consumer Skills', in D. Miller, ed., *Material Cultures— Why Some Things Matter,* London: UCL Press, 1998.

Clarke, S., 'Consumer Negotiations', *Business and Economic History,* 26/1 (1997), pp. 101–22.

Clarke, S., 'Managing Design: The Art and Colour Section at General Motors, 1927– 1941', *Journal of Design History,* 12/1 (1999), pp. 65–79.

Collins, P., *Changing Ideals in Modern Architecture: 1750–1950,* London: Faber and Faber, 1965.

Conway, H., ed., *Design History—A Student's Handbook,* London: Routledge, 1987.

Corn, J. J., 'Object Lessons/Object Myths? What Historians of Technology Learn from Things', in W. D. Kingery, ed., *Learning from Things—Method and Material of Material Culture Studies,* Washington, D.C.: Smithsonian Institution Press, 1996.

Coupland, D., *Generation X,* New York: St. Martin's Press, 1991.

Cowan, R. S., 'The Consumption Junction: A Proposal for Research Strategies in the Sociology of Technology', in W. E. Bijker, T. P. Hughes, and T. J. Pinch, eds., *The Social Construction of Technological Systems—New Directions in the Sociology and History of Technology,* Cambridge, Mass.: MIT Press, 1987.

Cowan, R. S., *More Work for Mother—The Ironies of Household Technology from the Open Hearth to the Microwave,* New York: Basic Books, 1983.

Cowan, R. S., *A Social History of American Technology,* New York: Oxford University Press, 1997.

Crowley, D., 'Building the World Anew: Design in Stalinist and Post-Stalinist Poland', *Journal of Design History,* 7/3 (1994), pp. 187–203.

Csikszentmihalyi, M., and Rochberg-Halton, E., *The Meaning of Things—Domestic Symbols and the Self,* Cambridge: Cambridge University Press, 1981.

Cummings, N., and Lewandowska, M., *The Value of Things,* London August/Birkhäuser, 2000.

Daston, L., ed., *Things That Talk—Object Lessons form Art and Science,* New York: Zone Books, 2004.

Davies, K., 'Scandinavian Furniture in Britain: Finmar and the UK Market, 1949–1952', *Journal of Design History,* 10/1 (1997), pp. 39–52.

DeLillo, D., *Underworld,* New York: Scribner, 1997.

Dilnot, C., 'The State of Design History, Part I', *Design Issues,* 1/1 (1984), pp. 3–23.

Dilnot, C., 'The State of Design History, Part II', *Design Issues,* 1/2 (1984), pp. 3–20.

Doordan, D., 'On History', *Design Issues,* 11/1 (1995), pp. 76–81.

Dorfles, G., 'Introduzione', in A. Pansera, ed., *Tradizione e Modernismo: Design 1918/1940—Atti del convegno,* Milan: L'Arca, 1988.

Dormer, P., *The Meanings of Modern Design,* London: Thames & Hudson, 1990.

Douglas, M., and Isherwood, B., *The World of Goods—Towards an Anthropology of Consumption,* London: Allen Lane, 1979.

Draper, P., ed., *Reassessing Nikolaus Pevsner,* Aldershot: Ashgate, 2004.

Edgerton, D., *The Shock of the Old—Technology and Global History Since 1900,* Oxford: Oxford University Press, 2007.

Edwards, S., 'Factory and Fantasy in Andrew Ure', *Journal of Design History,* 14/1 (2001), pp. 17–33.

Elzinga, A., 'Theoretical Perspectives: Culture as Resource for Technological Change', in M. Hård and A. Jamison, eds., *The Intellectual Appropriation of Technology, 1900–1939,* Cambridge, Mass.: MIT Press, 1998.

Er, H. A., 'Development Patterns of Industrial Design in the Third World: A Conceptual Model for Newly Industrialized Countries', *Journal of Design History,* 10/3 (1997), pp. 293–307.

Eriksen, T., 'Modernitet', in K. O. Eliassen and T. Brandt, eds., *Maskinkultur—Utsnitt fra fabrikkens tidsalder,* Trondheim: NTNU/Fabrikken, 2001.

Faldbakken, M. (under the pseudonym Abo Rasul), *The Cocka Hola Company—Skandinavisk misantropi,* Oslo: Cappelen, 2001.

Fallan, K., 'Architecture in Action—Traveling with Actor-Network Theory in the Land of Architectural Research', *Architectural Theory Review,* 13/1 (2008), pp. 80–96.

Fallan, K., 'De-scribing Design: Appropriating Script Analysis to Design History', *Design Issues,* 24/4 (2008), pp. 61–75.

Fallan, K., 'Form, Function, Fiction: Translations of Technology and Design in Product Development', *History and Technology,* 24/1 (2008), pp. 61–87.

Fallan, K., 'How an Excavator Got Aesthetic Pretensions—Negotiating Design in 1960s' Norway', *Journal of Design History,* 20/1 (2007), pp. 43–59.

Fallan, K., 'Modernism or Modern *ISMS*?—Notes on an Epistemological Problem in Design History', *Nordic Journal of Architectural Research,* 17/4 (2004), pp. 81–92.

Fallan, K., '"One Must Offer 'Something for Everyone'"—Designing Crockery for Consumer Consent in 1950s' Norway', *Journal of Design History,* 22/2 (2009), pp.133–49.

Fallan, K., 'The *Realpolitik* of the Artificial—Strategic Design at Figgjo Fajanse Facing International Free Trade in the 1960s', *Enterprise and Society,* 10/3 (2009), pp. 559–89.

Feyerabend, P., *Against Method—Outline of an Anarchistic Theory of Knowledge,* London: NLB, 1975.

Feyerabend, P., 'Consolations for the Specialist', in I. Lakatos and A. Musgrave, eds., *Criticism and the Growth of Knowledge,* Cambridge: Cambridge University Press, 1970.

Findeli, A., 'Design History and Design Studies: Methodological, Epistemological and Pedagogical Inquiry', *Design Issues,* 11/1 (1995), pp. 43–65.

Fisher, T. H., 'What We Touch, Touches Us: Materials, Affects, and Affordances', *Design Issues,* 20/4 (2004), pp. 20–31.

Flink, J. J., *The Automobile Age,* Cambridge, Mass.: MIT Press, 1988.

Flusser, V., *The Shape of Things—A Philosophy of Design,* London: Reaktion, 1999.

Forty, A., 'DEBATE: A Reply to Victor Margolin', *Journal of Design History,* 6/2 (1993), pp. 131–32.

Forty, A., *Objects of Desire—Design and Society Since 1750,* London: Thames and Hudson, 1986.

Fossati, P., *Il Design in Italia 1945–1972,* Turin: Einaudi, 1972.

Foucault, M., *The Archaeology of Knowledge,* London: Tavistock Publications, 1972.

Foucault, M., *The Order of Things—An Archaeology of the Human Sciences,* London: Routledge, 1989 [1st. Engl. ed. 1970].

Friedel, R., 'Some Matters of Substance', in S. Lubar and W. D. Kingery, eds., *History from Things—Essays on Material Culture,* Washington, D.C.: Smithsonian Institution Press, 1993.

Frobenius, N., *Teori og praksis*, Oslo: Gyldendal, 2004.

Fry, T., *Design History Australia*, Sydney: Hale & Iremonger, 1988.

Fry, T., 'Design History: A Debate?', *Block*, 5 (1981), pp. 14–18.

Fry, T., 'A Geography of Power: Design History and Marginality', *Design Issues*, 6/1 (1989), pp. 15–30.

Fry, T., 'Unpacking the Typewriter', *Block*, 7 (1982), pp. 36–47.

Galison, P., *How Experiments End*, Chicago: University of Chicago Press, 1987.

Galison, P., 'Image of Self', in L. Daston, ed., *Things That Talk—Object Lessons from Art and Science*, New York: Zone Books, 2004.

Gartman, D., *Auto Opium—A Social History of American Automobile Design*, London: Routledge, 1994.

Garvey, P. 'How to Have a 'Good Home'—The Practical Aesthetic and Normativity in Norway', *Journal of Design History*, 16/3 (2003), pp. 241–51.

Gay, P. du, Hall, S., Janes, J., Mackay, H. and Negus, K., *Doing Cultural Studies—The Story of the Sony Walkman*, London: Sage, 1997.

Gelfer-Jørgensen, M., 'Has Design History Anything to Do with Art History?', *Scandinavian Journal of Design History*, 11 (2001), p. 16–21.

Gelfer-Jørgensen, M., ed., *Nordisk Funktionalisme 1925–1950*, Copenhagen: Det danske Kunstindustrimuseum & Nordisk Forum for Formgivningshistorie, 1986.

Georgiadis, S., *Sigfried Giedion: An Intellectual Biography*, Edinburgh: Edinburgh University Press, 1989.

Giedion, S., *Mechanization Takes Command—a Contribution to Anonymous History*, New York: Oxford University Press, 1948.

Giedion, S., *Space, Time and Architecture: The Growth of a New Tradition*, Cambridge, Mass.: Oxford University Press, 1949.

Glennie, P., 'Consumption Within Historical Studies', in D. Miller, ed., *Acknowledging Consumption*, London: Routledge, 1995.

Goldstein, J., ed., *Foucault and Writing of History*, Oxford: Blackwell, 1994.

Goodall, P., 'Design and Gender', *Block*, 9 (1983), pp. 50–61.

Gorman, C. R., 'Reshaping and Rethinking: Recent Feminist Scholarship on Design and Designers', *Design Issues*, 17/4 (2001), pp. 72–88.

Graves, J., '"When Things Go Wrong . . . Inside the Inside": A Psychoanalytical History of a Jug', *Journal of Design History*, 12/4 (1999), pp. 357–67.

Grazia, V. de, ed., *The Sex of Things—Gender and Consumption in Historical Perspective*, Berkeley: University of California Press, 1996.

Guyatt, M., 'Better Legs: Artificial Limbs for British Veterans of the First World War', *Journal of Design History*, 14/4 (2001), pp. 307–25.

Habermas, J., 'Modernity—An Incomplete Project', in H. Foster, ed., *The Anti-Aesthetic—Essays on Post-Modern Culture*, Port Townsend, Wash.: Bay Press, 1983.

Hackett, E. J., Amsterdamska, O., Lynch, M., and Wajcman, J., eds., *The Handbook of Science and Technology Studies*, Cambridge, Mass.: MIT Press, 2008.

Hadjinicolaou, N., *Art History and Class Struggle*, London: Pluto Press, 1978.

Hannah, F., and Putnam, T., 'Taking Stock in Design History', *Block*, 3 (1980), pp. 25–33.

Hansen, P. H., *Da danske møbler blev moderne—Historien om dansk møbeldesigns storhedstid*, Odense: Syddansk Universitetsforlag & Aschehoug, 2006.

Hansen, P. H., 'Networks, Narratives, and New Markets: The Rise and Decline of Danish Modern Furniture Design, 1930–1970', *Business History Review*, 80/3 (2006), pp. 449–83.

Hård, M., 'Beyond Harmony and Consensus: A Social Conflict Approach to Technology', *Science, Technology and Human Values*, 18/4 (1993), pp. 408–32.

Hård, M., 'German Regulation: The Integration of Modern Technology into National Culture', in M. Hård and A. Jamison, eds., *The Intellectual Appropriation of Technology, 1900–1939*, Cambridge, Mass.: MIT Press, 1998.

Hård, M., and Jamison, A., *Hubris and Hybrids—A Cultural History of Technology and Science*, New York: Routledge, 2005.

Hård, M., and Jamison, A., eds., *The Intellectual Appropriation of Technology— Discourses on Modernity, 1900–1939*, Cambridge, Mass.: MIT Press, 1998.

Harris, J., *The New Art History—A Critical Introduction*, London: Routledge, 2001.

Hayward, S., ' "Good Design Is Largely a Matter of Common Sense": Questioning the Meaning and Ownership of a Twentieth-Century Orthodoxy', *Journal of Design History*, 11/3 (1998), pp. 217–33.

Hebdige, D., *Hiding in the Light—On Images and Things*, London: Routledge, 1988.

Hebdige, D., 'Object as Image: The Italian Scooter Cycle', *Block*, 5 (1981), pp. 44–64.

Heskett, J., 'Design in Inter-War Germany', in W. Kaplan, ed., *Designing Modernity—The Arts of Reform and Persuasion 1885–1945*, London: Thames & Hudson, 1995.

Heskett, J., *Industrial Design*, London: Thames & Hudson, 1980.

Heskett, J., 'Industrial Design' in H. Conway, ed., *Design History—A Student's Handbook*, London: Routledge, 1987.

Heskett, J., 'Modernism and Archaism in Design in the Third Reich', *Block*, 3 (1980), pp. 13–24.

Heskett, J., 'Some Lessons of Design History', in A. Skjerven, ed., *Designkompetanse— Utvkling, forskning og undervisning*, Oslo: Oslo National Academy of the Arts, 2005.

Highmore, B., 'A Sideboard Manifesto: Design Culture in an Artificial World', in B. Highmore, ed., *The Design Culture Reader*, London: Routledge, 2009.

Hodder, I., 'Theoretical Archaeology: A Reactionary View', in S. M. Pearce, ed., *Interpreting Objects and Collections*, London: Routledge, 1994.

Horowitz, R., and Mohun, A., eds., *His and Hers: Gender, Consumption, and Technology*, Charlottesville: University Press of Virginia, 1998.

Hubak, M., 'The Car as a Cultural Statement', in M. Lie and K. H. Sørensen, eds., *Making Technology Our Own?—Domesticating Technology into Everyday Life*, Oslo: Scandinavian University Press, 1996.

Hughes, T. P., *American Genesis—A Century of Invention and Technological Enthusiasm, 1870–1970*, New York: Viking, 1989.

Hughes, T. P., 'Edison and Electric Light', in D. MacKenzie and J. Wajcman, eds., *The Social Shaping of Technology*, 2nd edn., Maidenhead: Open University Press, 1999.

Hughes, T. P., 'The Evolution of Large Technological Systems', in W. E. Bijker, T. P. Hughes, and T. J. Pinch, eds., *The Social Construction of Technological Systems— New Directions in the Sociology and History of Technology*, Cambridge, Mass.: MIT Press, 1987.

Hughes, T. P., *Human-Built World—How to Think about Technology and Culture*, Chicago: Chicago University Press, 2004.

Hughes, T. P., *Networks of Power: Electrification in Western Society, 1880–1930,* Baltimore, Md.: John Hopkins University Press, 1983.

Hughes, T. P., 'The Seamless Web: Technology, Science, Etcetera, Etcetera', *Social Studies of Science,* 16/2 (1986), pp. 281–92.

Hunt, L., ed., *The New Cultural History,* Berkeley: University of California Press, 1989.

Hutchby, I., 'Technologies, Texts and Affordances', *Sociology,* 35/2 (2001), pp. 441–56.

Hvattum, M., 'Historisme og modernisme i moderne arkitekturhistorieskriving', *Nordic Journal of Architectural Research,* 19/1 (2006), pp. 85–90.

Ibsen, H. 'A Verse Letter,' www.ibsen.net, accessed 24 April 2009.

Iggers, G. G., *Historiography in the Twentieth Century—From Scientific Objectivity to the Postmodern Challenge,* Middletown, Conn.: Wesleyan University Press, 1997.

Ingram, J., Shove, E., and Watson, M., 'Products and Practices: Selected Concepts from Science and Technology Studies and from Social Theories of Consumption and Practice', *Design Issues,* 23/2 (2007), pp. 3–16.

Jackson, A., 'Labour as Leisure-The Mirror Dinghy and DIY Sailors', *Journal of Design History,* 19/1 (2006), pp. 57–67.

Jackson, F., 'The New Air Age: BOAC and Design Policy 1945–60', *Journal of Design History,* 4/3 (1991), pp. 167–85.

Jackson, S., 'Sacred Objects—Australian Design and National Celebrations', *Journal of Design History,* 19/3 (2006), pp. 249–55.

Jackson, S., 'The "Stump-jumpers:" National Identity and the Mythology of Australian Industrial Design in the Period 1930–1975', *Design Issues,* 18/4 (2002), pp. 14–23.

Jacob, M. C., 'Science Studies after Social Construction—The Turn toward the Comparative and the Global', in V. E. Bonnell and L. Hunt, eds., *Beyond the Cultural Turn—New Directions in the Study of Society and Culture,* Berkeley: University of California Press, 1999.

Jasanoff, S., Markle, G. E., Petersen, J. C., and Pinch, T., eds., *Handbook of Science and Technology Studies,* Thousand Oaks, Calif.: Sage, 1995.

Jencks, C. A., *The Language of Post-Modern Architecture,* London: Academy Editions, 1977.

Jones, C. A., 'Talking Pictures: Clement Greenberg's Pollock', in L. Daston, ed., *Things That Talk—Object Lessons form Art and Science,* New York: Zone Books, 2004.

Jones, M., 'Design and the Domestic Persuader—Television and the British Broadcasting Corporation's Promotion of Post-war "Good Design"', *Journal of Design History,* 16/4 (2003), pp. 307–18.

Jones, M., 'Why Fakes?', in S. M. Pearce, ed., *Interpreting Objects and Collections,* London: Routledge, 1994.

Julier, G., 'Barcelona Design, Catalonia's Political Economy, and the New Spain, 1980–1986', *Journal of Design History,* 9/2 (1996), pp. 117–27.

Julier, G., *The Culture of Design,* 2nd edn., London: Sage, 2008.

Katz, B. M., 'Intelligent Design', *Technology and Culture,* 47/2 (2006), pp. 381–90.

Katz, B. M., 'Technology and Design: A New Agenda', in *Technology and Culture,* 38/2 (1997), pp. 452–56.

Kelley, V., 'The Equitable Consumer: Shopping at the Co-Op in Manchester', *Journal of Design History,* 11/4 (1998), pp. 295–310.

Kingery, W. D., ed., *Learning from Things—Method and Material of Material Culture Studies,* Washington, D.C.: Smithsonian Institution Press, 1996.

Kingery, W. D., 'Technological Systems and Some Implications with Regard to

Continuity and Change', in S. Lubar and W. D. Kingery, eds., *History from Things—Essays on Material Culture,* Washington, D.C.: Smithsonian Institution Press, 1993.

Kinross, R., 'Herbert Read's "Art and Industry": A History', *Journal of Design History,* 1/1 (1988), pp. 35–50.

Kirkham, P., ed., *The Gendered Object,* Manchester: Manchester University Press, 1996.

Kline, R., and Pinch, T., 'Users as Agents of Technological Change: The Social Construction of the Automobile in the Rural United States', *Technology and Culture,* 37/4 (1996), pp. 763–95.

Koerner, J. L., 'Bosch's Equipment', in L. Daston, ed., *Things That Talk—Object Lessons form Art and Science,* New York: Zone Books, 2004.

Kopytoff, I., 'The Cultural Biography of Things: Commoditization as Process', in A. Appadurai, ed., *The Social Life of Things—Commodities in Cultural Perspective,* Cambridge: Cambridge University Press, 1986.

Kramer, L. S., 'Literature, Criticism, and Historical Imagination: The Literary Challenge of Hayden White and Dominick LaCapra', in L. Hunt, ed., *The New Cultural History,* Berkeley, Los Angeles: University of California Press, 1989.

Kubler, G., *The Shape of Time—Remarks on the History of Things,* New Haven, Conn.: Yale University Press, 1962.

Kuhn, T. S., *The Essential Tension—Selected Studies in Scientific Tradition and Change,* Chicago: University of Chicago Press, 1977.

Kuhn, T. S., 'Second Thoughts on Paradigms', in F. Suppe, ed., *The Structure of Scientific Theories,* Urbana: University of Illinois Press, 1977.

Kuhn, T. S., *The Structure of Scientific Revolutions,* 2nd edn. Chicago: University of Chicago Press, 1970.

LaCapra, D., *History & Criticism,* Ithaca, NY: Cornell University Press, 1985.

LaCapra, D., *Rethinking Intellectual History—Texts, Contexts, Language,* Ithaca, NY: Cornell University Press, 1983.

Lakatos, I., 'The History of Science and its Rational Reconstruction', in J. Worrall and G. Currie, ed., *Philosophical Papers,* Cambridge: Cambridge University Press, 1978.

Landström, C., 'National Strategies: The Gendered Appropriation of Household Technology', in M. Hård and A. Jamison, eds., *The Intellectual Appropriation of Technology, 1900–1939,* Cambridge, Mass.: MIT Press, 1998.

Lantry, D. N., 'Dress for Egress: The Smithsonian National Air and Space Museum's Apollo Spacesuit Collection', *Journal of Design History,* 14/4 (2001), pp. 343–59.

Latour, B., *Aramis, or The Love of Technology,* Cambridge, Mass.: Harvard University Press, 1996.

Latour, B., 'For Bloor and Beyond—A Reply to David Bloor's "Anti-Latour"', *Studies in History and Philosophy of Science,* 30/1 (1999), pp. 113–29.

Latour, B. (under the pseudonym Jim Johnson), 'Mixing Humans and Nonhumans Together: The Sociology of a Door-Closer', *Social Problems,* 35/3 (1988), pp. 298–310.

Latour, B., 'On recalling ANT', in J. Law and J. Hassard, eds., *Actor Network Theory and After,* Oxford: Blackwell, 1999.

Latour, B., *Politics of Nature,* Cambridge, Mass.: Harvard University Press, 2004.

Latour, B., *Reassembling the Social—An Introduction to Actor-Network-Theory,* Oxford: Oxford University Press, 2005.

Latour, B., *Science in Action,* Cambridge, Mass.: Harvard University Press, 1987.

Latour, B., *We Have Never Been Modern,* Cambridge, Mass.: Harvard University Press, 1993.

Latour, B., 'Where Are the Missing Masses? The Sociology of a Few Mundane Artefacts', in W. E. Bijker and J. Law, eds., *Shaping Technology/Building Society—Studies in Sociotechnical Change,* Cambridge, Mass.: MIT Press, 1992.

Law, J., 'After ANT: Complexity, Naming and Topology', in J. Law and J. Hassard, eds., *Actor Network Theory and After,* Oxford: Blackwell, 1999.

Law, J., *After Method—Mess in Social Science Research,* London: Routledge, 2004.

Law, J., *Organizing Modernity,* Oxford: Blackwell, 1994.

Law, J., and Hassard, J., eds., *Actor Network Theory and After,* Oxford: Blackwell, 1999.

Lees-Maffei, G., 'Studying Advice: Historiography, Methodology, Commentary, Bibliography', *Journal of Design History,* 16/1 (2003), pp. 1–14.

Lending, M., *Omkring 1900—Kontinuiteter i norsk arkitekturtenkning,* Oslo: Pax, 2008.

Levy, E., 'The Aesthetics of Power: High-Voltage Transmission Systems and the American Landscape', *Technology and Culture,* 38/3 (1997), pp. 575–607.

Lie, M. and Sørensen, K. H., eds., *Making Technology Our Own?—Domesticating Technology into Everyday Life,* Oslo: Scandinavian University Press, 1996.

Lowenthal, D., *The Past is a Foreign Country,* Cambridge: Cambridge University Press, 1985.

Lubar, S., 'Learning from Technological Things', in W. D. Kingery, ed., *Learning from Things—Method and Material of Material Culture Studies,* Washington, D.C.: Smithsonian Institution Press, 1996.

Lubar, S., and Kingery, W. D., eds., *History from Things—Essays on Material Culture,* Washington, D.C.: Smithsonian Institution Press, 1993.

Mácel, O., 'Avant-Garde Design and the Law: Litigation over the Cantilever Chair', *Journal of Design History,* 3(2/3) (1990), pp. 125–43.

MacKenzie, D., 'Missile Accuracy: A Case Study in the Social Processes of Technological Change', in W. E. Bijker, T. P. Hughes, and T. J. Pinch, eds., *The Social Construction of Technological Systems—New Directions in the Sociology and History of Technology,* Cambridge, Mass.: MIT Press, 1987.

MacKenzie, D., and Wajcman, J., eds., *The Social Shaping of Technology,* 2nd edn., Maidenhead: Open University Press, 1999.

Madge, P., 'Design, Ecology, Technology: A Historiographical Review', *Journal of Design History,* 6/3 (1993), pp. 149–66.

Madge, P., 'An Enquiry into Pevsner's "Enquiry"', *Journal of Design History,* 1/2 (1988), pp. 113–26.

Maguire, P., 'Craft Capitalism and the Projection of British Industry in the 1950s and 1960s', *Journal of Design History,* 6/2 (1993), pp. 97–113.

Maguire, P., 'Designs on Reconstruction: British Business, Market Structures and the Role of Design in Post-War Recovery', in *Journal of Design History* 4(1) (1991), pp. 15–30.

Maldonado, T., 'New Developments in Industry and the Training of Designers', *Architects' Yearbook,* 9 (1960), pp. 174–80.

Maldonado, T., 'Taking Eyeglasses Seriously', *Design Issues,* 17/4 (2001), p. 32–43.

Margolin, V., ed., *Design Discourse: History, Theory, Criticism,* Chicago: University of Chicago Press, 1989.

Margolin, V., 'Design History or Design Studies: Subject Matter and Methods', *Design Studies*, 13/2 (1992), pp. 104–116.

Margolin, V., 'Design in History', *Design Issues* 25/2 (2009), pp. 94–105.

Margolin, V., *The Politics of the Artificial: Essays on Design and Design Studies,* Chicago: University of Chicago Press, 2001.

Margolin, V. 'The Product Milieu and Social Action', in R. Buchanan and V. Margolin, eds., *Discovering Design: Explorations in Design Studies,* Chicago: University of Chicago Press, 1995.

Margolin, V., 'A Reply to Adrian Forty', *Design Issues*, 11/1 (1995), pp. 19–21.

Margolin, V., 'A World History of Design and the History of the World', *Journal of Design History*, 18/3 (2005), pp. 235–43.

Margolin, V., and Buchanan, R., eds., *The Idea of Design,* Cambridge, Mass.: MIT Press, 1995.

Masterman, M., 'The Nature of a Paradigm', in I. Lakatos and A. Musgrave, eds., *Criticism and the Growth of Knowledge,* Cambridge: Cambridge University Press, 1970.

McCarthy, T., *Auto Mania: Cars, Consumers, and the Environment,* New Haven, Conn.: Yale University Press, 2007.

McDonald, T., ed., *The Historic Turn in the Human Sciences,* Ann Arbor: University of Michigan Press, 1996.

McKellar, S., '"Seals of Approval"—Consumer Representation in 1930s' America', *Journal of Design History*, 15/1 (2002), pp. 1–13.

Megill, A., 'The Reception of Foucault by Historians', *Journal of the History of Ideas*, 48/1 (1987), pp. 117–41.

Meikle, J. L., *American Plastic—A Cultural History,* New Brunswick, NJ: Rutgers University Press, 1995.

Meikle, J. L., 'Design History for What?: Reflections on an Elusive Goal', *Design Issues*, 11/1 (1995), p. 71–5.

Meikle, J. L., *Design in the USA,* Oxford: Oxford University Press, 2005.

Meikle, J. L., 'Into the Fourth Kingdom: Representations of Plastic Materials, 1920–1950', *Journal of Design History*, 5/3 (1992), pp. 173–82.

Meikle, J. L., 'Material Virtues: on the Ideal and the Real in Design History', *Journal of Design History*, 11/3 (1998), pp. 191–99.

Meikle, J. L., *Twentieth Century Limited: Industrial Design in America, 1925–1939,* Philadelphia: Temple University Press, 1979.

Michael, V., 'Reyner Banham: Signs and Designs in the Time Without Style', *Design Issues*, 18/2 (2002), pp. 65–77.

Michl, J., 'Is There a Duty to be Modern?', in A. Pansera, ed., *Tradizione e Modernismo: Design 1918/1940—Atti del convegno,* Milan: L'Arca, 1988.

Michl, J., 'On Seeing Design as Redesign—An Exploration of a Neglected Problem in Design Education', *Scandinavian Journal of Design History*, 12 (2002), pp. 7–23.

Miller, D., ed., *Acknowledging Consumption,* London: Routledge, 1995.

Miller, D., *Material Culture and Mass Consumption,* Oxford: Blackwell, 1987.

Miller, D., ed., *Material Cultures—Why Some Things Matter,* London: UCL Press, 1998.

Miller, D., 'Things Ain't What They Used to Be', in S. M. Pearce, ed., *Interpreting Objects and Collections,* London: Routledge, 1994.

Mohun, A. P., 'Designed for Thrills and Safety: Amusement Parks and the Commodification of Risk, 1880–1929', *Journal of Design History*, 14/4 (2001), pp. 291–306.

Mom, G., 'Translating Properties into Functions (and Vice Versa): Design, User Culture and the Creation of an American and a European Car (1930–70)', *Journal of Design History*, 21/2 (2008), pp. 171–81.

Moriarty, C., 'A Backroom Service?—The Photographic Library of the Council of Industrial Design, 1945–1965', *Journal of Design History* 13/1 (2000), pp. 39–57.

Munch, A. V., *Den stilløse stil: Adolf Loos*, Copenhagen: Kunstakademiets Arkitekskoles Forlag, 2002.

Murphie, A., and Potts, J., *Culture & Technology*, Basingstoke: Palgrave Macmillan, 2003.

Narotzky, V., '"A Different and New Refinement"—Design in Barcelona, 1960–1990', *Journal of Design History*, 13/3 (2000), pp. 227–43.

Narotzky, V., 'Our Cars in Havana', in P. Wollen and J. Kerr, eds., *Autopia: Cars and Culture*, London: Reaktion Books, 2002.

Naylor, G., 'Theory and Design: The Banham Factor: The Ninth Reyner Banham Memorial Lecture', *Journal of Design History*, 10/3 (1997), pp. 241–52.

Nickles, S., '"Preserving Women": Refrigerator Design as Social Process in the 1930s', *Technology and Culture*, 43/4 (2002), pp. 693–727.

Nierop, O. A. van, Blankendaal, A. C. M., and Overbeeke, C. J., 'The Evolution of the Bicycle: A Dynamic Systems Approach', *Journal of Design History* 10/3 (1997), pp. 253–67.

Norman, D. A., *The Design of Everyday Things*, Cambridge, Mass.: MIT Press, 1998.

Norman, D. A., *Emotional Design—Why We Love (or Hate) Everyday Things*, New York: Basic Books, 2004.

Nydal, R, *I vitenskapens tid—Introduksjon til vitenskapsfilosofi etter Kuhn*, Oslo: Spartacus, 2002.

Nygaard, E., 'Arkitekturteorien—mellem manifester og videnskab', *Nordic Journal of Architectural Research*, 15/3 (2002), pp. 39–48.

O'Brien, P., 'Michel Foucault's History of Culture', in L. Hunt, ed., *The New Cultural History*, Berkeley: University of California Press, 1989.

Oldenziel, R., 'Object/ions—Technology, Culture, and Gender', in W. D. Kingery, ed., *Learning from Things—Method and Material of Material Culture Studies*, Washington, D.C.: Smithsonian Institution Press, 1996.

Oldenziel, R., Albert de la Bruhèze, A., and de Wit, O., 'Europe's Mediation Junction: Technology and Consumer Society in the 20th Century', *History and Technology*, 21/1 (2005), pp. 107–39.

Øllgaard, G., 'A Super-Elliptical Moment in the Cultural Form of the Table: A Case Study of a Danish Table', *Journal of Design History*, 12/2 (1999), pp. 143–57.

Olsen, B., 'Material Culture after Text: Re-Membering Things', *Norwegian Archaeological Review*, 36/2 (2003), pp. 87–104.

Østby, P., *Flukten fra Detroit: Bilens integrasjon i det norske samfunnet*, doctoral dissertation/STS rapport no. 24, Trondheim: University of Trondheim, 1995.

Østby, P., 'Escape from Detroit—The Norwegian Conquest of an Alien Artifact', in K. H. Sørensen, ed., *The Car and its Environments—The Past, Present and Future of the Motorcar in Europe*, Proceedings from the COST A4 (Vol. 2) Workshop in Trondheim, Norway, May 1993, Brussels: Commission of the European Communities, Directorate General XII, 1994, pp. 33–68.

Pacey, P., '"Anyone Designing Anything?" Non-Professional Designers and the History of Design', *Journal of Design History*, 5/3 (1992), pp. 217–25.

Palmer, R. R., and Colton, J., *A History of the Modern World*, 8th edn., New York: McGraw-Hill, 1995.

Pansera, A., *Storia del Disegno Industriale Italiano,* Bari, Italy: Laterza, 1993.

Pansera, A., ed., *Tradizione e Modernismo: Design 1918/1940—Atti del convegno,* Milan: L'Arca, 1988.

Pantzar, M., 'Domestication of Everyday Life Technology: Dynamic Views on the Social Histories of Artifacts', *Design Issues,* 13/3 (1997), pp. 52–65.

Pasca, V., and Trabucco, F., eds., *Design: Storia e Storiografia,* Bologna: Progetto Leonardo, 1995.

Patton, P., *Bug—The Strange Mutations of the World's Most Famous Automobile,* New York: Simon & Schuster, 2003.

Petroski, H., *The Evolution of Useful Things,* New York: Vintage Books, 1994.

Petroski, H., *The Pencil—A History of Design and Circumstance,* New York: Knopf, 1989.

Petroski, H., *To Engineer Is Human—The Role of Failure in Successful Design,* New York: St. Martin's Press, 1985.

Pevsner, N., *Pioneers of the Modern Movement—from William Morris to Walter Gropius,* London: Faber & Faber, 1936.

Pearce, S. M., ed., *Interpreting Objects and Collections,* London: Routledge, 1994.

Pearce, S. M., ed., *Museum Studies in Material Culture,* Leicester: Leicester University Press, 1989.

Pickering, A., *The Mangle of Practice—Time, Agency, and Science,* Chicago: University of Chicago Press, 1995.

Pinch. T., and Bijker, W., 'The Social Construction of Facts and Artefacts: or How the Sociology of Science and the Sociology of Technology Might Benefit Each Other', *Social Studies of Science,* 14/3 (1984), pp. 399–441.

Pinch, T. J., and Bijker, W. E., 'The Social Construction of Facts and Artifacts: Or How the Sociology of Science and the Sociology of Technology Might Benefit Each Other', in W. E. Bijker, T. P. Hughes, and T. J. Pinch, eds., *The Social Construction of Technological Systems—New Directions in the Sociology and History of Technology,* Cambridge, Mass.: MIT Press, 1987.

Popper, K., *The Logic of Scientific Discovery,* London: Hutchinson, 1959.

Popper, K., *Objective Knowledge—An Evolutionary Approach,* Oxford: Clarendon Press, 1972.

Porter, G., 'Cultural Forces and Commercial Constraints: Designing Packaging in the Twentieth-Century United States', *Journal of Design History,* 12/1 (1999), pp. 25–43.

Purbrick, L., 'The Dream Machine: Charles Babbage and His Imaginary Computers', *Journal of Design History,* 6/1 (1993), pp. 9–23.

Pursell, C., 'Seeing the Invisible: New Perspectives in the History of Technology', *ICON* 1 (1995), pp. 9–15.

Putnam, T., 'The Theory of Machine Design in the Second Industrial Age', *Journal of Design History,* 1/1 (1988), pp. 25–34.

Pye, D., *The Nature and Aesthetics of Design,* London: Barrie & Jenkins, 1978.

Raizman, D., *History of Modern Design—Graphics and Products since the Industrial Revolution,* London: Laurence King, 2003.

Raizman, D., and Gorman, C. R., 'Introduction', in D. Raizman and C. R. Gorman, eds., *Objects, Audiences, and Literatures—Alternative Narratives in the History of Design,* Newcastle: Cambridge Scholars Publishing, 2007.

Riccini, R., 'History from Things: Notes on the History of Industrial Design', *Design Issues,* 14/3 (1998), pp. 43–65.

Riccini, R., 'Innovation as a Field of Historical Knowledge for Industrial Design', *Design Issues* 17/4 (2001), pp. 24–31.

Ritzer, G., *Toward an Integrated Sociological Paradigm: The Search for an Exemplar and an Image of the Subject Matter*, Boston: Allyn and Bacon, 1981.

Rose, S. O., 'Cultural Analysis and Moral Discourses—Episodes, Continuities, and Transformations', in V. E. Bonnell and L. Hunt, eds., *Beyond the Cultural Turn—New Directions in the Study of Society and Culture*, Berkeley: University of California Press, 1999.

Rubin, E., 'The Form of Socialism without Ornament—Consumption, Ideology, and the Fall and Rise of Modernist Design in the German Democratic Republic', *Journal of Design History*, 19/2 (2006), pp. 155–68.

Rudofsky, B., *Architecture Without Architects: A Short Introduction to Non-pedigreed Architecture*, London: Academy Editions, 1964.

Schaanning, E., *Modernitetens oppløsning: Sentrale skikkelser i etterkrigstidens idéhistorie*, Oslo: Spartacus, 2000.

Schaffer, S., 'A Science Whose Business Is Bursting: Soap Bubbles as Commodities in Classical Physics', in L. Daston, ed., *Things That Talk—Object Lessons form Art and Science*, New York: Zone Books, 2004.

Schiffer, M. B., 'Cultural Imperatives and Product Development: The Case of the Shirt-Pocket Radio', *Technology and Culture*, 34/1 (1993), pp. 98–113.

Schiffer, M. B., 'Pathways to the Present—In Search of Shirt-Pocket Radios with Subminiature Tubes', in W. D. Kingery, ed., *Learning from Things—Method and Material of Material Culture Studies*, Washington, D.C.: Smithsonian Institution Press, 1996.

Schot, J., and Albert de la Bruheze, A., 'The Mediated Design of Products, Consumption, and Consumers in the Twentieth Century', in N. Oudshoorn and T. Pinch, eds., *How Users Matter—The Co-Construction of Users and Technology*, Cambridge, Mass.: MIT Press, 2003.

Scott, K., 'Art and Industry—A Contradictory Union: Authors, Rights and Copyrights during the *Consulat*', *Journal of Design History*, 13/1 (2000), pp. 1–21.

Seddon, J., 'The Architect and the "Arch-Pedant": Sadie Speight, Nikolaus Pevsner and "Design Review"', *Journal of Design History*, 20/1 (2007), pp. 29–41.

Selle, G., *Die Geschichte des Design in Deutschland von 1870 bis heute—Entwicklung der industriellen Produktkultur*, Cologne: DuMont, 1978.

Selle, G., 'There Is No Kitsch, There is Only Design!', *Design Issues*, 1/1 (1984), pp. 41–52.

Sewell, W., Jr., 'The Concept(s) of Culture', in V. E. Bonnell and L. Hunt, eds., *Beyond the Cultural Turn—New Directions in the Study of Society and Culture*, Berkeley: University of California Press, 1999.

Silverstone, R., 'Domesticating Domestication. Reflections on the Life of a Concept', in T. Berker, M. Hartmann, Y. Punie, and K. J. Ward, eds., *Domestication of Media and Technology*, Maidenhead: Open University Press, 2006.

Silverstone, R., Hirch, E. and Morley, D., 'Information and Communication Technologies and the Moral Economy of the Household', in R. Silverstone and E. Hirsch, eds., *Consuming Technologies. Media and Information in Domestic Spaces*, London: Routledge, 1992.

Simon, H., *The Sciences of the Artificial*, 3rd edn., Cambridge, Mass.: MIT Press, 1996.

Sismondo, S., *An Introduction to Science and Technology Studies*, Oxford: Blackwell, 2004.

Skinner, Q., 'Meaning and Understanding in the History of Ideas', in J. Tully, ed., *Meaning and Context: Quentin Skinner and His Critics*, Princeton, NJ: Princeton University Press, 1988.

Smith, C. S., 'Material Culture and Mass Consumption' [book review], *Journal of Design History*, 1/2 (1988), pp. 149–50.

Somers, M. R., 'The Privatization of Citizenship—How to Unthink a Knowledge Culture', in V. E. Bonnell and L. Hunt, eds., *Beyond the Cultural Turn—New Directions in the Study of Society and Culture*, Berkeley: University of California Press, 1999.

Sparke, P., *As Long as it's Pink—The Sexual Politics of Taste*, London: Pandora, 1995.

Sparke, P., *A Century of Car Design*, London: Mitchell Beazley, 2002.

Sparke, P., *Consultant Design—The History and Practice of the Designer in Industry*, London: Pembridge Press, 1983.

Sparke, P., 'Cookware to Cocktail Shakers: The Domestication of Aluminum in the United States, 1900–1939', in S. Nicols, ed., *Aluminum by Design*, Pittsburgh/New York: Carnegie Museum of Art/Abrams, 2000.

Sparke, P., 'Imagining Consumers—Design and Innovation from Wedgwood to Corning. By Regina Lee Blaszczyk' [book review], *Technology and Culture* 42/29 (2001), pp. 345–46.

Sparke, P., *An Introduction to Design and Culture in the Twentieth Century*, London: Allen & Unwin, 1986.

Stafford, S., et al., eds., *The BLOCK Reader in Visual Culture*, London: Routledge, 1996.

Stanfield, P., 'Heritage Design: The Harley-Davidson Motor Company', *Journal of Design History*, 5/2 (1992), pp. 141–55.

Staudenmaier, J. M., *Technology's Storytellers: Reweaving the Human Fabric*, Cambridge, Mass.: MIT Press, 1985.

Steadman, P., *The Evolution of Designs: Biological Analogy in Architecture and the Applied Arts*, Cambridge: Cambridge University Press, 1979.

Steadman, P., 'The History and Science of the Artificial', *Design Studies*, 1/1 (1979), pp. 49–58.

Steedman, C., 'Culture, Cultural Studies and the Historians', in S. During, ed., *The Cultural Studies Reader*, London: Routledge, 1993.

Suppe, F., ed., *The Structure of Scientific Theories*, Urbana: University of Illinois Press, 1977.

Sørensen, K. H., 'Domestication: The Enactment of Technology', in T. Berker, et al., eds., *Domestication of Media and Technology*, Maidenhead: Open University Press, 2006.

Sørensen, K. H., *Technology in Use. Two Essays on the Domestication of Artefacts*, STS Working Paper 2/94, Trondheim, Norway: University of Trondheim, 1994.

Sørensen, K. H., Aune, M. and Hatling, M., 'Against Linearity—On the Cultural Appropriation of Science and Technology', in M. Dierkes and C. von Grote, eds., *Between Understanding and Trust—The Public, Science and Technology*, Amsterdam: Harwood Academic, 2000.

Thompson, M., *Rubbish Theory—The Creation and Destruction of Value*, Oxford: Oxford University Press, 1979.

Tournikiotis, P., *The Historiography of Modern Architecture*, Cambridge, Mass.: MIT Press, 1999.

Tucker, M. 'Norge I Form: Kunsthåndverk og Design under Industrikulturen' [book review], *Journal of Design History* 2(2/3), p. 237.

Uriarte, L. F., 'Modernity and Postmodernity from Cuba', *Journal of Design History*, 18/3 (2005), pp. 245–55.

Vattimo, G., *La fine della modernità*, Milan: Garzanti, 1985.

Venturi, R., *Complexity and Contradiction in Architecture*, New York: Museum of Modern Art, 1966.

Verbeek, P.-P., *What Things Do—Philosophical Reflections on Technology, Agency, and Design*, University Park: Pennsylvania State University Press, 2005.

Volti, R., 'A Century of Automobility', *Technology and Culture*, 37/4 (1996), pp. 663–785.

Vyas, H. K., 'The Designer and the Socio-Technology of Small Production', *Journal of Design History*, 4/3 (1991), pp. 187–210.

Walker, J. A., *Design History and the History of Design*, London: Pluto, 1989.

Werne, F., *Arkitekturens ismer*, Stockholm: Arkitektur Förlag, 1998.

Wick, R., 'Critical Observations and General Remarks about Design History', in A. Pansera, ed., *Tradizione e Modernismo: Design 1918/1940—Atti del convegno*, Milan: L'Arca, 1988.

Wilde, O., *The Picture of Dorian Gray*, 1891, repr. London: Penguin, 1994.

Wildhagen, F., 'Flodhesten, Gullfisken og Kristine Valdresdatter—Streamlining og designhistorien', in M. Gelfer-Jørgensen, ed., *Nordisk Funktionalisme 1925–1950,* Copenhagen: Det danske Kunstindustrimuseum & Nordisk Forum for Formgivningshistorie, 1986.

Wildhagen, F., *Norge i Form—Kunsthåndverk og design under industrikulturen*, Oslo: J.M. Stenersen, 1988.

Wildhagen, F., 'Towards a Methodology of Design History', in A. Pansera, ed., *Tradizione e Modernismo: Design 1918/1940—Atti del convegno*, Milan: L'Arca, 1988.

Wittgenstein, L., *Philosophical Investigations*, 3rd edn., Oxford: Blackwell, 1967.

White, H., *The Content of the Form: Narrative Discourse and Historical Representation,* Baltimore: Johns Hopkins University Press, 1987.

Whiteley, N., 'Design History or Design Studies?', *Design Issues*, 11/1 (1995), pp. 38–42.

Whiteley, N., *Reyner Banham: Historian of the Immediate Future,* Cambridge, Mass.: MIT Press, 2002.

Wolfe, T., *From Bauhaus to Our House,* New York: Farrar, Straus & Giroux, 1981.

Wolfe, T., *The Kandy-Kolored Tangerine-Flake Streamline Baby,* 1965, repr. New York: Bantam Books, 1999.

Wolfe, T., *I am Charlotte Simmons,* New York: Farrar, Straus, Giroux, 2004.

Woodham, J. M., 'British Modernism between the Wars: An Historical "Léger de main"?', in A. Pansera, ed., *Tradizione e Modernismo: Design 1918/1940—Atti del convegno,* Milan: L'Arca, 1988.

Woodham, J. M., 'Designing Design History: From Pevsner to Postmodernism', Paper delivered at the Digitisation and Knowledge conference at Auckland University of Technology, February 2001.

Woodham, J. M., *A Dictionary of Modern Design,* Oxford: Oxford University Press, 2004.

Woodham, J. M., *The Industrial Designer and the Public,* London: Pembridge, 1983.

Woodham, J. M., 'Local, National and Global: Redrawing the Design Historical Map', *Journal of Design History*, 18/3 (2005), pp. 257–67.

Woodham, J. M., 'Managing British Design Reform II: The Film 'Deadly Lampshade': An Ill-Fated Episode in the Politics of "Good Taste"', *Journal of Design History*, 9/2 (1996), pp. 101–15.

Woodham, J. M., 'Resisting Colonization: Design History Has Its own Identity', *Design Issues,* 11/1 (1995), pp. 22–37.

Woodham, J. M., *Twentieth-Century Design,* Oxford: Oxford University Press, 1997.

Woodhouse, E., and Patton, J. W., 'Design by Society: Science and Technology Studies and the Social Shaping of Design', *Design Issues,* 20/3 (2004), pp. 1–12.

Woolgar, S., 'What Happened to Provocation in Science and Technology Studies?', *History and Technology,* 20/4 (2004), pp. 339–49.

Worden, S., and Seddon, J., 'Women Designers in Britain in the 1920s and 1930s: Defining the Professional and Redefining Design', *Journal of Design History,* 8/3 (1995), pp. 177–93.

Yagou, A., 'Rethinking Design History From an Evolutionary Perspective: Background and Implications', *The Design Journal,* 8/3 (2005), pp. 50–60.

INDEX